African Americans and the Politics of Congressional Redistricting

race and politics
volume 2
garland reference library of the social sciences
volume 1439

RACE AND POLITICS
TONI-MICHELLE C. TRAVIS, *Series Editor*

RACE, POWER, AND POLITICAL
EMERGENCE IN MEMPHIS
by Sharon D. Wright

AFRICAN AMERICANS AND THE
POLITICS OF CONGRESSIONAL
REDISTRICTING
by Dewey M. Clayton

AFRICAN AMERICANS AND THE POLITICS OF CONGRESSIONAL REDISTRICTING

DEWEY M. CLAYTON

GARLAND PUBLISHING, INC.
A MEMBER OF THE TAYLOR & FRANCIS GROUP
NEW YORK & LONDON / 2000

Published in 2000 by
Garland Publishing, Inc.
A member of the Taylor & Francis Group
19 Union Square West
New York, NY 10003

10 9 8 7 6 5 4 3 2 1

Library of Congress Cataloging-in-Publication data

Clayton, Dewey M.
    African Americans and the politics of congressional redistricting / Dewey
M. Clayton
        p.   cm. — (Race and Politics ; 2) (Garland reference library of social
    science ; v. 1439)
    Includes bibliographical references and index.
    ISBN 0-8153-3455-9 (alk. paper)
    1. United States. Congress. House—Election districts.   2. Apportionment
(Election law)—United States.   3. Election districts—United States.   4. Afro-
Americans—Politics and government.   I. Title.   II. Series.   III. Series:
Garland reference library of social science ; v. 1439

JK1341.C55 1999
328.73'07347'08996073—dc21
                                                                                99-049527

Printed on acid-free, 250-year-life paper
Manufactured in the United States of America

To my parents,
Christine and Dewey,
who by example taught me the difference between right and wrong
and the importance of fighting for social justice

Contents

Preface   xi
Acknowledgments   xiii
Tables and Figures   xv

Chapter 1 Introduction   1
           Newly Acquired Black Political Power   *1*
           Overview of the Book   *5*

Part I   **Politics of Exclusion and Politics of Congressional
           Redistricting**

Chapter 2 History of the Exclusion of Blacks from the American
           Political Process   11
           The Racial Gap: A Contrast in Black and White   *11*
           History of the Black Struggle for Equality   *13*
           Radical Reconstruction   *15*
           Second Reconstruction   *18*
           The Congressional Black Caucus   *20*
           Representation Theory   *23*
           The Urban Underclass   *24*
           Conservative Opposition to Race-Based Districting   *25*

Chapter 3 Pander, Slander, Gerrymander   33
           The Census and Reapportionment   *34*
           Federal and State Redistricting Requirements   *36*

Voting Rights Act of 1965	*37*
North Carolina Redistricting in the 1990s	*40*
Republican Strategy	*41*
Black Political Empowerment in North Carolina	*42*
Adoption of the First Congressional Plan	*45*

Chapter 4 Redistricting, Round Two: North Carolina
Legislators Are Required to Create a Second
Majority-Minority District   57
*The Department of Justice's Response to the
Enacted Plan*   *59*
Public Reaction to the Adopted Plan   *60*
Department of Justice's Rejection of the Enacted Plan   *61*
State Legislators Go Back to the Drawing Board   *63*
*Two Majority Black District Alternatives Presented
to the Legislature*   *64*
Origin of the I–85 District   *65*
Submission of Plan to U.S. Department of Justice   *69*

Part II **Court Litigation Surrounding Redistricting and
Standards of Congressional Redistricting**

Chapter 5 Legal Issues Surrounding North Carolina's Redistricting
Process   93
U. S. Supreme Court Decisions in the 1980s   *93*
*Voting Rights Act of 1982 and Administrative
Regulations Issued*   *94*
*Background to Redistricting Lawsuits in North
Carolina in the 1990s*   *95*
Lawsuits Arising out of the Initially Adopted Plan   *96*

Chapter 6 Subsequent Court Challenges in the South   113
*Southern States That Have Created Majority-Minority
Districts for the First Time This Century*   *114*
*Recent Court Challenges to Majority-Minority Districts
Around the Country*   *121*
*U.S. Supreme Court Rulings on Majority-Minority
Districts Throughout the South*   *122*

Chapter 7 Standards of Congressional Redistricting   133
Population Equality, Compactness, and Contiguity   *133*

Equal Population   *134*
Respect for Political Boundaries   *135*
Contiguity and Compactness   *136*
Compactness   *137*
Communities of Interest   *141*
Alternative Plans Presented to the General Assembly   *144*

Chapter 8   Calculating Compactness in North Carolina Plans   149
Measures of Compactness   *150*
Results of Calculations   *154*

Chapter 9   Conclusion: The Case for Majority Black Districts
    Remains Compelling   167
Incumbency Effect and Racially Polarized Voting   *172*
The Myth of Contiguity and Compactness   *174*
The Unfinished Business of Racial Equality   *177*

Bibliography   181
Index   191

Preface

I believe that representation strikes at the core of democracy. The number of African Americans in the U.S. Congress is at 39. This is due, in large part, to the creation of 13 majority black districts prior to the 1992 elections. As a result of these new districts, black representation jumped from 26 to 39, a 50 percent increase. Of these 13 newly created majority black districts, 12 were located in the South. All elected blacks to Congress in the 1992 elections. However, a conservative U.S. Supreme Court has attacked the interpretation of the Voting Rights Act, which led to the creation of these congressional districts. Others have argued that we have moved beyond race to a "color-blind" society. I share that lofty goal, but we have not yet reached that point. Majority black districts are still necessary in the South to ensure black representation in the U.S. Congress. They are a temporary solution to a complex problem. Due to continued residential segregation patterns, the existence of racially polarized voting, and lack of minority success absent race-conscious remedies, the case for majority black districts remains compelling.

Many political observers have stated that the creation of majority black districts around the South in the early 1990s resulted in bizarrely shaped districts because legislators had to go where black voters lived in order to draw the districts. What has been overlooked is that the irregularly shaped districts are not unique to majority black districts. Oddly shaped majority white districts have been a part of America's political landscape for quite some time. Furthermore, many of the majority black districts created throughout the South in the 1990s were a result of partisan gerrymandering by state legislators in their efforts to protect incumbents.

I expect people reading this book to gain an understanding of congressional redistricting and how this process, which has always been highly partisan, is now affected by the added dimension of race. The important issues of race, representation, and redistricting have been very much neglected by political analysts, who have been preoccupied with representation of majority interests. Consequently, little attention has been paid to the issue of representation for an entrenched minority population. This book demonstrates that race matters because without the creation of majority black districts, black representation in Congress would be substantially diminished.

Acknowledgments

There are several people I wish to acknowledge in helping me complete this book. I am deeply indebted to the staff at the North Carolina General Assembly, Information Systems Division, and, in particular, Kelly Stallings, Systems Analyst, who supplied me with endless data and maps. Dan Frey, Senior Geographic Information-Redistricting Analyst Programmer, provided me with numerous redistricting maps. Research Analyst Amy Childs was patient and expert at retrieving maps. Cathy Martin, the North Carolina General Assembly Legislative Librarian, made available numerous data, newspaper articles, and maps. I thank the members of the North Carolina General Assembly who were gracious enough to grant me interviews. I owe special gratitude to my former colleague, Mary Hawkesworth, Ph.D., who gave intellectual guidance as well as encouragement and support. She read the chapters in draft form and allowed me course release, which enabled me to complete this project. Angela Stallings was invaluable as a proofreader and someone to take issue with some of my intellectual arguments. Michael Hicks was a tireless source in helping me shape the manuscript into final form with his computer skills. Diane O'Regan was extremely timely and resourceful with the indexing. Susan Salsburg provided excellent copyediting and constructive criticism. I thank Suzanne Malone for proofreading and for her emotional support.

Tables and Figures

TABLES

3.1	North Carolina Congressional Districts, 1992	37
3.2	Black Population of North Carolina Congressional Districts, 1981	41
3.3	Three Alternative Congressional Redistricting Plans Presented to the North Carolina Legislature During Regular Session, 1991	51
4.1	Percentage Black Voting Age Population, by District	71
4.2	New Black Congressional Districts, 1992	76
8.1	Polygon Area Test: Comparison of Polygon Area of the Urban Districts of the Alternative Plans with the Enacted Plan in North Carolina	155
8.2	Polygon Perimeter Test: Comparison of the Urban Districts of the Alternative Plans with the Enacted Plan in North Carolina	155
8.3	Comparison of Urban District of the Enacted Plan with the Urban Districts of the Alternative Plans (Grofman Test)	156
8.4	Comparison of Urban District of the Enacted Plan with the Urban Districts of the Alternative Plans (Schwartzberg Test)	157
8.5	Comparison of Urban District of the Enacted Plan with the Urban Districts of the Alternative Plans (Reock Test)	158
8.6	Polygon Area Test: Comparison of Polygon Area of the Rural Districts of the Alternative Plans with the Enacted Plan in North Carolina	160

8.7 Polygon Perimeter Test: Comparison of the Rural Districts
of the Alternative Plans with the Rural District of the
Enacted Plan in North Carolina 160
8.8 Comparison of Rural District of the Enacted Plan
with the Rural Districts of the Alternative Plans
(Grofman Test) 161
8.9 Comparison of Rural District of the Enacted Plan
with the Rural Districts of the Alternative Plans
(Schwartzberg Test) 162
8.10 Comparison of Rural District of the Enacted Plan
with the Rural Districts of the Alternative Plans
(Reock Test) 163
8.11 Matrix of the Most Compact Rural and Urban Districts
Under All Five Tests of Compactness 165
9.1 Congressional Districts Represented by Blacks, 1991 175

FIGURES

4.1 Balmer 6.2 80
4.2 Justus Plan 81
4.3 Congressional Base Plan #6 82
4.4 Balmer Congress 8.1 83
4.5 Kimbrough Plan 84
4.6 92 Congress 1 85
4.7 Optimum II—Zero 86
4.8 Compact 2—Minority Plan 87
4.9 Flaherty Plan 88
4.10 Congressional Base Plan #10 89
6.1 South Carolina Congressional District Map, 1992 114
6.2 Florida Congressional District Map, 1992 116
6.3 Georgia Congressional District Map, 1992 117
6.4 Louisiana Congressional District Map, 1992 119
6.5 Texas Congressional District Map, 1992 120
7.1 Redistricting Criteria for Congressional Seats, 1991 135
9.1 California Congressional District Map, 1982 176
9.2 Tennessee Congressional District Map, 1992 177

African Americans and the Politics of Congressional Redistricting

CHAPTER 1

Introduction

African Americans and the Politics of Congressional Redistricting addresses one of the most profound political issues confronting the American public: the equitable representation of African Americans. This is a book about one of the most hotly debated issues in American politics today: majority black congressional districts. Created by state legislatures across the South in response to a variety of judicial, legislative, and administrative mandates, these districts literally changed the face of the United States Congress and created a new battleground over race, politics, and power.

In this work, I explore the reasoning for, and strategies behind, race-based congressional districting. Focusing on developments in North Carolina as emblematic of the redistricting process in the South, I expose the internal dynamics surrounding race-based redistricting. My methodology offers a sustained analysis of the subtleties and political complexities of the redistricting process that have thus far been overlooked by other scholars and the press. It is a story of political intrigue of seemingly strange political bedfellows—black Democrats and white Republicans—who jockeyed behind the scenes to gain political advantage. The stakes were and remain high and will ultimately affect the participation of blacks in shaping laws and the political debate on the national level. It will also impact their very enfranchisement in the political system.

NEWLY ACQUIRED BLACK POLITICAL POWER

The political experience of blacks in the United States has always suffered, and continues to suffer, from the politics of backlash. Up until the

Civil War, over 200 years after the first arrival of blacks in America, Southern blacks had no citizenship rights and were denied the right to vote. However, with passage of the Civil War Amendments (the Thirteenth, Fourteenth, and Fifteenth Amendments to the U.S. Constitution), blacks were freed from slavery, acquired citizenship rights, and gained the right to vote. During this brief period (1867–1877) after the Civil War, referred to as Radical Reconstruction, blacks voted and held elective office at the local, state, and national levels. Federal troops were withdrawn from the South following the Hayes-Tilden Compromise of 1876. Without that federal presence, the South reverted to its antebellum ways. Southern states employed numerous tactics such as literacy tests, poll taxes, grandfather clauses, and racial gerrymandering of their legislative districts to deny blacks the recently gained full rights of citizenship and effectively to disenfranchise them. Post–Civil War Reconstruction ended with blacks once again relegated to second-class citizenship in America.

From the end of Reconstruction until passage of the Voting Rights Act of 1965, blacks in southern states were largely preoccupied with securing the right to vote and full citizenship rights. With passage of the Civil Rights Act of 1964 and the Voting Rights Act of 1965, the Second Reconstruction was in full swing. Passage of the Voting Rights Act of 1965 did the following: (1) it allowed for the effective voter registration of blacks throughout the South; (2) it outlawed literacy tests; and (3) it stipulated that southern states had to submit any election changes to the U.S. Justice Department for approval. As a result, increased black political mobilization led to a significant rise in the number of black registered voters as well as the number of black elected officials at the local and state levels, but not at the congressional level. Black representation in Congress from the South would remain minimal until 1992. Renewal of the Voting Rights Act in 1982, coupled with judicial actions in the 1980s and the census of 1990, set the stage for the creation of 13 new majority black congressional districts, 12 of which were located in the South.* This redistricting resulted in the election of 13 blacks to Congress in 1992—the largest number since Reconstruction.

Two of these majority black districts were created in North Carolina, a state with a 22 percent black population. North Carolina was typical of most southern states in that its black residents had been denied the right

---

*Twelve of these majority black districts were created in the South—defined as the 11 former states of the Confederacy—and the 13th was drawn in Maryland.

to vote and locked out of political power for most of the twentieth century. Black candidates running for congressional seats after 1965 were repeatedly unsuccessful in majority white districts.

Following each decennial U.S. Census, Congress reapportions congressional seats to reflect immigration and population shifts. Redistricting occurs in those states that have gained or lost congressional seats during the reapportionment process. State legislatures are then charged with the task of redrawing congressional district boundaries based on those gains or losses. Redistricting has always been about power. As a process, it has always been controlled by the majority party in the state legislature. In the twentieth-century South, this has almost always meant that the Democrats, who were usually in the majority, would draw district boundaries to the disadvantage of Republicans. Moreover, Democrats, the majority of whom were white, would also normally draw boundaries that diluted black voting strength—even that of black Democrats—by not creating majority black districts. Several Southern states with substantial black populations—North Carolina, South Carolina, Florida, Alabama, and Virginia—failed in this century to create a majority black district that would allow black voters to elect a candidate of their choice; simultaneously, they created majority white districts that clearly gave white voters that opportunity. White Democrats had enjoyed a position of power in drawing congressional districts in the South throughout most of the century. But the political winds were changing. Following the 1990 census and reapportionment, southern white legislatures were forced to make significant changes in how they drew district boundaries. Due to a series of judicial decisions in the 1980s and the Department of Justice's interpretation of the Voting Rights Act of 1965, the Department of Justice issued one simple mandate to all southern states regarding their redistricting process: Create a majority black district wherever one can feasibly be drawn.

The state of North Carolina provides an excellent case study because it typifies the black struggle to acquire political power in the South and because it has been at the center of the redistricting controversy throughout the 1990s. By 1992, the state had never elected a black to Congress during the twentieth century despite the attempts of several qualified black candidates. After the creation of two majority black districts in 1992, two black congressional representatives were elected from these districts. Following the election, however, dissatisfied voters mounted legal challenges to the constitutionality of these majority black districts. One such challenge, *Shaw v. Reno* (1993), was ultimately decided by the

U.S. Supreme Court. Other southern states were waiting anxiously to see how the Court would rule because they too had drawn controversial majority black districts for the first time.

Blacks have continually suffered from the politics of vacillation: one step forward, two steps back. Today, majority black congressional districts are under attack in both the political and judicial arenas. In 1993, a conservative U.S. Supreme Court stated that these race-based districts balkanize us as a society and create enclaves of black voters akin to political apartheid.

Conservative scholars, both black and white, support that view. Carol Swain argues in *Black Faces, Black Interests* (1995) that the creation of majority black districts is a negative consequence of the Voting Rights Act. Furthermore, she believes these districts are not in the interest of minorities and that they harm prospects for blacks to enter into biracial coalitions. In *America in Black and White: One Nation, Indivisible* (1997), Abigail Thernstrom and Stephan Thernstrom paint an overly optimistic view of blacks and the political process in America. They are opponents of the creation of race-based districts. In their view, these districts do nothing more than limit the number of blacks in Congress. Moreover, they assert that these districts are not needed. In their opinion, majority black districts create an unnecessary safe haven for black candidates who, if they simply ran in majority white districts and formed biracial coalitions, would win elections.

This book will refute these arguments on political and legal grounds. It explores those questions that are still debated concerning race-based districting: Was it a victory for blacks; a compromise by Democrats; a major coup for Republicans? Was it a long-range strategy or a short-term tactic? Can it be defended as good policy as well as good politics?

This book demonstrates that race still matters in drawing congressional districts. Due to continued residential segregation, the existence of racial-bloc voting on the part of whites, and lack of minority success absent race-conscious remedies, the case for majority black congressional districts remains compelling.

Scholars such as Swain and the Thernstroms construct a narrative of progress when discussing blacks' political experience in the United States. Recent successes by blacks in majority white districts have created a false belief that majority black districts are no longer needed. But black successes in majority white districts have been rare. *In the entire history of the United States Congress, only 10 blacks have ever won election from majority white districts.* Without majority black districts, the number of blacks in Congress would be substantially reduced and, in my view, democracy would be diminished.

OVERVIEW OF THE BOOK

Part I examines the historical exclusion of blacks from the American political process and the politics behind congressional redistricting. To understand why the creation of majority black districts is important, one must examine the systematic denial to blacks of full participation in the political process in American society. Chapter 2 begins with a discussion of the racial gap in American society. There is a stark contrast between the social, economic, and political well-being of black and white Americans. What role, if any, does the representation of blacks in America have in narrowing this gap? This chapter chronicles Radical Reconstruction, a period immediately following the Civil War in which black males were granted the right to vote and held elective office at the local, state, and national levels. Once federal troops were withdrawn from the South, however, southern states began disenfranchising black voters, and by 1900 Radical Reconstruction was over. Almost as quickly as blacks were given the right to vote, it was taken away from them; thus began the politics of vacillation in America. The chapter culminates with the rise of the Congressional Black Caucus, followed by a discussion of representation theory and the relationship between black political power and representation in America today. It ends with a discussion of conservative opposition to race-based districting.

Chapter 3 begins with a detailed investigation of the politics behind redistricting to assess whose interests were being served. To gain a systematic understanding of these political maneuvers, I focus on partisan politics as well as on legislative action in North Carolina, a state that serves as a model for subsequent developments in other states throughout the South. This chapter includes a discussion of the history of the Voting Rights Act of 1965 and its subsequent amendments, which lay the groundwork for the Justice Department's scrutiny of state redistricting proposals. I examine some of the political dynamics that developed between black and white legislators of both political parties, dynamics that led to the creation of the first congressional plan by the state legislature in North Carolina.

Chapter 4 examines the rejection of North Carolina's first congressional plan in 1991 by the U.S. Department of Justice. What were the factors that influenced a Republican Justice Department to deny approval of North Carolina's initially ratified plan? Were there political motives behind the Justice Department's ruling that the state of North Carolina should have created two majority-minority districts instead of one?

Part II focuses on the court litigation surrounding redistricting and standards of congressional redistricting. Chapter 5 begins with a discussion of the lawsuits filed as a consequence of North Carolina's Democratically controlled legislature creating a second districting plan that would double Democratic seats compared to those of Republicans. This chapter culminates with the U.S. Supreme Court ruling in *Shaw v. Reno* (1993), a redistricting case involving North Carolina and the first major case challenging race-based districting in the 1990s.

Shaw v. Reno (1993) set the parameters on congressional redistricting for the 1990s. The nation as a whole, and the southern states in particular, watched to see whether the high court would allow these newly created majority black districts in North Carolina to stand. Chapter 6 chronicles the legal challenges brought in other southern states as a result of *Shaw v. Reno* (1993). Disgruntled voters in Georgia filed a challenge to two newly created majority black congressional districts that was ultimately decided by the U.S. Supreme Court in *Miller v. Johnson* (1995).

Constitutional standards pertaining to congressional redistricting are examined in Chapter 7. I discuss compactness, contiguity, and communities of interest as guidelines for the creation of congressional districts. I point out that most of the controversy surrounding the newly created majority black districts concerned their awkward shapes. Many political observers felt that the plan created by the North Carolina legislature violated traditional notions of compactness and contiguity.

I identify several widely accepted measures of compactness in Chapter 8. Using these measures, I analyze the final plan enacted by the legislature in North Carolina against the major alternative plans presented to the legislature that created two majority-minority districts. I conduct these tests to determine if the state legislature in North Carolina could have adopted a plan with two majority-minority districts that was more compact than the enacted plan.

In Chapter 9, I conclude that majority black congressional districts are under attack today, as are prospects for inclusive democracy in America. Opponents of majority black districts are engaged in high-minded discussions of "race-blind" redistricting. A conservative U.S. Supreme Court has attacked the newly created majority black districts in the South because of the bizarreness of their shapes. Moreover, conservative scholars have attacked the Voting Rights Act that led to the creation of these districts. What has been overlooked in this discourse is that irregularly shaped districts are not unique to the phenomenon of creating majority black districts; rather, they have been the result of partisan gerrymandering by state legislators in their efforts to protect incumbents. Indeed, bizarrely shaped districts have been a regular part of the political landscape for quite some time. Too much attention to this superficial discussion and the failure to see the mistakes and distortions that lie beneath will leave blacks in a worse position.

Theoretically, this book causes us to reexamine our concept of representation and majority rule under single-member voting districts. Currently, the American view of representation rewards the majority and relegates the minority to the permanent status of disaffected voter. The legitimacy of our system and inclusive democracy are both at stake.

PART I

Politics of Exclusion and Politics of Congressional Redistricting

CHAPTER 2

History of the Exclusion of Blacks from the American Political Process

The question of political representation lies at the core of democratic theory. One way of examining whether democracy works at the end of the twentieth century in America is by observation of a population sector that was disenfranchised for nearly two centuries after the founding of this nation.

This chapter begins by providing a historical overview of the plight of black Americans and their efforts to gain political and social equality in America. It traces black representation in Congress from the Reconstruction era (1867–1877) to the Second Reconstruction era (1940–present). Included in this discussion is the rise of the Congressional Black Caucus. This chapter closes with an examination of black representation and political power in American politics. If descriptive representation in American politics gives a voice to those previously denied access to the body politic, then how do redistricting and the creation of majority-minority districts fit into the overall contours of American politics generally and black politics specifically?

THE RACIAL GAP: A CONTRAST IN BLACK AND WHITE

Black Americans are the largest and most visible minority group in the country. By 1998 they numbered approximately 34.5 million of the estimated 271 million Americans, comprising roughly 12.7 percent of the population.

Almost all objective indicators point out that blacks still lag behind whites on most measures of socioeconomic status. Blacks are three times as likely as whites to live in single-parent families. Blacks are less likely to earn college degrees than whites. Twenty-four percent of whites age 25 and older have completed four years of college or more, but only 13.2 percent of blacks age 25 and older have completed four or more years of college. The Department of Labor reports that blacks make up only 4.2 percent of the doctors, 5 percent of the college professors, 3.7 percent of the engineers, 3.3 percent of the lawyers, and 1.4 percent of the architects in the United States. Blacks' incomes are still likely to be less than those of whites with comparable education. In 1996, the median income for blacks with a high school education was $14,881, 19.3 percent less than the median white income for high school graduates. For those with a bachelor's degree or more, there is only a slight improvement. The white median income for those who have a bachelor's degree or more is $36,193, and the median for blacks is $30,519, a 15.6 percent difference.[1] In 1994, the median income of black families was $26,522, just over half of the $47,023 median income for white families. As of 1995, only 11.2 percent of whites had incomes below $7,763, compared to 29.3 percent of blacks—which means that more than one-fourth of blacks live in poverty. The median household net worth of individuals (defined as the total value of assets, including homes and cars) shows a particularly stark contrast between blacks and whites: In 1993, the median household net worth of white Americans was $45,740, whereas the median household net worth of blacks was only $4,418; thus, white net worth is an astounding 10.4 times greater than that of blacks.[2]

Blacks lag significantly behind whites in major health care indices. For example, the infant mortality rate for whites is 6.3 per 1,000 live births; for blacks, the rate is 14.6 per 1,000 live births. Moreover, although the gap between blacks and whites is narrowing, blacks continue to have a lower life expectancy than whites. The life expectancy of white men is 73.8 years, versus 66.1 years for black men—a gap of 7.7 years. White women have a life expectancy of 79.6 years, while black women's life expectancy is 74.2 years, a gap of 5.4 years.[3] During 1996, the rate of new acquired immune deficiency syndrome (AIDS) cases per 100,000 population was 89.7 among blacks and 13.5 among whites, a rate nearly seven times higher for blacks than for whites.[4]

The outlook in the criminal justice system is particularly alarming. The portrayal by the mass media of crimes as being perpetrated by young black males has led to the creation of public policy from the national to the local level that reinforces the existing tough approach to crime, evidenced by such measures as "three strikes, you're out" and a "zero tolerance" stance. Political scientist Andrew Hacker writes in *Two Nations: Black and White, Separate, Hostile, Unequal* (1992) that "in virtually all spheres—offenders, victims, prisoners, and arrests by the police—the rates for black men and women account for 47.0 percent of the individuals awaiting trial in local jails or serving short terms there."[5] Of the 1.5 million people incarcerated in 1997, a disproportionate 46 percent were African American men.[6] Moreover, 40 percent of all prisoners on death row are black Americans, and one in three African American men are in prison, on parole, or on probation.[7] African Americans provide fodder for the burgeoning correctional-industrial complex in America, which has capitalized on the incarceration of young black males in particular. This is the sad result of the hegemony of white America over black America and the superordinate–subordinate power relationship that has existed between these two groups for almost 400 years.

The struggle for political representation by black Americans in this country has been an arduous task with victories and setbacks alike. As this nation moves into the twenty-first century, it remains to be seen whether or not black Americans will become full players in the power game of politics in America.

While government alone cannot solve many of the seemingly intractable problems in the black community, it can play a vital role. Public policies in the areas of equal employment opportunity, education, employment training, and health care can improve the employment opportunities and the well-being of millions. Government policy in these areas, however, has shifted over the years. It is ironic that at a time when the national government should be taking a more active role in implementing public policies to improve the quality of life for so many, our political leaders are drastically reducing the role of the federal government and devolving power to the states.

As a form of representative democracy, the American republic is dedicated to the principle that government should be responsive to the needs of all the people, not just certain populations within society. Why, then, are conditions so deplorable for so many black Americans? One key to government responsiveness to blacks is the representation of black interests by those formally in positions to make policy decisions.

HISTORY OF THE BLACK STRUGGLE FOR EQUALITY

When the Constitution of the United States was drafted in 1776, the majority of blacks in this country were enslaved. Under the institution of slavery, they were considered as chattel or property and had neither the right to vote nor the right to political representation. The Declaration of Independence, which was drafted by the Continental Congress in 1776, proclaimed that

> We hold these truths to be self-evident, that all men are created equal, that they are endowed by their Creator with certain unalienable Rights, that among these are Life, Liberty, and the pursuit of Happiness.

Obviously, there was an inconsistency between these lofty ideals and reality for the black person in America. The founding fathers (some of whom knew that slavery was morally wrong) were reluctant even to mention black Americans in the Constitution and to use the term "slave." Ironically, black Americans who were enslaved and had no political rights figured prominently in one of the major debates that occurred during the Constitutional Convention of the spring and summer of 1787. This debate was finally resolved by an agreement known as the Three-fifths Compromise, which stated that each slave would count as equal to three-fifths, or 60 percent, of a free white person in determining representation in the House of Representatives and in apportioning direct taxes. Article 1, Section 2, of the U.S. Constitution states, in part, that

> Representatives and direct taxes shall be apportioned among the several States which may be included within the Union, according to their respective numbers, which shall be determined by adding to the whole number of free persons, including those bound to service for a term of years and excluding Indians not taxed, three-fifths of all other persons.[8]

Two points are to be noted here. One is that enslaved black Americans were implicated at the center of the most contentious debate of the Constitutional Convention, a debate that dealt with none other than the question of representation in the U.S. House of Representatives. Second, the founding fathers, who sanctioned the institution of slavery, for one reason or another refrained from using the term anywhere in the Constitution. The term "slave" is sanitized by usage of the phrase "all other persons."

The Emancipation Proclamation issued by President Lincoln on January 1, 1863, outlawed the institution of slavery in the areas of the country under rebellion. Moreover, the Thirteenth Amendment to the Constitution, ratified in 1865, outlawed slavery and involuntary servitude anywhere else in the United States or in any place subject to its jurisdiction. One sad chapter of American history had finally come to a close. However, the "peculiar institution" has had an enduring legacy for both black and white Americans.

Not all black Americans were denied participation in the electoral process prior to the end of the Civil War. Blacks were participants in the political process in 10 of the original 13 states. Only Georgia, South Carolina, and Virginia originally denied free black men the right to vote. From 1792 until the Civil War, however, a number of states revised their constitutions and new states adopted constitutions to deny blacks suffrage. Consequently, by the start of the Civil War in 1861, blacks were denied the right to vote in 85 percent of the states.[9]

RADICAL RECONSTRUCTION

During the period known as Reconstruction, which began after the Civil War in 1865, black males were active participants in the electoral process in America. This was largely due to congressional passage of the Fourteenth Amendment in 1868 and the Fifteenth Amendment in 1870. These two amendments, along with the Thirteenth Amendment, were an attempt by the U.S. federal government to bestow the full rights and privileges of citizenship on all Americans. The Fourteenth Amendment granted citizenship rights to former enslaved Americans, and the Fifteenth Amendment gave former enslaved American males the right to vote.

In addition to these acts of the national government, the Reconstruction governments in the South were actively engaged in bestowing full citizenship privileges on black men. As historian John Hope Franklin writes in *From Slavery to Freedom* (1980):

> The state constitutions drawn up in 1867 and 1868 were the most progressive the South has ever known. Most of them abolished property qualifications for voting and holding office; some of them abolished imprisonment for debt. All of them abolished slavery, and several sought to eliminate race distinctions in the possession or inheritance of property.[10]

When Congress passed the Reconstruction Act of 1867, a little over 90 percent of the total black population in the United States resided in the South.[11] The states of Alabama, Florida, Louisiana, Mississippi, and South Carolina had majority black populations at this time. Black men voted in large numbers during the period of Reconstruction, and many blacks were elected to public office at all levels of government. They served in state legislatures, they became lieutenant governors, and one even became acting governor.[12] But perhaps the greatest political representation by blacks was achieved when blacks won election to the U.S. Congress.

The first black men were elected to the Congress in 1870. Between 1870 and 1901, 22 blacks were elected to the national legislature. Two of them were elected to the Senate and 20 were elected to the House of Representatives. Not surprisingly, they all were from the South, and, still owing their allegiance to the political party that emancipated them, they were all Republicans. It was not until 1929 that the first black was elected to the Congress from a non-southern state.

Carol Swain has noted that over 92 percent of the blacks elected to Congress during the period of Reconstruction were from majority black districts. Emphasizing a point made by V. O. Key in his classic work, *Southern Politics in State and Nation* (1949), Swain states that far fewer blacks were elected to Congress from the South than one would have expected given the size of the black populations in those states. Furthermore, three former slave states—Arkansas, Tennessee, and Texas—never elected a black to Congress during the period of Reconstruction.[13] Several of the first blacks elected to Congress were denied their seats by those objecting to black political power. According to Congressman William Clay, "Five of the first twenty blacks elected to the House [of Representatives] were denied their seats, and ten others had their terms interrupted or delayed."[14] Moreover, Clay noted that the charges against the newly elected blacks were "frivolous . . . [and] frequently fabricated, often having to do with alleged voting irregularities."[15]

Carol Swain argues that far more important than unity and political skill was the percentage of blacks within each electoral district. Black votes were diluted by concentrating blacks in a few districts. North Carolina's Second Congressional District, for example, was created by the Democrats in 1878 in order to neutralize the power of the state Republicans. According to historian Eric Anderson:

> In drawing borders that were friendly to their party, the Democrats created one extraordinary district they could never hope to carry, but a district in which thousands of Republican votes would be neutralized.[16]

This district included ten counties along the coastal plain of North Carolina. These counties were Warren, Northampton, Halifax,

Edgecombe, Wilson, Wayne, Lenoir, Craven, Greene, and Jones. Eric Anderson notes:

> According to the more reliable 1880 census, three of the counties were more than two-thirds black, and with the exception of Wayne and Wilson all had black majorities. Even the two "white" counties were more than 45 percent black. Indeed, more than one fifth of the total Negro population of North Carolina lived in the second district.[17]

The Second Congressional District was a Republican and black stronghold for the next 28 years—until the state disenfranchisement amendment of 1900. The four blacks that North Carolina elected to Congress during Reconstruction—John A. Hyman, James E. O'Hara, Henry P. Cheatham, and George H. White—all represented the Second Congressional District.

George H. White of North Carolina was the last black to sit in the U.S. Congress in the nineteenth century. In fact, when White was sworn in on March 15, 1897, he was the only black serving in the U.S. Congress. White managed to win reelection in 1898, but he chose not to run for reelection in 1900. It would be 28 years before the U.S. Congress seated another black American.

Reconstruction did not end or begin at one particular time. However, most scholars point to the Hayes-Tilden Compromise of 1876 as the catalyst for sounding the death knell for Reconstruction. Rutherford B. Hayes assumed the presidency after a controversial election against Samuel Tilden that was decided ultimately by a committee of 15 from the U.S. Senate, the U.S. House of Representatives, and the U.S. Supreme Court. Hayes withdrew federal troops from the South, allowing it to revert to its antebellum ways. The South began to deny blacks the political and social rights that they only recently had begun to enjoy. John Hope Franklin writes that "not even the Supreme Court postponed the overthrow of Radical Reconstruction. As a matter of fact, its decisions had the effect of hastening the end."[18]

Franklin was referring to a set of U.S. Supreme Court decisions that called into question the Fifteenth Amendment's guarantee to citizens of the right to vote. This was the beginning of a sweeping era of intimidation and violence in the South directed at black Americans by the Ku Klux Klan, the Jayhawkers,[19] and other white hate groups determined to gain back white supremacy, some of which they felt was lost during Reconstruction. It was an attempt to regain total control over blacks in the South.

When George H. White left his seat in Congress in 1901 as the lone black, he saw it as useless to remain in a legislative body as a representative of North Carolina when he no longer had the support of many of the white Republicans in his home state. The state had already passed a constitutional amendment disenfranchising black voters.[20] And the congressional district boundaries were redrawn in 1901 in order to destroy any opportunity for a black to get elected to Congress.

The *Raleigh News and Observer* summed up the pervasive racial climate in North Carolina. In a cartoon that appeared in 1900, Congressman White is depicted as some sort of monster with a human head, a long tail, and an elephant's trunk attached to a container representing the public till. The caption states: "He doesn't like to let go, but most people think our only negro congressman has had it about long enough."

George H. White found himself in an increasingly hostile environment in his final term in Congress. Maurine Christopher writes in *America's Black Congressmen* (1971) that in one speech given in response to a southern state's discourse on racial supremacy, White retorted:

> Yes, by force of circumstances, we are your inferiors. Give us 240 years the start of you, give us your labor for 240 years without compensation, give us the wealth that the brawny arm of the black man made for you, give us the education that his unpaid labor gave your boys and girls, and we will not be begging, we will not be in a position to be sneered at as aliens or members of an inferior race.[21]

White supremacists devised numerous legal and illegal tactics to deny blacks political and social equality. Tactics such as the grandfather clause, literacy tests, white primaries, racial gerrymandering, and poll taxes were used to deny blacks the right to vote. In 1896, in the landmark decision *Plessy v. Ferguson*,[22] the U.S. Supreme Court upheld the doctrine of "separate but equal," which legally segregated American society and effectively reduced black Americans to second-class citizens in all facets of American life. Reconstruction was a critical period in America: *It was the first real effort on the part of the American government to provide full social and political rights to black Americans.*

SECOND RECONSTRUCTION

Throughout the first half of the twentieth century, blacks and whites for the most part lived in separate worlds. From 1901 to 1928, there was not a single black elected to Congress from any congressional district in this nation. Amid its lack of representation, by 1928 the black population in the United States had risen to 11 million.

Oscar DePriest, a Republican, was the first black elected to Congress in the twentieth century. In 1928, he defeated a white incumbent and a black independent in a majority black district in Chicago, Illinois. Though DePriest had broken the color line in Congress for this century, it would be another 17 years before there was another black in Congress, and then two blacks would serve at the same time.[23] In 1945 Adam Clayton Powell, a Democrat, was elected from a majority black district in the New York borough of Manhattan. Nevertheless, it would be 27 years before the South would again elect a black American as a member of the country's largest representative body.

Jim Crow had an extended career during the first half of the twentieth century in the American South. The term "Jim Crow" is a pejorative that refers to the laws that required segregation of the races and supported the doctrine of white supremacy. Blacks and whites remained isolated from each other throughout World War I, the Great Depression, the New Deal, and World War II. Blacks fought in separate units in World War II against the superiority of Hitler's Aryan race, only to return home to fight oppression and degradation of the American system of racial apartheid.

But change was just over the horizon. In 1948, President Truman appointed a committee of blacks and whites to examine the problem of integration in the armed services and to make recommendations for their improvement. Based on the recommendations of the committee, the army adopted a hiring policy in 1949 that opened all jobs to qualified personnel irrespective of the color or race of the applicant.[24] The armed services served as a model for the rest of the nation as to how integration could be achieved in other segments of American society.

Only five years later, the U.S. Supreme Court struck down the doctrine of "separate but equal" in elementary and secondary public education in the landmark decision *Brown v. Board of Education* (1954).[25] The *Brown* decision marked a watershed in the dismantling of de jure racial discrimination in America. A decade later, Congress passed the Civil Rights Act of 1964. This act has been considered by many as the most comprehensive legislation outlawing racial discrimination in America.

In 1965, Congress passed the Voting Rights Act, and there was renewed hope in the black community that the doors to political empowerment for black Americans were finally open. The intense voter registration drives by civil rights workers in the South to register blacks, taken in conjunction with the Civil Rights Act of 1964, which outlawed segregation in all areas of public accommodations and employment, constituted the "Second Reconstruction." C. Vann Woodward coined the term "Second Reconstruction" to describe the period in America that began with the *Brown* decision in 1954,[26] when blacks began to match Reconstruction precedents concerning black representation in Congress.

THE CONGRESSIONAL BLACK CAUCUS

By 1966, there were only six black American members of Congress. They were William Dawson, Chicago (1943–1970); Adam Clayton Powell, Jr., New York (1945–1967, 1969–1971); Charles C. Diggs, Detroit (1955–1980); Robert Nix, Philadelphia (1958–1979); Augustus Hawkins, Los Angeles (1963–1991), and John Conyers, Jr., Detroit (1965–present). By 1969, three more blacks joined the Congress: Louis Stokes, Cleveland (1969–1999); William Clay, St. Louis (1969–present); and Shirley Chisholm, New York City (1969–1983), the first black woman to serve in Congress. Nine blacks were serving in the U.S. Congress—an unprecedented number. Previously, the largest contingent of blacks that served in the Congress at the same time was in 1875, when seven blacks held seats in the U.S. House of Representatives.

All seven of the black Americans who served in the U.S. House of Representatives in 1875 represented districts from the South and were Republicans. The nine blacks serving in the U.S. Congress in 1969 were all from Northern or border states and were all Democrats.[27]

By 1971, the black membership in Congress had risen to 13 members. That year the black members of the House of Representatives formed the Congressional Black Caucus (CBC). The CBC was created partially as a response to the conservative attack on the Great Society programs of the 1960s. In his book *Just Permanent Interests* (1992), Congressman William Clay, one of the founders of the CBC, writes: "Blacks benefited tremendously from these government programs, and what the new administration offered as replacement was more ideological than substantive."[28] The CBC has always considered itself as having a national black constituency. Its members adopted as their motto: "Black people have no permanent friends, no permanent enemies . . . just permanent interests."[29]

The CBC gained national attention from its inception, when Congressman Charles Diggs made a formal request to the White House that

Republican President Richard Nixon meet with them because of their growing alarm concerning the state of black America. Nixon flatly refused. Addressing the House of Representatives, Congressman William Clay stated that the CBC wanted to meet with President Nixon for the following reasons:

> To make known at this time our outright disgust with the president's policies and his refusal to give us an audience . . . there is no doubt where Mr. Nixon has placed his priorities . . . He has travelled more than 35,000 miles in foreign countries. He has entertained hundreds of foreign dignitaries but refuses to meet with elected representatives of the Black "nation" within this country.[30]

Approximately three months later, on March 25, 1971, Nixon finally met with the CBC.

As the CBC grew in membership, so did its influence. By 1973, 16 blacks held seats in the U.S. Congress. They included four women and one U.S. senator, Edward Brooke, a Republican from Massachusetts (1967–1979). In November 1972 the South had elected its first blacks to Congress in this century. Barbara Jordan, a Democrat, represented Texas (1973–1979), and Andrew Young, a Democrat, represented Georgia (1973–1977).

The number of blacks in Congress reached an all-time high of 41 members in 1994. In 1999, there are 39 members serving in the U.S. House of Representatives. No blacks are currently serving in the U.S. Senate. The CBC presently has a total of 38 members. (J. C. Watts, a black Republican from Oklahoma, was first elected in 1994 but has declined membership in the CBC.) Its increasing size is matched by increasing diversity. No longer is the CBC the monolithic voice of 1971 that requested that the president of the United States allow it a forum from which to express its concerns. Presently, CBC members are diverse in age, background, occupation, gender, political experience, and the constituencies that they represent. When President Nixon refused to meet with the CBC in 1971, all of its members represented metropolitan areas across America—cities with the same set of urban problems. By 1992, the black members elected to Congress were no longer being elected exclusively from urban areas in the North, Midwest, and West. Increasingly, black congresspeople are representing districts that are rural and southern.

Furthermore, not only has the geographical nature of their districts changed, but the racial composition has changed dramatically. No longer are black congresspeople elected solely from heavily black majority districts; many are increasingly elected from districts with only a slight black majority, and some represent majority white districts.

For example, Gary Franks, a black Republican member of the U.S. House of Representatives from Waterbury, Connecticut, represented a district that was 96 percent white. When he was first elected to his seat in 1990, he was the first black Republican in the U.S. House of Representatives in 56 years. Franks was reelected for two more terms but failed to win reelection in 1996. Alan Wheat, a black Democratic member of the U.S. House of Representatives from Kansas City, Missouri, represented a district that was 71.1 percent white. Wheat held that seat from 1982 until 1994, when he ran for an open U.S. Senate seat from Missouri. In 1994, J. C. Watts became only the third black Republican elected to the U.S. House this century when he won election from the Fourth District of Oklahoma, which has an 83 percent white population. In 1996, Julia Carson was elected from the Tenth Congressional District of Indiana, which has a 69 percent white population. Today, the CBC has expanded its membership to include not only the black members currently serving in Congress, but also nonblack associate members.

The creation of majority-minority districts has helped increase the representation of African Americans at the congressional level. The CBC, although representing a more diverse constituency than ever, still serves to protect the interests of black Americans. With the increase of CBC members to 38, it has established itself as a formidable caucus now able to form coalitions with other informal groups in Congress. The CBC can help pass legislation critical to the black community: housing, education, unemployment, and crime. Furthermore, although the Republicans became the majority party in both houses of Congress in 1994, the CBC has shown its political mettle in persuading President Clinton to continue to adopt policies favorable to the African American community.

The increase in the number of blacks serving in Congress is the result of a variety of factors. The migration of black America has played a critical role in shaping the political landscape of America. Much of the out-migration of blacks after the Civil War was from the South to the cities of the Northeast. Gradually, this out-migration occurred from the South to the north-central and later to the western states. In *Blacks in the United States: A Geographic Perspective* (1975), George Davis observes:

> At the end of the Civil War just over 90 percent of the total black population remained in the South, much as it had since 1790. This proportion dropped slowly at first and decreased dramatically later. Until 1920 the

South still contained virtually nine out of ten of the black people in this country.[31]

By 1970, however, 19 percent of blacks lived in the Northeast, 20 percent in the Midwest, and 8 percent in the West.[32] Much of this out-migration was fueled by economic opportunity in factories in the cities of the Northeast and Midwest, coupled with the wretched social climate for blacks in the South and the low pay of tenant farming. Moreover, advances in technology lessened the need for labor-intensive crop cultivation.

Much of the out-migration of blacks from the South, which began at a gradual pace in the 1860s, had increased so significantly by 1915 that it was referred to as the "great migration." Davis writes:

> It was this great migration that marked a significant change in the distribution of Blacks in the United States. Most, if not all, of this increase in the northern, urban black population originated in the rural areas of the South.[33]

As a result of the out-migration from the South by blacks and in-migration to the Northeast and Midwest, in addition to legal residential segregation patterns in the urban cities of these regions, blacks became concentrated in many inner cities throughout America in areas referred to as "ghettos." However, although blacks still faced discrimination outside the South, they now had the right to vote. The increase in black numbers and political power became apparent when the first blacks elected to the U.S. Congress this century were elected from majority black congressional districts in the Northeast and Midwest regions of the country: inner-city areas that had a large enough majority black concentration to constitute a single congressional district. Black congressional representation in the South today, for the most part, has been the result of the Voting Rights Act of 1965 and subsequent congressional legislation and court decisions involving redistricting and reapportionment (see Chapter 5).[34]

REPRESENTATION THEORY

The desire for black electoral success is grounded in representation theory. Much of the discussion about representation theory has involved descriptive and substantive representation. On the topic of descriptive representation, Carol Swain writes that there is "an assumption that someone of the same race, gender, or religion will be more sensitive to the needs and concerns of members of their categorical group."[35] Various scholars have argued the merits of descriptive representation versus substantive representation—the degree to which a representative is able to understand the needs and wishes of his constituency and to act in the interest of those constituents, regardless of racial, gender, or religious similarity (see Pitkin, 1967; Swain, 1995; Clayton, 1995; Lublin, 1997; Whitby, 1997).

However, because blacks and other minorities traditionally have been excluded from political representation in America, many blacks feel that any representation is better than no representation. Clarence Thomas provides a case in point. Although major civil rights groups opposed Thomas's nomination by President George Bush to the Supreme Court in 1991 (most notably the National Association for the Advancement of Colored People), the National Urban League decided to remain neutral—neither to oppose nor advocate Thomas. Thomas's nomination left blacks with the dilemma of whether to support him; although his judicial philosophy was inconsistent with the views of many civil rights organizations, if Thomas were not confirmed to the Supreme Court, then there would be no black representation on the Court. In *Blacks and American Government* (1991), political scientists J. Owens Smith, Mitchell Rice, and Woodrow Jones, Jr., point to the inherent good or the independent and symbolic value of descriptive black representation. Moreover, they assert that black representation can increase overall support for government by these groups:

> A few blacks and other minorities placed in positions in government is for some in society of the same race and background [the affirmation] that government is representative of their interests.[36]

THE URBAN UNDERCLASS

Historically and contemporaneously, blacks and whites in America have lived in two totally separate worlds. As black Americans continually left the South after the Civil War and migrated to the inner cities of the Northeast, Midwest, and West in search of economic opportunity—especially following the "dramatic 'great migration' of 1915"—whites who were living in the cities began moving into other neighborhoods within the cities.[37] As black migration to the cities increased, whites began fleeing to the urban rim or the suburbs. Segregated residential housing patterns restricted the movement of blacks to limited areas in the central cities, and often they were confined to ghettos (see Davis & Donaldson, 1975). Many of the largest cities in America still reflect this movement in their substantial black populations. The national housing policies of the U.S. government made sure that public housing projects would be confined to the inner cities and not allowed in the suburbs (see Lowi, 1979). The majority of black and white Americans live in metropolitan areas today; however, they do not live in the same communities.[38] White flight to the suburbs continued at a steady pace, and in 1970, for the first time in American history, the majority of urban dwellers lived outside the central cities. Moreover, as jobs were increasingly located in the suburbs, many inner-city blacks remained trapped in the inner cities miles from these jobs.

William Julius Wilson, a sociologist, and Cornel West, a theologian, have written about an ever-increasing segment of urban black Americans—the underclass who are unemployed and no longer seeking employment. This group has become so substantial that the Bureau of Labor Statistics has created a category called "discouraged workers," who are not counted as part of the unemployed in the official unemployment statistics. West refers to this condition of hopelessness among many blacks in urban America as nihilism, for many of them have grown fatalistic and feel as though their condition in society is immutable.

A government loses its legitimacy among individuals who feel that they are powerless in society. These individuals often cease to be law-abiding citizens, engaging in lawless behavior. Moreover, the value of life is lessened for them—both their own and anyone else's. This is, in fact, a condition that exists across urban America today. West writes in *Race Matters* (1993):

> The exodus of stable industrial jobs from urban centers to cheaper labor markets here and abroad, housing policies that have created "chocolate cities and vanilla suburbs" . . . white fear of black crime . . . all have helped erode the tax base of American cities just as the federal government has cut its supports and programs. The result is unemployment, hunger, homelessness, and sickness for millions.[39]

CONSERVATIVE OPPOSITION TO RACE-BASED DISTRICTING

Many scholars have felt that race-conscious districting and other remedies such as voting rights legislation would lead to increased participation by and representation of minority communities, which in turn would lead to increased legitimacy of the system. However, not everyone has supported this line of thinking. One such critic, conservative scholar Abigail Thernstrom, has long been an opponent of the interpretation of the Voting Rights Act of 1965. In *Whose Votes Count?* (1987), she writes that the civil rights leaders of the day laid out an argument that Congress was persuaded to buy. According to Thernstrom, "We are racially gerrymandering the whole country, on the assumption that the law requires the maximum number of safe black and Hispanic districts."[40]

Thernstrom admits that federal intervention was needed to enfranchise southern blacks amid a hostile environment, and she contends that the Voting Rights Act has accomplished just what it was meant to do—enfranchise blacks. According to Thernstrom, what has been substituted is "a standard of proportional representation that can only lead to a covert system of reserved seats."[41] Thernstrom and other critics of race-based legislative districts have struck a nerve with middle-class, white America. Many view race-based districts as granting a special privilege to blacks and other minorities.

Political scientist Bruce Cain sums up this position quite effectively when he states that

> Abigail Thernstrom and other critics did not object to the initial applications of the Voting Rights Act when the purpose was to vote *per se.* After all, that was a right the majority already enjoyed. Rather what disturbs them is the . . . right of blacks . . . to an undiluted vote, but that is not a right . . . the [Supreme] Court, had recognized or protected for other political groups and individuals . . . In short, critics believe racial and ethnic minorities are getting a special new right, thereby violating the second principle of democracy, political equality.[42]

An example of rising opposition to race-conscious remedies in the voting rights arena was President Clinton's nomination in early 1993 of law professor Lani Guinier as Assistant Attorney General of the Civil Rights Division, which enforces the Voting Rights Act. Clinton withdrew her nomination several months later after a rising conservative tide of opposition that believed Guinier to be the advocate of a racial spoils system. The opening shot was fired by Clint Bolick, a conservative activist who labeled Guinier as a proponent of a racial quota system. The headline that appeared in the *Wall Street Journal* on April 30, 1993, read, "Clinton's Quota Queen." In his article, Bolick stated the following about Guinier:

She demands equal legislative outcomes, requiring abandonment not
only of the "one person, one vote" principle, but majority rule itself.[43]

Robert Dole, then Minority Leader of the U.S. Senate, sardonically
quipped:

If nothing else, Ms. Guinier has been consistent in her writings—consistently hostile to the principle of one person, one vote; consistently
hostile to majority rule; and a consistent supporter, not only of quotas,
but of vote-rigging schemes that make quotas look mild.[44]

However, some defended Guinier and her writings. Law professor
Stephen Carter wrote in the foreword of Guinier's book, *The Tyranny of
the Majority* (1994), that

when groups identify collective interests and vote them, elections become winner-take-all. Minorities—whether defined by race or geography or income or what have you—wind up losers. This is not Lani
Guinier's discovery, nor is it what she advocates. But she recognizes
the problem and wants to do something about it. The obsession of her
scholarship therefore turns out to be precisely the reverse of what her
critics ascribe to her. She believes in democracy and opposes the democratic spoils system.[45]

Much of the underlying criticism directed at Guinier was simply because her writings on representation deal directly with race. Critics attacked her as a proponent of proportional representation. In fact, Guinier
has been a critic of proportional representation. She discusses shortcomings of proportional representation, particularly its failure to realize the
potential of political equality.[46]

According to Guinier, proportional descriptive representation does
not in and of itself guarantee political equality. Guinier's concern is that
more representation is not "necessarily more responsive government."[47]
Guinier states that she can understand the need for race-conscious districting. She argues that in a society as deeply cleaved by issues of racial
identity as ours, there is no one race. Moreover, in the presence of such
racial differences, a system of representation that fails to provide group
representation loses legitimacy.[48] Furthermore, notes Guinier, the representation of groups or individuals is not well achieved by the winner-take-all system. She writes that "winner-take-all territorial districting

imperfectly distributes representation based on group attributes and disproportionately rewards those who win the representational lottery."[49] For example, Candidate A receives 51 percent of the vote, while Candidate B receives 49 percent. Under the winner-take-all single member district, Candidate A's supporters receive all the power, whereas Candidate B's supporters and other disaffected voters have essentially wasted their votes.

Guinier has explored alternatives to winner-take-all redistricting. One such alternative, cumulative voting, is a modification of the current winner-take-all, at-large voting system.[50] Guinier argues that there is nothing antidemocratic or un-American in this proposal. She asserts, moreover, that it is consistent with the doctrine of one person, one vote. Guinier exclaims that "my focus is not on guaranteed equal results, but on an equal opportunity to influence those results."[51]

CONCLUSION

African Americans, shut out of the political process for most of the twentieth century, have had to find ways in which they could exert influence on the American political process to affect political and social change. During this period, democracy lost much of its legitimacy for that segment of society. Representation is at the core of democracy. Descriptive representation, although not guaranteeing substantive representation, still has symbolic value. Increased representation of African Americans at all levels of government, brought about by race-conscious remedies, has made democracy more inclusive and at the same time has restored faith in the democratic process.

Eva Clayton, an African American congresswoman from North Carolina, emphasized the importance of increased black electoral representation:

> We have seen over the past several years increased diversity of the city councils, boards of county commissioners, State legislatures, judicial appointments and the Congress as a direct result of district representation. This increased representation by blacks and other ethnic minorities has strengthened the true meaning of representative government. Because of this, we have witnessed an active increase in government at all levels. People are viewing government not as an abstract, unrelated entity but as an institution that is responsive and sensitive to the needs of people. There is an increased desire to want to serve and be a part of the

democratic process. All of this is happening because of the renewed hope in government caused by a more representative government of the people.[52]

NOTES

[1]"Total Money Income in 1996 of Persons 25 Years Old and Over, by Educational Attainment, Sex, Region, and Race (Persons as of March 1997)," United States Department of Commerce, Bureau of the Census <http://www.census.gov/population/socdemo/race/black/tabs97/tab09B.txt>. July 30, 1998.

[2]Leslie Scanlon, "Jobs, Money, Education Divide Americans," *Louisville Courier-Journal*, June 11, 1997: 15A.

[3]Sheryl Gay Stolberg, "U.S. Life Expectancy Hits New High," National Center for Policy online <http://www.public.policy.org>. September 19, 1998.

[4]Centers for Disease Control and Prevention. *HIV/AIDS Surveillance Report*, 1996; vol. 8, No. 2: 1–40.

[5]Andrew Hacker, *Two Nations: Black and White, Separate, Hostile, Unequal* (New York: Macmillan Publishing Co., 1992) 180.

[6]Joe Davidson, "Caged Cargo," *Emerge*, October 1997: 36–46.

[7]Michael Fletcher. "Kerner Prophecy on Race Relations Came True, Report Says," *Washington Post* online edition <http://www.washingtonpost.com>. March 1, 1998.

[8]Article 1, Section 2, paragraph 3, United States Constitution.

[9]William L. Clay, *Just Permanent Interests: Black Americans in Congress, 1870–1991* (New York: Amistad Press, 1992) 10.

[10]John Hope Franklin, *From Slavery to Freedom: A History of Negro Americans,* 5th ed. (New York: Knopf, 1980) 217.

[11]George A. Davis, *Blacks in the United States: A Geographic Perspective* (Boston: Houghton Mifflin, 1975) 30.

[12]Franklin, *From Slavery to Freedom*, 218.

[13]Carol Swain, *Black Faces, Black Interests: The Representation of African Americans in Congress* (Cambridge: Harvard University Press, 1993) 23.

[14]Clay, *Just Permanent Interests,* 23.

[15]Clay 23.

[16]Eric Anderson, *Race and Politics in North Carolina: 1872–1901* (Baton Rouge: Louisiana State University Press, 1981) 4.

[17]Anderson 4.

[18]Franklin, *From Slavery to Freedom,* 230.

[19]Franklin 226.

[20]Anderson, *Race and Politics in North Carolina*, 310.

[21]Maurine Christopher, *America's Black Congressmen* (New York: Cromwell, 1971) 164.

[22]*Plessy v. Ferguson*, 163 U.S. 537 (1896).

[23]Clay, *Just Permanent Interests*, 53.

[24]Franklin, *From Slavery to Freedom*, 412.

[25]*Brown v. Board of Education*, 347 U.S. 483 (1954).

[26]C. Vann Woodward, *The Strange Career of Jim Crow*, 3rd. ed. (New York: Oxford University Press, 1966) 122–147.

[27]Clay, *Just Permanent Interests*, 108.

[28]Clay 126.

[29]Clay ix.

[30]Clay 140.

[31]Davis, *Blacks in the United States*, 30.

[32]William P. O'Hare et al., *African Americans in the 1990s* (Washington, D.C.: Population Reference Bureau, Inc., 1991) 7.

[33]Davis, *Blacks in the United States*, 31.

[34]Swain, *Black Faces, Black Interests*, 36.

[35]Swain 11.

[36]J. Owens Smith, Mitchell Rice, and Woodrow Jones, Jr., *Blacks and American Government* (Dubuque, Iowa: Kendall Hunt, 1991) 128.

[37]George A. Davis and O. Fred Donaldson, *Blacks in the United States: A Geographic Perspective* (Boston: Houghton Mifflin Company, 1975) 31.

[38]William P. O'Hare et al., *African Americans in the 1990s* (Washington, D.C.: Population Reference Bureau, 1997) 8.

[39]Cornel West, *Race Matters* (Boston: Beacon Press, 1993) 5.

[40]Robert Pear, "Under the Voting Law, Citizens' Rights Get More Than Lip Service," *New York Times*, July 21, 1991: E4.

[41]Quoted in Bernard Grofman and Chandler Davidson, "What Is the Best Route to a Color-Blind Society?" *Controversies in Minority Voting*, ed. Bernard Grofman and Chandler Davidson (Washington, D.C.: Brookings Institution, 1992) 305.

[42]Bruce Cain, "Voting Rights and Democratic Theory: Toward a Color-Blind Society?" *Controversies in Minority Voting*, ed. Bernard Grofman and Chandler Davidson (Washington, D.C.: Brookings Institution, 1992) 268.

[43]Quoted in Stephen Carter, Foreword, *The Tyranny of the Majority*, by C. Lani Guinier (New York: Free Press, 1994) ix.

[44]Quoted in Stephen Carter, Foreword, ix.

[45]Stephen Carter, Foreword, ix.

[46]C. Lani Guinier, "Voting Rights and Democratic Theory: Where Do We Go From Here?" *Controversies in Minority Voting*, ed. Bernard Grofman and Chandler Davidson (Washington, D.C.: Brookings Institution, 1992) 286.

[47]C. Lani Guinier, "Voting Rights and Democratic Theory," 287.

[48]Guinier, *The Tyranny of the Majority* (New York: Free Press, 1994) 121.

[49]Guinier 121.

[50]Guinier 95.

[51]Guinier, "Who's Afraid of Lani Guinier?" *New York Times Magazine*, February 27, 1994: 54.

[52]United States, Congressional Record, "1965 Voting Rights Act Under Attack," 103rd Cong., 2nd Sess., March 22, 1994: H1876.

CHAPTER 3

Pander, Slander, Gerrymander

The redistricting process that unfolded in each southern state in the early 1990s was characterized by its own unique set of political machinations. However, there were similarities common to states throughout the South. With the exception of Tennessee and Arkansas, the remaining nine states in the region were covered by the Voting Rights Act of 1965, in whole or in part. In addition, 112 congressional seats were up for grabs in these states for the 1992 congressional elections. These "covered" states (see Chapter 5) were required by the U.S. Department of Justice to create majority-minority congressional districts where possible. Despite having a sizable black population, many of these states had not sent a black to Congress in the twentieth century.

Congressional redistricting is traditionally under the authority of state legislatures, and Democrats were the majority party in every southern state legislature in the early 1990s. Therefore, white Democrats, as usual, controlled the redistricting process. However, for this round of redistricting, a unique coalition formed in some of the state legislatures around the South: Republicans and black Democrats joined forces for the purpose of creating majority black districts. White Democrats wanted to draw district lines to protect congressional Democratic incumbents, and black Democrats wanted to create majority black districts to increase the chances of blacks being elected to Congress. Republicans, outnumbered, saw that their only opportunity to gain congressional seats was to ally themselves with blacks in support of the creation of majority black districts. They reasoned that by creating new majority black districts, black voters would be removed from existing Democratic districts, which would leave the remaining Democratic incumbents vulnerable because the districts would be more white and more Republican-leaning.

The redistricting process that occurred throughout the South in the 1990s presents an interesting study in general of how state legislators make decisions within the institutional restrictions placed on them by the U.S. Justice Department and the policy outputs that result from those decisions. North Carolina presents an ideal case study in particular because it is representative of the political jousting occurring in state legislatures throughout the South.

North Carolina was the 12th of the original 13 states to ratify the U.S. Constitution. It did so on November 21, 1789. The state sent 5 representatives to the first Congress in 1789. Those 5 congressmen were chosen from districts created by the state legislature. The number of the state's congressional delegation in the ensuing years has fluctuated from as low as 0 to as high as 13. During the Civil War period, North Carolina sent no representatives to the U.S. Congress. However, it did send 10 representatives to the Confederate Congress as part of the Confederate States of America from 1861 to 1865. For three decades, from 1812 to 1843, it sent 13 representatives to the United States Congress.

North Carolina has always chosen its congressional delegation from single-member districts. It was not until 1967 that Congress outlawed the use of multimember congressional districts in all states entitled to two or more members of Congress.

THE CENSUS AND REAPPORTIONMENT

The number of congressional seats each state is accorded is determined by the population of each state. The U.S. Constitution provided for a count of the population "within three years after the first meeting of the Congress of the United States, and within every subsequent term of ten years." The first census was taken in 1790. After each decennial census, the Census Bureau determines the number of representatives to which each state is entitled. States that have increased their population significantly over the previous 10-year period gain a congressional seat, and states that have a substantially smaller population than that of 10 years earlier lose a congressional seat. The remaining states retain the same number of House seats that they previously held. This process is undertaken to account for immigration and population shifts that have occurred throughout the country during the previous 10 years.

Since 1941, the number of seats in the U.S. House of Representatives has been set at 435. Reapportionment is the process of allocating or apportioning those 435 seats in the U.S. House of Representatives among the 50 states. Each state receives its number of representatives based on a complex formula utilized by the Census Bureau after it determines the total population of the nation. It divides that number by 435 to determine the average congressional district size. From there, the congressional delegations are determined based on how many districts of the average size could be apportioned to a state. For example, in 1990, the Census Bureau determined that the total population in this country was 249,022,783, an increase of roughly 10 percent over the previous count. The average figure used for reapportionment for 1990 is roughly 572,466 (249,022,783 divided by 435 roughly equals 572,466).

North Carolina's population grew from 5,881,766 in 1980 to 6,657,630 in 1990. Because its population increased by nearly 800,000, North Carolina became eligible for a one-seat gain in the U.S. Congress. Although the average population of each of the 11 congressional districts in North Carolina was 534,706 in 1981, the average population of each of the 12 districts in 1991 had increased to 552,386. North Carolina's increase in population reflects a continuing trend in demographics around the country: There has been a consistent population movement from states in the Northeast and Midwest (snowbelt) to states in the South and West (sunbelt).

This population shift is reflected in the reapportionment process conducted by the Bureau of the Census in 1990. As a result of the 1990 census, a total of 19 seats were shifted in the U.S. House of Representatives. Eight states gained representation for the 103rd Congress that convened in January 1993. All of these states were located in the South or the West. California had the largest increase, with a gain of seven seats. Florida followed with a gain of four seats. Texas gained three seats, and Arizona, Georgia, North Carolina, Virginia, and Washington each gained one seat.

Conversely, those states that lost representation were for the most part in the Northeast and Midwest. Thirteen states lost at least one seat in their congressional delegation. New York lost three seats, and Illinois, Michigan, Ohio, and Pennsylvania each lost two seats. Eight states lost only one seat; they were Iowa, Kansas, Kentucky, Louisiana, Massachusetts, Montana, New Jersey, and West Virginia.[1]

The U.S. Census Bureau must furnish the results of the census by April 1 of the year following the census so that each state may begin the redistricting process.[2] Each state must redraw its congressional districts based on whether it gained or lost seats during the reapportionment process. Each individual state determines the procedures and guidelines for its redistricting process.

FEDERAL AND STATE REDISTRICTING REQUIREMENTS

In North Carolina, redistricting is a duty of the state legislature. This body, also known as the General Assembly, is a bicameral legislature. The General Assembly must follow federal and state guidelines in carrying out its congressional redistricting. It has been over 30 years since the U.S. Supreme Court handed down its ruling in the landmark case *Baker v. Carr* (1962).[3] In this case involving the Tennessee state legislature, the U.S. Supreme Court ruled that legislative redistricting (and, by implication, congressional redistricting) was within its scope of jurisdiction under the Equal Protection Clause of the Fourteenth Amendment to the U.S. Constitution.

For many years, the Supreme Court had refused to hear redistricting cases, relying on the precedent established in *Colegrove v. Green* (1946).[4] In that case, the Supreme Court had taken the position that disparities that arose concerning redistricting were political questions and, therefore, should be resolved by the political branches of government (legislative and executive), not the judicial branch.

However, egregious population disparities between urban and rural districts drawn by state legislators caused an activist Supreme Court to make redistricting ripe for judicial scrutiny. Article 1, Section 2, of the U.S. Constitution states that "Representatives . . . shall be apportioned among the several States which may be included within this Union, according to their respective numbers" and be "chosen by the people of the several states."

The U.S. Supreme Court has interpreted this language to mean that congressional districts within a state are to be drawn as nearly equal as possible. The decision handed down in *Wesberry v. Sanders* (1964) held that "as nearly as is practicable, one person's vote in a congressional election is to be worth as much as another's."[5] In *Wesberry,* the Supreme Court declared unconstitutional a Georgia congressional district map that had not been revised since 1931 and had a population disparity of 550,000 between the most populated and least populated districts. By requiring that the congressional districts within each state have approximately the same number of citizens, the Supreme Court in *Wesberry* was eliminating severe vote dilution.

The principle of one person, one vote is a fundamental tenet of political equality in this country. It has its roots in the U.S. Constitution's congressional reapportionment clause. It is also because of this clause that the population equality standard for congressional districts is much

Table 3.1. North Carolina Congressional Districts, 1992 (Average Population: 552,386)

District	Incumbent	Population
1	Eva Clayton (D)	552,386
2	Tim Valentine (D)	552,386
3	Martin Lancaster (D)	552,387
4	David Price (D)	552,387
5	Stephen Neal (D)	552,386
6	Howard Coble (R)	552,386
7	Charlie Rose (D)	552,386
8	W.G. Hefner (D)	552,387
9	Alex McMillan (R)	552,387
10	Cass Ballenger (R)	552,386
11	Charles Taylor (R)	552,387
12	Melvin Watt (D)	552,386

Source: Compiled from data from the North Carolina General Assembly, Information Systems Division, and North Carolina State Board of Elections, 1992.

stricter than for other legislative bodies. Table 3.1 shows the 1992 election results, the population size of each of the 12 districts, and the average population of each district after the 1990 census.

VOTING RIGHTS ACT OF 1965

Two other federal guidelines for redistricting center around the Voting Rights Act (VRA) of 1965, extended in 1970, 1975, and 1982 for 25 years (until 2007), and partisan gerrymandering. The history of the Voting Rights Act has been remarkable. It has done more than guarantee minorities the right to vote. It also prohibits subtle tactics of governing bodies used to dilute the voting potential of black communities. Most recently, the 1982 amendments to the Voting Rights Act prohibit redistricting plans from diluting minority voting strength. These amendments were passed by Congress in response to a landmark U.S. Supreme Court case. In *City of Mobile v. Bolden* (1980),[6] the U.S. Supreme Court ruled that it was not enough for minorities to prove that a districting plan had a discriminatory effect, unless there was evidence that it was created with discriminatory intent as well. Congress, angered that its intent had been circumvented, passed a 1982 amendment to the Voting Rights Act stating that any districting practice that had the effect of discriminating against minorities—regardless of intent—was unconstitutional.

Once the Voting Rights Act was passed by Congress in 1965, many public officials, particularly in southern states, changed their tactics from those that denied minorities access to the ballot box to those that diluted the minority vote. Minority vote dilution may occur in a variety of ways, most notably through the processes of stacking, cracking, and packing voting districts.[7]

- Stacking occurs when heavily concentrated minority districts or concentrations of minority populations, large enough for separate representation, are combined with majority districts or population concentrations.
- Cracking occurs when a substantial minority population, large enough to constitute one or more majority-minority districts, is divided among several majority districts, which effectively dilutes minority voting strength.
- Packing is the practice of drawing district lines so as to create districts that are 70, 80, or 90 percent minority. This procedure wastes minority votes that could have either created another minority district or strongly influenced a majority district.[8]

A redistricting plan is deemed unconstitutional if it dilutes minority voting strength. Under Section 5 of the Voting Rights Act, the state of North Carolina must bear the burden of proof that its congressional plan has neither the intent nor the effect of diluting minority voting strength in the 40 counties of the state that are subject to Section 5 preclearance requirements.

Section 2 of the Voting Rights Act, amended by Congress in 1982, places the responsibility on the plaintiff to prove only that a redistricting plan has the effect of diluting minority voting strength. Prior to 1982, the plaintiff had to prove discriminatory intent in a redistricting plan. Unlike Section 5, which only applies to selected states in whole and parts of others, Section 2 applies to all states.

Partisan gerrymandering is another guideline that states must abide by when redistricting. The term "gerrymander" was coined after Elbridge Gerry, an early governor of Massachusetts, sought to protect his political party by drafting an election district that was said to resemble a salamander because of its winding shape. The term now refers to the drawing of a legislative district to give unfair advantage to one group or another in elections. The Supreme Court has stated explicitly that redistricting plans may be challenged in a court of law for discriminating against political parties.

In *Davis v. Bandemer* (1986),[9] the U.S. Supreme Court held that

> claims of political gerrymandering were justifiable in federal court . . . A plurality of the court ruled that the Democrats challenging the plan had not proven "a sufficiently adverse effect" to demonstrate that they had been "unconstitutionally denied [their] chance to effectively influence the political process."[10]

A political party must prove that the other party intended to discriminate and that the plan resulted in actual discrimination. The courts have yet to provide guidance as to how to measure intent. The irony here is that the federal courts have always looked on redistricting as a highly partisan affair. It was not until the early 1960s that the federal courts determined that disputes of this nature were ripe for judicial intervention. Today, the federal courts have clearly indicated that partisan gerrymandering is within the scope of their jurisdiction.

Historically, the state of North Carolina has attempted to observe the traditional notions of contiguity of territory and compactness of districts. A congressional district is generally considered to be contiguous if all of the counties within are touching one another. However, according to the state constitution, congressional districts are not explicitly required to contain contiguous districts.[11]

On the issue of compactness of districts, neither the North Carolina state constitution nor the U.S. Constitution mandates that congressional districts be compact. The lack of compactness is often cited by critics as an indication of political gerrymandering, but the federal courts have yet to strike down a redistricting plan simply because of the irregularity of its shape. There are several geometric standards for measuring compactness (see Chapter 7); however, these have never become judicial standards.

It should be noted that for state legislatures to create congressional districts that are approximately equal in population, compact, and contiguous, the integrity of county divisions is violated more often than not. Moreover, in North Carolina, the county lines that have been used as the boundaries for district lines are increasingly being split into more than one district. North Carolina's state constitution does not expressly forbid dividing counties in congressional redistricting. However, the state legislature attempts to avoid doing so when feasible. Other factors that the state legislature takes into consideration but are not requirements under law are district homogeneity and cohesiveness. These factors may be identified through such means as transportation patterns, mass communication (newspaper, television, telephone) coverage areas, and historical ties. All lend themselves to a sense of community.

NORTH CAROLINA REDISTRICTING IN THE 1990s

Long before the president pro tempore of the North Carolina Senate appointed the Senate Redistricting Committee and the Speaker of the House of Representatives appointed two House committees on redistricting in the General Assembly in 1991, there was speculation that due to population growth, North Carolina would likely gain a seat in Congress. Even before the final census figures were released by the Census Bureau, black state legislators had discussed the idea that this new seat could be occupied by the state's first black congressional representative since 1901.

Representative H. M. "Mickey" Michaux (Democrat), dean of the black state legislators in North Carolina, quipped in 1990:

Although redistricting won't begin until next summer, there is a move afoot to create a new congressional district or adjust an existing one to better concentrate black voters.[12]

The black population of the state was 1,456,323, 22 percent of the population, in 1990. That was an increase of 137,269, from 1,319,054 in 1980. However, of the 11 congressional districts in the state that were created after the 1981 redistricting process, only two districts had more than a 30 percent black population: the First District, 35 percent; and the Second District, 40 percent. In none of those districts was the total of black registered voters higher than 30 percent. Rep. Michaux remarked in 1990 that "some legislators want to create at least one district with 40 percent black registered voters."[13]

Michaux and other black legislators in North Carolina who wanted at least a black influence district would receive support in their efforts to that end from an unlikely entity: the U.S. Justice Department under the Republican administration of George Bush.

Table 3.2. Black Population of North Carolina Congressional Districts, 1981

District	Black Population	Percent Black
1	187,676	35.2
2	214,484	40.1
3	144,694	27.3
4	106,716	19.9
5	85,633	16.2
6	105,927	20.7
7	145,544	27.3
8	107,105	20.1
9	123,354	23.3
10	532,954	10.6
11	265,572	5.5

Source: Compiled from data from the North Carolina General Assembly, Information Systems Division, 1982.

REPUBLICAN STRATEGY

According to John Dunne, Assistant Attorney General during the Bush administration and head of the 1991 redistricting process, the Voting Rights Act (Section 2 in particular) meant that whenever a state legislature could feasibly create a minority congressional district, it should do so. Although John Dunne headed the Civil Rights Division of the Justice Department, it was the Republican National Committee's chief counsel, Ben Ginsberg, who was the real tactician of this bold Republican strategy.[14] At that time the Republican Party had been extremely successful at the presidential level, having won the presidency in all but one election between 1968 and 1988. However, Republicans had not been nearly as successful at the congressional level as they had been at the presidential level. In fact, as of 1990, the Republican party in the House of Representatives had been the minority party since 1954, a total of 36 years. In the Senate, Democrats had been in the majority from 1954 to 1990, for all but one senatorial term (1981–1987), a total of 30 years. Eager to end Democratic congressional dominance, Ginsberg crafted a scheme whereby minorities and civil rights organizations would become strange political bedfellows with the Republican National Committee and conservative organizations. Both blacks and Republicans had something to gain from the creation of majority black districts: increased representation. Their strategy has been referred to as "the pizza pie versus doughnut theory":

> Blacks and minorities are generally concentrated in the center of cities . . . If the city and surrounding suburbs are districted into pizza-like slices, then Democrats have a core base in each district, but there is no guarantee that a black or Hispanic will be elected. If instead, the center city areas are turned into a separate district like the center of a doughnut, the suburban, more-Republican vote ringing the city is fortified.[15]

The Republican strategy was not devised out of altruism. Republicans knew that packing blacks and other minorities into supermajority black districts would potentially benefit Republican candidates. Because blacks vote overwhelmingly Democratic, by creating heavily black majority districts, the remaining districts will be more white and more favorable to Republican candidates. This strategy caused concern for white Democrats. According to Thomas Edsall,

> For Democrats, the problem with such districts is regularly reflected in statewide elections in the South. In close contests, the Democratic Party depends on a coalition of solid black support and a minority—often about 40 percent—of the white vote. Such coalitions are difficult to achieve in districts that are overwhelmingly white or black.[16]

The irony here is that the Republican party, traditionally reluctant to embrace the Voting Rights Act, was now using it as an instrument to advance its own agenda. Obviously, the stakes were higher for this round of redistricting than ever before. The prospects for continued congressional dominance by white congressional Democrats throughout the South seemed to be in jeopardy. The Voting Rights Act and a series of Supreme Court rulings in the 1980s (see Chapter 5) seemed to position blacks and the Republican party as the big winners in congressional elections in the 1990s.

BLACK POLITICAL EMPOWERMENT IN NORTH CAROLINA

Blacks in North Carolina were aware of the partisan nature of redistricting. However, they saw a new opportunity opening up for them—one of political empowerment. They saw a realistic chance for the first time in the twentieth century for a black American in the state of North Carolina to represent them in the body politic at the national level. *This was politics—this was about power.*

Nevertheless, there was no guarantee that when the next redistricting battle occurred in the year 2001 the U.S. Justice Department and the U.S. Supreme Court would interpret the Voting Rights Act as they had in the past.

It was the redrawing of state legislative districts in North Carolina in the 1980s that led to increased black political clout in the state legislature. Black Democrats were able to form a biracial coalition with key white Democrats to elect Democrat Dan Blue as the first black Speaker of the House of Representatives in 1991. In 1980, blacks held only 3 House seats out of 120 (2.5 percent) and one Senate seat out of 50 (2 percent). By 1991, they held 14 House seats (12 percent) and 5 Senate seats (10 percent). Those increases were due in large part to court litigation that originated in North Carolina after the 1981 House and Senate legislative redistricting.

The case of *Thornburg v. Gingles* (1986) began in September 1981 and alleged, among other things, that the House and Senate redistricting plans diluted minority voting strength in several districts. The case was heard by the U.S. Supreme Court in 1986.[17] The Court had to decide whether the use of multimember districts had the effect of diluting minority voting strength when a group of black voters was sufficiently large and geographically compact to constitute a majority in a single-member district. In 1984, prior to when *Gingles* reached the U.S. Supreme Court, a federal district court ruled in favor of the black plaintiffs. The district court also required the state legislature to redraw the House and Senate districts in 1984. Linwood Jones, a staff member in the Research Division of the General Assembly, said the following about the district court ruling:

> In 1984, after several special sessions and plan revisions, the General Assembly enacted its final [state] House and redistricting plans. The plans created most of the minority districts sought by the plaintiffs in the suit, but with the proviso that the old 1981 plans would go back into effect if the Supreme Court reversed the district court. The district court further modified the legislature's plan by splitting a multimember House district in Nash, Wilson, and Edgecombe Counties into 3 single-member districts and making adjustments to a single-member district created by the legislature in those counties.[18]

The case reached the U.S. Supreme Court on appeal from the federal district court. By applying a results test of Section 2 of the Voting Rights

Act to the districts in question in North Carolina, the Court found that all but one of the multimember districts violated this test.

That decision let stand the creation of the single-member legislative districts by the state legislature in North Carolina in 1984 and allowed for the increase of black legislators. The number of black state legislators increased from one senator and 11 representatives in 1983–1984 to 3 senators and 13 representatives in 1985–1986.

Moreover, the end result of the *Gingles* decision was the Supreme Court ruling that a minority legislative district should be drawn if the following conditions were met:

1. The minority group is sufficiently large and geographically compact to be a majority of the population in a single-member electoral district.
2. The minority group is politically cohesive.
3. The white majority votes as a bloc to the degree that it usually can defeat candidates preferred by the minority.[19]

The *Gingles* decision, coupled with other legal developments in the 1980s, created an environment that saw the Voting Rights Act foster the creation of more majority-minority districts. In addition to legal changes, the U.S. Justice Department with John Dunne as Assistant Attorney General for the Civil Rights Division clearly would be more vigilant in its enforcement of the Voting Rights Act than the Reagan administration had been.

Dunne had made public comments that he and his staff were primarily concerned that those redistricting plans submitted to him for approval not have the effect of diluting minority voting strength.

Similarly, Phil Duncan wrote in the *Washington Times* that goals that had guided map-drawers in the past, making districts compact and preventing the drawing of district lines that slice through community boundaries, would "take a back seat to the imperative that minorities must be served first when new boundaries are drawn."[20]

It is interesting to note that Gerry Cohen, director of legislative drafting for the North Carolina General Assembly Legislative Services Office, who assisted in the submission of the 1991 congressional plan to the Department of Justice, stated that:

> In fact, there is really no conclusive evidence that the Voting Rights Act required any predominantly black congressional district to be drawn, but legislative leadership decided early on that there would be a congressional district in which minorities would be able to be elected.[21]

Many blacks in North Carolina and in the other southern states saw this as an opportunity of a lifetime. The question had become one of empowerment; an opportunity now existed for blacks to gain what had been denied or stolen from them. The time had come for political representation for blacks at the congressional level in North Carolina. The only real question that remained for the Democratic majority in the state legislature was how to strike a balance between protecting incumbents and ensuring minority representation.

Redistricting, often a highly partisan battle fought in the state legislature in North Carolina, for the first time this century had an old variable but with a new twist. Whereas in the past congressional districts had been gerrymandered to exclude blacks, now the districts would be drawn for the purpose of including blacks.

ADOPTION OF THE FIRST CONGRESSIONAL PLAN

The redistricting process in North Carolina in 1991 began in normal fashion. In April, the Senate and House Redistricting Committees met jointly and adopted various criteria for congressional redistricting. Later that month, the General Assembly's computer software for redistricting was made available for public use. North Carolina had been one of the first states to allow its citizens access to computer terminals to create their own redistricting plans for submission to the legislature. In an article entitled, "Computers Allow Public Access into Redistricting," Hunter Kome states:

> In the past, legislators told staff members what they wanted districts to look like. Then staff, in a painstaking process using hundreds of U.S. Census maps for cross-reference, drew erasable lines with markers on state maps with Mylar overlays.[22]

Kome, who interviewed Glenn Newkirk, head of Legislative Automated Services for the North Carolina Legislative Services Office, went on to state:

> Since the last census, 10 years ago, the Census Bureau teamed up with the U.S. Geologic Survey to create a computer data base that combines census information with geographic information.[23]

The use of computers was heralded for two reasons, according to Newkirk. First, they allowed a degree of detail down to the smallest geographic unit, something that had never been achieved before. And second, the time required to create a plan became extremely shorter than what it used to be. Kome said:

> Now, what took days, takes hours. Staff members can work on a plan until 3 A.M., then have maps, 100 pages of statistics and a proposed bill ready for legislators at the start of the business day. Likewise, people proposing an alternative plan can have things ready on short notice.[24]

Because of the new computer technology, North Carolina's redistricting process became even more democratic. Anyone in the state who could make it to Raleigh could draw a congressional plan.

The General Assembly had computer experts who trained the legislative staff, counsel, and committee leaders on how to create the congressional plans using the computer technology. Subsequently, all of the legislators were given training on use of the computers. Public access hours were established initially for 20 hours per week in one-hour slots and later expanded to 40 hours per week in four-hour slots.

By May 1991, no congressional plans had been generated by the public and presented to the redistricting committees in their opening meetings. In May 1991, the first public hearing was held on congressional redistricting by the Joint Senate and House redistricting committees. The meeting was held in the auditorium of the State Legislative Building, and no one offered to speak or presented a congressional plan.

It was not until the end of May 1991 that the congressional redistricting process showed renewed signs of life. That was when the cochairmen of the House and Senate redistricting committees unveiled Congressional Base Plan #1 at a joint meeting of the House and Senate redistricting committees. This plan created one majority black district and one Republican district. The majority black district, the first created since 1891, was drawn from Durham, in the Piedmont, across the northeast portion of the state and to the coast. In the new district, the Twelfth, Republicans enjoyed a 48.9 percent to 45.3 percent advantage over Democrats in terms of registered voters. Political observers noted that some of the districts in this plan were bizarre and awkwardly shaped. Republicans criticized the plan, stating that it "diluted the political strength of minorities and Republicans."[25] However, the Democratic leadership defended the plan as necessary "to meet several goals: creating a district with a black majority, avoiding placing two incumbent congressmen in the same district, and getting all the districts as close as possible to the ideal population."[26]

Only four days later, on June 6, 1991, the House and Senate Redistricting co-chairmen presented Congressional Base Plan #2 (which was only a slight variation from Base Plan #1) to a meeting of the House Congressional Redistricting Committee. Representative David Balmer (Republican) presented Balmer Congress 6.2 (a Republican alternative) at that same House committee meeting. The number of Balmer's plans corresponded with the month and day that they were generated. The two plans presented thus far by the House and Senate co-chairmen had created one district that was majority black in voter registration. However, Balmer's 6.2 contained one majority-minority district that stretched from Charlotte in the western Piedmont all the way east to Wilmington on the coast. The majority-minority district was 45.32 percent black and 7.5 percent Native American in voting-age population. Its characterization as a minority district depended on the supposition that the black and Native American population in that district voted as a cohesive bloc.

There was evidence to the contrary, however. State House Speaker Dan Blue contacted the Robeson County Board of Elections, where the majority of Lumbee Indians resided, and requested election returns for all local, countywide elections from 1986 through 1990 where there were either black or Indian candidates. An examination of the general election results revealed that although "both black voters and Native American voters tended to vote Democratic in general elections, no matter what the race of the candidate, Native American voters did not tend to support black candidates who were supported by black voters in primary elections."[27]

In the meantime, the Senate Congressional Redistricting Subcommittee met and adopted Congressional Base Plan #1 and referred it to the full Senate Redistricting Committee. They planned to present this plan at an upcoming public hearing. The House Redistricting Committee met in early June and adopted Congressional Base Plan #2. A motion was made to present the Balmer plan as well, but that motion was defeated.

In mid-June 1991, the Joint House and Senate Redistricting Committee held a public hearing in the auditorium of the State Legislative Building. The public hearing was held to elicit reaction to the various plans thus far submitted and to hear criticisms and suggestions from the public. Maps of Base Plans #1 and #2 had been mailed to county courthouses and boards of election across the state. Representative Larry Justus (Republican) presented his congressional plan at this public hearing. Justus's congressional plan created one majority black district in the northeastern part of the state with 51.12 percent black registered voters. It would have created an 8–4 Republican majority in the congressional districts based upon results from the 1990 Helms-Gantt Senate race.

Unlike the first public hearing on congressional redistricting held almost four weeks earlier where no one spoke, this time numerous individuals rose to comment on the two plans submitted thus far or on other matters concerning the congressional redistricting process. Many objections were raised by white representatives of several counties in the state to the splitting of counties into more than one congressional district. Several members of the North Carolina Black Leadership Caucus expressed satisfaction with public access to the redistricting computers but objected to the lack of evening or weekend access time. Moreover, some members of the Black Leadership Caucus stated: "Instead of considering one minority district, why not make it a possibility of two."[28]

Bob Hunter, who had been asked to speak by Rep. David Balmer, introduced into the record a letter from the four Republican congressmen representing North Carolina. The letter objected to the committee plans adopted thus far. These same four congressmen had sent a letter dated June 5, 1991, to Senator Dennis Winner, chairman of the North Carolina Senate Redistricting Committee. In this letter, they stated:

> According to population statistics released by the U.S. Census Bureau, it appears that there should be two minority districts in North Carolina, and we would urge you to redraw the district lines to accomplish this result.[29]

Moreover, in a letter written to John Dunne at the U.S. Department of Justice, these same four congressmen, U.S. Representatives Howard Coble, Cass Ballenger, Alex McMillan, and Charles Taylor, asked Dunne to investigate North Carolina's congressional redistricting process. They were quoted in several North Carolina newspapers as charging that Congressional Base Plan #2 weakened minority voting concentrations "by splitting minorities among the 8th, 7th, and 3rd districts."[30] Furthermore, the congressmen claimed that "the new plan perpetuates the racial inequities caused by the configuration drawn in 1980 and approved by the Justice Department."[31]

However, Charlie Rose, a Democratic congressman from North Carolina who represented the Seventh District, accused the Republicans of trying to gain influence and strengthen their own districts under the guise of supporting minority rights. Queried Rose:

> But where were these four evangelists last week when the Civil Rights
> Act moved through Congress and they could have done something
> meaningful for minorities?[32]

Former State Representative Trip Sizemore, who assisted in the submission of the letter by the Republican congressmen at the public hearing, even acknowledged that the creation of two majority black districts
would help Republicans.

No one at the public hearing supported Congressional Base Plan #1
or #2. Willie Lovett, head of the North Carolina Black Leadership Caucus (NCBLC), stated, "The two plans' primary objective appears to be
the protection of Democratic incumbents . . . It appears to have been
done on the backs of blacks."[33]

Jack Hawke, state Republican party chairman, was quoted after the
public hearing as saying "Both plans are illegal because they dilute Republican voting power and divide communities that should be together. If
either one passes, Republicans will sue."[34] Oddly enough, Republicans
joined with members of the Black Leadership Caucus in North Carolina,
the National Association for the Advancement of Colored People
(NAACP), and the American Civil Liberties Union (ACLU) in objecting
to Base Plans #1 and #2.

Representative Sam Hunt (Democrat), co-chairman of the House
Redistricting Committee, also received a letter from the North Carolina
Republican congressional delegation that objected to the congressional
plans drafted to date. He asserted that very few people had been pleased
with the plans. Furthermore, he stated that the state's Democratic
congressional delegation had also complained about the plans. Hunt,
who was about the only one who could glean humor from the situation,
said:

> That's the first time I've heard the complaints from the Republican
> congressmen . . . All our complaints had come before from the Demo-
> cratic congressmen. Usually if both sides are a little bit unhappy,
> you've probably been fair.[35]

But Senator Dennis Winner (Democrat), chairman of the Senate
Redistricting Committee, felt that the public hearing would definitely
affect the redistricting process. Winner stated, "There'll be some
changes because of it, I'm sure."[36] Winner went on to argue, however,
that

legislators are under pressure from federal courts to draw districts that
are as close to the ideal district population as possible, and to create districts where blacks have a realistic chance of being elected . . . we've
got to follow the law. You cannot do that without dividing counties.[37]

On June 18, 1991, Congressional Base Plan #3 was presented to and
adopted by the Senate Redistricting Committee. On June 20, 1991, Congressional Base Plan #3 subsequently passed in the full Senate. That
same day, Congressional Base Plan #4 was presented to the House Redistricting Committee. On the following day, June 21, the House Congressional Redistricting Committee adopted Congressional Base Plan #4
as a committee substitute. The committee also rejected Balmer Congress
Block Level, which was simply a refinement of Balmer Congress 6.2;
Representative Justus's Congressional Plan; and an updated plan from
Representative Wilson on that same day.

On June 27, 1991, the Senate failed to agree on Congressional Base
Plan #4 and the matter was taken up by conferees. The chairmen of the
conference committee presented Congressional Base Plan #5 to the conferees on July 3, 1991. After making minor adjustments, the conferees
ultimately approved the plan, which became Congressional Base Plan
#6. The Senate approved the conference report on Congressional Base
Plan #6 on July 4, 1991. All of the black senators who voted were in
favor of this plan.

On July 8, 1991, Representative Balmer filed his second plan, Balmer
Congress 7.8, which created two districts with a substantial minority
population. District 2 had a 54.11 percent black voting-age population,
and District 3 had a 53.03 percent black voting-age population. However,
the number of black registered voters totaled 49.66 percent in District 2
and 52.59 percent in District 3. Although District 2 had less than a 50
percent black voting-age population, it included the military bases in
both Cumberland and Onslow counties. In a tactical maneuver, Balmer
made a motion to suspend the rules so that Balmer 7.8 could be given
first reading. That motion failed, and the House of Representatives subsequently approved Congressional Base Plan #6, with no racial minorities voting against it.

On July 9, 1991, Balmer 7.8 was referred to the House Congressional Redistricting Committee, which did not meet again. Balmer 7.8
was never presented to the Senate. On that same day, Congressional Base
Plan #6 was ratified. It was adopted in the House of Representatives with
the full support of the Speaker of the House, Dan Blue, Democrat from
Wake, and all of the minority members of the House who were present

and voted. It was adopted in the Senate with the full support of all black and Native American senators who were present and voted.

It is noteworthy that prior to the adoption of Congressional Base Plan #6, only three plans were offered as alternative plans to those six presented by the committee chairmen. They were all presented to the redistricting committees by Republican state legislators. All three plans would have created at least an 8–4 Republican advantage in the congressional delegation, based upon results from the 1990 Helms-Gantt U.S. Senate race. None had the slightest chance of passing in a Democratic majority legislature. It was extremely odd that only three alternative plans were presented, considering all the notice that was given that the redistricting process in North Carolina would be open to the public to create plans for the first time. As a matter of fact, on May 15, 1991, after giving public notice that the Senate and House redistricting committees would receive congressional redistricting plans from any member of the public, the Senate subcommittee and House committee held a joint public meeting to receive proposed plans. When no plans were presented, there was concern that no one from the public had had adequate time to create a congressional plan.

It was announced at that public hearing that the public would be able to present congressional plans at any meeting that the committee held prior to June 9, 1991. At all subsequent committee meetings held before

Table 3.3. Three Alternative Congressional Redistricting Plans Presented to the North Carolina Legislature During Regular Session, 1991

Plan	Date Presented	Minority Districts	Percent Black VR	Percent Am In VR	Black Support
Balmer 6.2	6/3/91	2	D2 53.52 D12 46.80	D12 7.79	None
Justus	6/13/91	1	D2 51.12	D2 0.84	None
Balmer 7.8	7/9/91	2	D2 54.11 D3 53.03		None

VR—Registered Voters
Am In—American Indian
D—District

Source: North Carolina Legislative Services Office, 1991

the adoption of Congressional Base Plan #6, not one person from the public presented a congressional plan. Furthermore, at the public hearing held on June 13, 1991, representatives of the National Association for the Advancement of Colored People (NAACP), the North Carolina Black Leadership Caucus, and the Republican party all commented on the current redistricting plans being debated. More than one black speaker rose during that public hearing and called for the creation of more than one majority black congressional district in North Carolina. However, Kathleen Wilde, staff counsel for the ACLU Southern Regional Office, argued that public input was lacking for a reason. Wilde, who submitted a letter to the U.S. Justice Department asking it to reject the initial congressional plan that had been submitted, said that the public was denied meaningful access to participation in the congressional redistricting process. She claimed that the North Carolina Black Leadership Caucus and the NAACP had complained repeatedly about the lack of computer time. According to Wilde, this was one of the main reasons why no public plans were presented to the House or Senate committees on congressional redistricting.[38]

Moreover, Representative David Balmer seemed to be the only one interested in drafting congressional plans that created more than one majority black district. In an interview with Representative Balmer, he informed me that the Democrats were not willing to look at the possibility of two minority districts and he wanted to show them that it could be done.[39] Balmer claimed that political motivation had nothing to do with his creation of these plans. However, the two plans he had introduced thus far would have created either a 9–3 (Balmer 6.2) or 8–4 (Balmer 7.8) Republican majority based on voter election results from the 1990 Helms-Gantt Senate race. Representative Balmer wanted to run for the U.S. Congress, so he likely had partisan and personal motivations for producing his plans.

Not surprisingly, both political parties proposed plans that protected their incumbents and increased their chances of gaining party representation. The redistricting plan in existence in North Carolina after the 1980 census consisted of 11 congressional districts. The congressional delegation from 1982 until 1992 stood at seven Democrats and four Republicans. According to Gerry Cohen, Congressional Base Plan #6, which created one black district, was a seven Democrat and five Republican plan.[40] In other words, the Democratically controlled legislature was willing to cede the new district that the state had gained to the Republicans.

Representative Toby Fitch (Democrat), a black co-chairman of the House Redistricting Committee, acknowledged that there was criticism placed on the House leadership for accepting a congressional plan that created only one majority black district. Fitch exclaimed:

> Yes, there was criticism. There was criticism of myself individually as a black legislator. There was criticism toward the Speaker coming from the community and some of the leadership. Purely, from a political standpoint and looking at and anticipating what we thought the moves of [the Department of] Justice would be. [We had to be realistic about] not only Justice but what we could get through the House or through the Senate, the real politics of it.[41]

Fitch appeared to be saying that the black members of the state legislature had to be realistic and attempt to pass a plan that would be accepted by a majority of the white Democrats. It was not simply a matter of creating as many majority black districts as was possible: The reality of the situation was that the white Democratic majority wanted to protect the incumbents as much as possible. Fitch went on to assert that

> whites in general to a large degree wanted to cluster [blacks] and in the true clustering what you were doing was limiting any influence that you had elsewhere. And while the law does not speak towards influence districts it is now beginning to involve or evolve where influence districts, in my opinion, will be more the norm than the exception in the days to come. And we were concerned about not having one representative or having just two representatives but having what we could realistically achieve at the same time being able to be a sizable force on ten others or on eight others.[42]

So Fitch saw the potential trade-off of blacks controlling one or two districts but having almost no influence in the remaining districts. Moreover, although all signs from the U.S. Department of Justice were pointing to the creation of majority black districts where possible, according to Fitch, this was not a certainty in North Carolina. He stated that the Senate redistricting leadership had come to the House redistricting committee members and told them that it was the Senate's position that no minority seats be created because as they understood the law, they were not mandated to do so.

It appears that the black leadership in the legislature was trying to increase black representation while remaining loyal to the Democratic party. Though members of the NAACP and others criticized the plan adopted by the legislature, none of them presented alternative plans to the legislature. Carolyn Coleman, state director of the NAACP, said that gaining access to the computers to draw alternative plans was a real problem.[43]

On August 28, 1991, the State Board of Elections, on behalf of the State of North Carolina, submitted its congressional redistricting plan to the U.S. Department of Justice. The submission was made in accordance with the preclearance requirement under Section 5 of the Voting Rights Act.

NOTES

[1]United States, Department of Commerce, Bureau of the Census, "1990 Census Population for the United States is 249,632,692; Reapportionment Will Shift 19 Seats in the U.S. House of Representatives," *United States Department of Commerce News*, Press Release (Washington, D.C.: U.S. Governmental Printing Office, 1990) 2.

[2]*1991–1992 Redistricting and Reapportionment Community Education Handbook* 2nd ed. (Washington, D.C.: National Coalition on Black Voter Participation, 1991) 2.

[3]*Baker v. Carr*, 369 U.S. 186 (1962)

[4]*Colegrove v. Green*, 328 U.S. 549 (1946)

[5]*Wesberry v. Sanders*, 376 U.S. 1 (1964)

[6]*City of Mobile v. Bolden*, 446 U.S. 55 (1980).

[7]Lisa Handley, "The Quest for Minority Voting Rights: The Evolution of a Vote Dilution Standard and Its Impact on Minority Representation," diss., George Washington University, 1991, n.p.

[8]*1991–1992 Redistricting and Reapportionment Community Education Handbook* 2nd ed. (Washington, D.C.: National Coalition on Black Voter Participation, 1991) 82–84.

[9]*Davis v. Bandemer*, 478 U.S. 109 (1986).

[10]Frank R. Parker, "Changing Standards in Voting Rights Law," *Redistricting in the 1990s: A Guide for Minority Groups*, ed. William P. O'Hare (Washington, D.C.: Population Reference Bureau, Inc., 1989) 65.

[11]*Redistricting 1991: Legislator's Guide to North Carolina Legislative and Congressional Redistricting* (Raleigh: North Carolina General Assembly Research Division, 1991) 12.

[12]Quoted in Kevin O'Brien, "New District Could Boost Blacks' Chance," *Charlotte Observer* September 3, 1990: B1.

[13]Quoted in Kevin O'Brien, "New Seat Could Aid Black Voice," 1.

[14]Beth Donovan, "Redistricting: Political Dance Played Out through Legal Wrangling," *Congressional Quarterly Weekly Report*. December 21, 1991: 3693–3694.

[15]Thomas B. Edsall, "GOP Goal: Gain Ground by Fostering 'Majority Minority' Districts," *The Washington Post*. July 7, 1990: A6.

[16]Edsall A6.

[17]*Thornburg v. Gingles*, 478 U.S. 30 (1986).

[18]*Redistricting 1991*, 10.

[19]Peter Bragdon, "Democrats' Ties to Minorities May Be Tested by New Lines," *Congressional Quarterly Weekly Report*. June 2, 1990: 1740.

[20]Phil Duncan, "Race-based Congressional Districts?" *The Washington Times* August 13, 1990: D3.

[21]Gerry Cohen, Memorandum to the U.S. Department of Justice, October 14, 1991.

[22]Hunter Kome, "Computers Allow Public Access into Redistricting," *Hendersonville Times-News*, July 7, 1991: C1.

[23]Kome C1.

[24]Kome C1.

[25]Van Denton, "Redistricting Plan Defended, Derided," *Raleigh News and Observer*, May 30, 1991: 1.

[26]Denton 1.

[27]North Carolina, Department of Justice, "Section 5 Submission for North Carolina Congressional Redistricting," Chapter 601 (Raleigh: GPO, 1991) C–28D.

[28]Van Ellisen, "Transcript of Congressional Redistricting Public Hearing," June 13, 1991.

[29]Cass Ballenger, Howard Coble, J. Alex McMillan, and Charles Taylor, Letter to Dennis J. Winner, June 5, 1991.

[30]Matthew Davis, "Republicans Attack State Redistricting," *Wilmington Morning Star*, July 15, 1991: B3.

[31]Davis B3.

[32]Quoted in Davis B3.

[33]Quoted in Charles Hoskinson, "Congressional Redistricting Plans Draw Jeers," *Greenville Daily Reflector* June 14, 1991: A–2.

[34]Quoted in Charles Hoskinson, "Republicans See Political Gains in Redistricting," *Greenville Daily Reflector* June 16, 1991: B–1.

[35]Quoted in Seth Effron, "U. S. House Members Write Letter Opposing North Carolina Redistricting Plan," *Greensboro News and Record*, June 11, 1991: 1.

[36]Quoted in Charles Hoskinson, "Congressional Redistricting Plans Draw Jeers," *Greenville Daily Reflector*, June 14, 1991: A–2.

[37]Quoted in Charles Hoskinson, "Congressional Redistricting." A–2.

[38]Kathleen Wilde, Letter to Assistant U. S. Attorney General John Dunne, September 25, 1991.

[39]Interview with David Balmer, June 2, 1992, Raleigh, North Carolina.

[40]Interview with Gerry Cohen, May 27, 1992, Raleigh, North Carolina.

[41]Interview with Toby Fitch, June 3, 1992, Raleigh, North Carolina.
[42]Interview with Toby Fitch.
[43]Interview with Carolyn Coleman, May 27, 1992, Raleigh, North Carolina.

CHAPTER 4

Redistricting, Round Two: North Carolina Legislators Are Required to Create a Second Majority-Minority District

Prior to North Carolina's submission of its redistricting plan to the U.S. Department of Justice, forces were at work attempting to undermine that process. Representative David Balmer had corresponded with the Justice Department on August 5, 1991. In a letter addressed to John Dunne, Assistant U.S. Attorney General, Balmer enclosed copies of the congressional plans that he introduced into the North Carolina state legislature and that were defeated either by legislative action on the floor of the House or in the House Congressional Redistricting Committee. Balmer asserted that under Congressional Base Plan #6, black concentrations were divided in such a way "that neutralizes black voting potential in the state."[1]

Because of this, Balmer insisted that the North Carolina plan was not in compliance with Section 5 of the Voting Rights Act (VRA) of 1965. In addition, he stated that he had introduced plans that did comply with the VRA, and he enclosed those plans with the letter. Balmer submitted three plans to the Justice Department: Balmer Congress 6.2, Balmer Congress Block Level (a refinement of 6.2), and Balmer Congress 7.8. All three plans included two minority congressional districts.

After North Carolina's submission to the Justice Department, other organizations filed official comment letters with the Justice Department objecting to North Carolina's Congressional Redistricting Plan. The most detailed objection letter came from the ACLU Southern Regional Office. On September 25, 1991, Kathleen Wilde, staff counsel for the ACLU in the Atlanta office, submitted a letter to the Department of Justice objecting to North Carolina's congressional plan. Wilde stated that her comment letter was submitted "on behalf of black voters in North Carolina whom I represent with respect to racially discriminatory plans . . . which were recently submitted to the United States Attorney General."[2] Wilde went on to strongly urge the U.S. Department of Justice to object to North Carolina's congressional plan.

She insisted that blacks in North Carolina were not consulted concerning the alternative congressional plans placed before the legislature:

> Nor were any minority voters (or the organizations which represent them, including the NAACP and ACLU) contacted, consulted or included by the various plans being considered by the state legislature. To the extent any decisions were had with the black community concerning the proposed districts in various parts of the state, those conversations were almost exclusively had with incumbent black legislators, who in many instances had personal and/or partisan interests not necessarily consistent with those of their constituents—black voters protected under the VRA.[3]

Wilde summed up the actions by the state accordingly:

> North Carolina simply cannot have it both ways. Having failed to provide the minority community meaningful access to the reapportionment process, it cannot then claim that it is "off the hook" because the community did not present plans, or support alternatives that were never presented by the state's committees.[4]

Moreover, Wilde contended that there were at least three alternative congressional plans proposed that created two minority districts. She noted how the state had defended its objection against those plans by saying that they would have substantially decreased the black influence in Congressional Districts 4, 7, 8, and 9. Her reply to this was that "protection of white Democratic incumbents is not a valid reason for refusal to create a majority minority district."[5] Furthermore, Wilde alleged that Congressional Base Plan #6 was intended to dilute minority strength, which she said was in violation of Section 5 of the VRA. It was her contention that the congressional plan adopted by the state legislature was done primarily to protect Democratic incumbents and to secure Democratic seats. "And I don't have a problem with that, except that it should not be done on the backs of the black population in this state."[6]

She concluded her objections by insisting that North Carolina had failed to meet its burden of proof by showing that its congressional plan was free of racially discriminatory intent in clear violation of Section 2 of the VRA.[7]

On September 27, 1991, Representative David Balmer sent a detailed comment letter to John Dunne at the U.S. Department of Justice urging him not to preclear Congressional Base Plan #6 because, according to Balmer, "it unfairly discriminates against blacks and American Indians by diluting their voting strength."[8] Balmer included copies of the three plans (Balmer Congress 6.2, Balmer Congress 7.8, and Balmer Congress 8.1) that he had introduced into the legislative record and sent to Assistant Attorney General Dunne with his letter of August 5, 1991. Balmer outlined a detailed analysis of the black congressional district population in his three plans vis-à-vis the black congressional district population in the ratified version.

On September 30, 1991, the leadership of the North Carolina House and Senate redistricting committees and the North Carolina Speaker of the House went to Washington, D.C., and met with the U.S. Department of Justice staff in regard to both the North Carolina congressional redistricting plan and the state House and Senate redistricting plans.

Gerry Cohen, head of legislative drafting for the state legislature, prepared a written response for the Department of Justice to the comments made by Kathleen Wilde on behalf of the ACLU and the comments made by Representative Balmer. The main purpose of the comments submitted by North Carolina was to refute the assertions made by Wilde and Balmer. Cohen made his submission to the U.S. Department of Justice on October 15, 1991.

THE DEPARTMENT OF JUSTICE'S RESPONSE TO THE ENACTED PLAN

On October 18, 1991, the U.S. Department of Justice asked the North Carolina state legislature to provide it with more information on North Carolina's redistricting plans. This request meant that the Justice Department would have an additional 60 days before responding to North Carolina's redistricting plans. The Justice Department noted in its request that failure by the state of North Carolina to respond within 60 days could result in an objection to the ratified plan.

The Justice Department wanted the state of North Carolina to provide a variety of documentation with respect to the congressional redistricting plan. First, it wanted an estimate of the mileage distance and the travel time by automobile from the two most distant points for each of the 12 districts. Second, it requested voter registration data and election returns that may have been used to arrive at the conclusion that the second minority district in Balmer's Congressional Plan 6.2 did not have a cohesive voting bloc of blacks and Native Americans.

It also requested election returns for Robeson, Hoke, Scotland, Cumberland, and Guilford counties for the years 1982–1988 by county and precinct. Finally, it requested a breakdown of the offices to be filled, method of election, candidates, name and race, vote breakdown for each candidate, and the number of registered voters for the same time period.[9]

PUBLIC REACTION TO THE ADOPTED PLAN

Many Republicans in the state legislature in addition to Representative Balmer had been outraged at the adoption of Congressional Base Plan #6. They screamed foul play and partisan gerrymandering. Many newspapers across the state expressed the frustration felt on the part of many Republicans. The *Winston-Salem Journal* quoted Representative Art Pope (Republican), chairman of the Joint Legislative Caucus, in an article entitled, "Districts Debated In Angry Assembly: Plan Is Partisan, Republicans Say." Pope said, "It's the most partisan, blatant gerrymandering we've seen in the General Assembly."[10]

An article that appeared in a local paper in Gastonia, North Carolina, near Charlotte, asserted that with the newly created plan, the Democrats were hoping for a 10–2 majority in the congressional delegation after the 1992 elections. The article stated, "You can bet that fairness and common sense weren't even considered when the Democrats redrew the map. Getting the maximum number of Democrats from North Carolina in Congress was top priority."[11]

Furthermore, on November 1, 1991, a group of Republican state legislators filed suit in federal district court in North Carolina challenging the state House, state Senate, and congressional redistricting plans as unconstitutional. In their complaint, they asked the court to assume full responsibility for the redistricting process in North Carolina. The conventional wisdom all along was that the Republicans would probably try to get as many redistricting plans tied up in the federal court system as possible. This was because North Carolina's state legislature, as well as all other state legislatures throughout the South, was Democratically controlled and most of the federal judges were Republicans appointed by former Republican President Reagan or President Bush. The logic clearly was that Republican legislators would stand a better chance with

Republican judges in achieving redistricting plans that were more favorable to them. The suit, *Daughtry v. State Board of Elections* (1991), brought by State Senator N. Leo Daughtry (Republican), was filed in the U.S. Middle District Court in North Carolina.

DEPARTMENT OF JUSTICE'S REJECTION OF THE ENACTED PLAN

On December 18, 1991, Assistant Attorney General John Dunne sent a letter on behalf of the U.S. Department of Justice to the North Carolina Attorney General listing objections to the congressional redistricting plan. In the letter, he remarked, among other things, about the unusual shape of the one majority black congressional district that was drawn in the northeastern part of the state. However, the Justice Department determined that the district "did not have the purpose or effect of minimizing minority voting strength in that region."[12]

Furthermore, Dunne stated that North Carolina was well aware of the significant interest on the part of the minority community in creating a second majority-minority congressional district in North Carolina. Dunne noted:

> For the south-central to southeast area, there were several plans drawn providing for a second majority-minority congressional district, including at least one alternative presented to the legislature. No alternative plan providing for a second majority-minority congressional district was presented by the state to the public for comment. Nonetheless, significant support for such an alternative has been expressed by the National Association for the Advancement of Colored People (NAACP) and the American Civil Liberties Union (ACLU).[13]

Although Dunne claimed that his sole interest was enforcement of the VRA, others questioned his motivation. Leslie Winner, who served as special counsel to the North Carolina House Redistricting Committee, for example, informed me that North Carolina House Speaker Dan Blue and Representative Toby Fitch, House leaders, along with Senator Dennis Winner, Senate Redistricting Chairman (and brother of Leslie Winner), a staff person, and Winner herself, all went to the Department of Justice and met with Assistant Attorney General John Dunne the day before Dunne sent the objection letter to North Carolina. Winner stated:

> We didn't know it was the day before the objection was rendered or
> whatever you call it and took maps and tried to explain to him the rea-
> sons for not creating two districts, two majority black districts. And,
> then his letter said that all of our reasons were pretextual and we really
> had a racially discriminatory purpose which I found to be bizarre. That
> he would look at Dan Blue and Toby Fitch and me and Dennis and de-
> cide that we really had a racially discriminatory purpose, I don't think
> he believed that.[14]

Winner felt that Dunne's actions were politically motivated. She
stated that all of the maps the Republicans submitted to the North Carolina General Assembly had eight Republican districts and four Democratic districts. It is particularly interesting to note that Winner said the
strong push by blacks for two minority districts in the North Carolina
congressional plan did not occur until after Dunne's objection.

> Now, after Dunne objected, I sensed a change. There was an evolution
> in attitude. Particularly, after some black constituents, many black con-
> stituents appeared and said that they wanted to have some black dis-
> tricts. And the NAACP and the ACLU came in and I think the black
> legislators' opinions about it changed after that. I think it's true that I
> never heard a black constituent support having two majority black dis-
> tricts until after some objected. I can't promise you. It may have been
> one or two but there were no black leaders.[15]

Winner was chief counsel for the plaintiffs in the North Carolina
case *Thornburg v. Gingles* (1986), outlawing multimember districts in
the North Carolina state legislature.

North Carolina House Speaker Dan Blue recalled that the staff
people in the U.S. Justice Department were interested in enforcing the
VRA but that Dunne and his assistants "were more concerned about the
political implications of what the redistricting held."[16]

Nonetheless, the U.S. Department of Justice objected to the congressional plan on the grounds that North Carolina failed to create a second majority-minority congressional district when it could have done so.
Moreover, by not creating the second minority district, the state's action
"will have the expected result of minimizing or canceling out the voting
strength of black and Native American minority voters."[17]

The U.S. Justice Department informed the state of North Carolina
that it could ask the U.S. Attorney General to reconsider its objections or

seek a declaratory judgment from the U.S. District Court for the District of Columbia.

North Carolina Governor James G. Martin, who opposed the congressional plan, could not veto it because at that time North Carolina was the only state in the Union that did not give its governor any form of veto power.* Nevertheless, the Justice Department's preclearance denial had state Republicans elated. State Republican Chairman R. Jack Hawke, Jr., said:

> The Democrats in their usual arrogance, thought they could ignore the law of the land. They get away with that in North Carolina, but they can't get away with that when it involves a federal law.[18]

STATE LEGISLATORS GO BACK TO THE DRAWING BOARD

On December 20, 1991, Governor Martin called for the General Assembly to meet in extra session to decide what course of action it would take in response to the ruling and to postpone the filing period for congressional candidates that was set by law to begin January 6, 1992, and to end February 3, 1992.

No one knew exactly how the state legislature would react to the rejection letter. Five Democratic congressmen from North Carolina, who thought that blacks should not be confined to only a few minority districts, asked the Democratic leadership in the state legislature to challenge the Justice Department's rejection in federal court. However, the state's four Republican congressmen asked the state legislature to revise its congressional plan rather than to attempt to defend it in court.[19]

The state legislature convened in extra session on December 30, 1991, but the only action that it took was to postpone the filing period for the elections from February 10 to March 2, 1992. Representative David Balmer introduced four bills, all different congressional plans that created either two black or two minority districts out of 12. Balmer named these four plans Balmer Congress 8.1, Balmer Congress 9.1, Balmer Congress 10.1, and Balmer Congress Final Version. Balmer 8.1 contained two majority black districts: one located in the eastern portion of the state and the other located in the central Piedmont portion of the state. This particular plan stood out because of the unusual shape of the district located in the Piedmont section of the state. It stretched from Mecklenburg County on the South Carolina border north following Interstate 85 to Granville

County on the Virginia border, picking up black voters in urban areas along the way. This district would serve as the prototype for what would become the Interstate 85 corridor district.

The state legislature was not scheduled to convene its regular ression until January 13, 1992. On that day and the next, announcements were sent to North Carolina State House and Senate members of meetings and public hearings that would be held prior to the regular session convening. Notices were also sent to the media and minority groups announcing the public hearing to be held in Raleigh on January 8, 1992, concerning congressional redistricting.

TWO MAJORITY BLACK DISTRICT ALTERNATIVES PRESENTED TO THE LEGISLATURE

The North Carolina House Congressional Redistricting Committee and the North Carolina Senate Congressional Redistricting Committee held a public hearing in Raleigh to entertain comments about the congressional redistricting plan. At the public hearing, numerous citizens spoke about black representation and supported the creation of two majority black districts.

Curiously, Republicans who spoke at the public hearing endorsed the idea of two black majority districts and the plan created by Representative Balmer in which one of the majority black districts was located in the northeastern part of the state while the second minority district was in the southeastern part of the state. This particular plan had been referred to by the Justice Department in its rejection letter to the state of North Carolina.

Most representatives of black interest groups who spoke at the public hearing favored the creation of two majority black districts but did not endorse any particular plan.

At the public hearing, Scott Kimbrough, a white chemist from Alamance County, presented a congressional plan that contained two minority districts. Kimbrough said:

> First, I want to confirm what most North Carolinians have suspected
> since June of last year, that Congressional district boundaries can be
> drawn mainly along county lines, creating districts that respect regional
> integrity and identity, and avoid what some have called political
> pornography, while still empowering—empowering minorities.[20]

*The state legislature granted the governor veto power effective January 1997.

Of significance were comments at the public hearing made by Mary Peeler, Executive Director of the North Carolina State Conference of Branches of the NAACP. Peeler stated that all along her organization had attempted to "maximize the voting strength of African Americans and other minorities in this state."[21] She presented a congressional plan that she believed accomplished just that. In effect, Peeler's congressional plan created two black districts: one district with a majority of blacks in rural eastern North Carolina, the First, and another district that included blacks along urban centers throughout the Piedmont portion of the state, the Twelfth.

The NAACP plan became known as the "Interstate 85" corridor plan because the Twelfth District meandered along the interstate just north of the South Carolina border all the way to the Virginia. It had initially been submitted to the House and Senate Redistricting Committees' co-chairmen for their consideration by several of North Carolina's Democratic congresspeople. Curiously, the two black districts in this plan are similar to the two black districts in Balmer's 8.1.

The district that contained mostly black population areas in eastern North Carolina had been drawn with only slight variations from almost all of the previous plans that had created a majority black district. This area of the state, historically referred to as the "black belt" by V. O. Key in his seminal work, *Southern Politics in State and Nation*,[22] had the largest concentration of blacks in the state. Congressional Base Plan #6, the plan rejected by the U.S. Justice Department, contained a majority black district in this portion of the state, a district to which the Justice Department did not object.

ORIGIN OF THE I–85 DISTRICT

The origin of the Interstate 85 corridor black district in urban Piedmont North Carolina was not as geographically clear-cut. After North Carolina made its submission of Congressional Base Plan #6 to the U.S. Justice Department, State Representative Thomas Hardaway (Democrat), a young, black legislator from Enfield in eastern North Carolina, paid a visit to several staff members of the North Carolina General Assembly. Hardaway approached Bill Guilkeson, a staff attorney for the Research Division of the General Assembly, and inquired about alternatives for two black districts besides Balmer's plan, which created the majority-minority district that stretched over 200 miles from Charlotte in the Piedmont and to Wilmington on the coast. Guilkeson informed Hardaway that a number of plans drawn up on the public access terminal or by Guilkeson created two black districts, and Hardaway identified a plan that created a black district from Charlotte to Durham along the Interstate 85 corridor. According to an interview with Gerry Cohen, Hardaway saw this plan as

> one that would unify both the black and the Democratic interests. Plus, it did another thing for him. He was against Mickey Michaux in the Democratic primary. It also had the effect of putting him and Michaux in different congressional districts.[23]

According to Cohen, Hardaway's request was for a plan that not only had two black districts but also a 7–5 Democratic-Republican balance, "so that the effect of adding a second black district would not affect the partisan balance of the delegation."[24]

Hardaway asked Guilkeson to model the plan after Balmer 8.1. This plan was entitled "Optimum II–Zero." Furthermore, according to Cohen, Hardaway had Guilkeson mail a copy of the plan to the U.S. Department of Justice and to Congressman Tim Valentine, who represented the Second Congressional District in North Carolina.[25]

Cohen noted, additionally, that the press had criticized this plan as originating with Tom Merrit, an aide to North Carolina Democratic Congressman Charlie Rose. But in a sworn deposition, Merrit stated that he met Representative Hardaway at the Howard Johnson's in Gold Rock, North Carolina, where Hardaway handed him the plan. *Congressional Quarterly Weekly Report* had this to say about Hardaway in a special issue in April 1992:

> Though he is one of the state's youngest legislators, Hardaway, 35, proved his political mettle by playing a key role in creating the First. He met with Justice Department officials, contacted members of Congress and plotted line drawing strategy with an aide to the 7th District Democratic Representative Charlie Rose, who was integral in shaping the district.[26]

The chairman of the North Carolina Legislative Black Caucus (NCLBC), state senator James T. Richardson (Democrat), announced publicly that the state's black legislators as a group "had agreed to seek a second minority congressional district but did not endorse any specific plan."[27] Moreover, the NCLBC had a meeting with members of the state chapter of the NAACP and the ACLU. Kathleen Wilde, lead attorney for the ACLU's Voting Rights Project based in Atlanta, was quoted as warning legislators that "to go to litigation would require a court to draw an interim plan."[28] Wilde contended that the consequences of this would be to hold elections in 1992 under one plan, only to see elections in 1994 based on another plan.[29]

Of note here is the change in the position of the NCLBC. Previously, not one of the members of the NCLBC had voted in favor of any of the congressional plans that created more than one black or minority congressional district. Furthermore, there appeared to have been a split between the rank-and-file black members of the state legislature and the black members of the legislature who headed the congressional redistricting process. Apparently, pressure from black interest groups that overwhelmingly supported the creation of two majority black districts had caused the NCLBC to do an about-face. One of the local papers, *The Raleigh News and Observer*, ran a story on January 7, 1992, that highlighted the ongoing controversy. In an article entitled "Party Loyalty, Black Gains Clash in Redistricting," several black leaders were quoted as saying that the increase in black political power is paramount to all other concerns. Reverend Thomas Walker, a black Democratic county commissioner from Edgecombe County in the eastern part of the state, said:

> It's a sad commentary on white Republicans and white Democrats, but we are not going to get any blacks elected unless we have majority black districts. We have to look after our interests first and the party second.[30]

However, other black leaders were more cautious. Representative Toby Fitch (Democrat), cochairman of the House Congressional Redistricting Committee, was quoted in the same article as saying:

> If blacks go too far they will find themselves confined to "political reservations" with less political influence than they have today.[31]

Howard Clement III, a black Republican member of the Durham City Council, had this to say about the black legislative leadership:

> I think that these folks are more concerned about their standing in the Democratic Party than they are concerned about the needs and aspirations of the minority community. If we get the numbers, at least we

have people there who can articulate more clearly the needs and aspirations of the minority community. At this stage in our history, that is very important.[32]

It was now clear that the task before the General Assembly was to create a congressional plan that contained at least two minority districts. The only real question that remained was where the districts would be located.

Because of complaints during the first round of redistricting about the lack of access to the computer terminals, the House and Senate leadership expanded the hours of the Public Access Terminal to include evening and weekend hours.

Mary Peeler's plan was entered into the computer by General Assembly staff as "92 Congress 1." The legislature chose to begin its work on congressional redistricting only after the state House and Senate legislative redistricting was completed. Because of this, both chambers did not plan on meeting to begin work on the congressional redistricting plan until January 22, 1992. During the interim, the House Congressional Redistricting Committee met once.

At that meeting, Representative Larry Justus (Republican) presented a Republican plan with two minority districts that was called "Compact 2–Minority Plan." This plan contained two districts that had a majority of either blacks (District 2) or blacks and Native Americans (District 6). No votes were taken on this plan at the meeting. The Senate Congressional Redistricting Subcommittee canceled two scheduled meetings prior to January 22, 1992.

However, on the weekend of January 18–19, the leadership of the House and Senate released separate redistricting plans to House members and the public. The House plan, referred to as 1992 Congressional Base Plan #7, created two majority black congressional districts, District 1 and District 12. The Senate plan, referred to as Congressional Base Plan #8, was almost identical to Base Plan #7. It also created two majority black congressional districts, District 1 and District 12, and contained almost the same population totals for each district as Base Plan #7. Both plans were only slight variations of Mary Peeler's 92 Congress 1, with each plan having a rural black district in the eastern portion of the state and an urban black district running along the Interstate 85 corridor in the Piedmont region.

When the House Congressional Redistricting Committee finally met on January 21, members discussed Base Plan #7. State Representative David Flaherty (Republican) presented an alternative to the Democratic plan known as "Representative Flaherty's Congress Plan." The plan contained two districts where blacks were in the majority, District 2 and 12, and an influence district where the black and Native American population combined was slightly less than 50 percent in total population.

The Senate Congressional Redistricting Subcommittee met the next day and decided that the Senate would delay further discussion of congressional redistricting until the House passed a plan.

The House Congressional Redistricting Committee co-chairmen presented Base Plan #9 to the House Congressional Redistricting Committee on the following day. Base Plan #9 contained minor changes to Base Plan #7 that had been proposed by committee members. The committee voted down amendments that would have substituted Representative Justus's plan and Representative Flaherty's plan. However, a significant amendment that was approved was one offered by Rep. Walter Jones, Jr., a white Democrat. Jones made a motion to move four Pitt County precincts from the Second Congressional District to the First Congressional District. This had the effect of placing Jones' residence, as well as that of his father, Congressman Walter B. Jones, Sr., in the First Congressional District. The initial ratified plan sent to the U.S. Justice Department (Base Plan #6) had placed the residences of Jones, Jr., and his father in the First District, but all subsequent plans had placed the two in the Second Congressional District.

SUBMISSION OF PLAN TO U.S. DEPARTMENT OF JUSTICE

The full House took up Congressional Base Plan #9 on January 23, 1992, and defeated the same amendments Flaherty and Justus had offered in committee. The House passed Congressional Base Plan #9. The following day, the full Senate passed Congressional Base Plan #9 as well. The plan that was sent to the U.S. Department of Justice on January 28, 1992, was known as Congressional Base Plan #10. It was essentially the same as Congressional Base Plan #9 except it increased the total black population in District 1 from 57.16 percent to 57.26 percent.

Congressional Base Plan #10 was based in large part on the plan presented by Mary Peeler of the NAACP at the public hearing (see Figures 4.1–4.10 on pages 80–89 at the end of this chapter for a display of the maps presented to the General Assembly). In fact, all of the congressional base plans presented by the leadership of the House and Senate from Congressional Base Plan #7 through Base Plan #10 were based on the Peeler prototype.

Representative David Balmer (Republican), who became somewhat of a statewide celebrity for the Republican party during the first round of congressional redistricting and who introduced four different plans on December 20, 1991, which created two minority districts, never presented any of these plans to either the House or Senate redistricting committees during the extra session or the regular session. None of those plans had support from the black community. Of note, it was a Republican legislator, Representative David Balmer, who had originally created the Interstate 85 corridor district. Table 4.1 lists plans that were either major contenders for acceptance or provided a unique redistricting perspective during the 1991–1992 redistricting session and shows the percentage of the black voting-age population for all of the districts in each plan.

Upon examination, it is clear that even some of the earliest plans presented, such as Balmer 6.2, had bizarrely shaped districts. Even the two plans accepted by the state legislature (Base Plan #6 and Base Plan #10) had irregularly shaped districts. In Base Plan #6, the black majority district—the First—sprawls east from the Piedmont almost to the North Carolina coast. However, the shape of the Second is even more bizarre. It resembles a multiarmed creature with tentacles spreading in all directions. All of these plans violate the notion of compact and contiguous districts. In both Base Plan #6 and Base Plan #10, there are districts that are contiguous only because they touch at points.

On February 6, 1992, the U.S. Justice Department notified the North Carolina Attorney General that its congressional redistricting plan had been precleared under Section 5 of the VRA. Shortly after the U.S. Justice Department notified state officials of its action, leaders of the state NAACP and ACLU suggested that they were considering lawsuits to make the state draw even more minority congressional districts. Republican party stalwarts in the state were not particularly pleased with the precleared plan. State Republican party Chairman R. Jack Hawke, Jr., said that Republicans

> might challenge the congressional plan on other grounds, including partisan gerrymandering, a failure to draw compact districts and a lack of consideration for "communities of interest."[33]

Hawke went on to accuse the Democrats of creating an idiotic congressional redistricting plan drawn for the sole purpose of protecting Democratic incumbents.

But Senator Herbert Hyde (Democrat) saw it differently. He observed that it was the U.S. Department of Justice's rejection of the first

Table 4.1. Percentage Black Voting-Age Population, by District

District Plan	1	2	3	4	5	6	7	8	9	10	11	12
Balmer 6.2	21.42	**53.71**	19.39	15.76	12.98	20.03	18.28	12.38	9.98	10.32	4.21	**45.32**
Balmer 7.8	17.83	**49.65**	**52.60**	14.92	8.05	8.81	18.09	13.94	22.62	22.20	10.43	4.19
Balmer 8.1	21.45	**54.87**	18.22	14.76	8.61	8.23	22.87	16.72	10.09	10.42	3.92	**53.75**
Justus's Plan	20.16	**52.55**	28.35	22.56	15.22	19.79	22.48	14.55	22.71	12.31	7.49	4.76
Compact 2—Minority Plan	20.19	**52.37**	22.85	17.35	15.82	**44.79**	14.06	19.79	9.87	14.55	7.50	4.75
Flaherty's Plan	16.60	**53.05**	19.04	13.58	7.25	9.59	**38.61**	12.89	9.02	9.51	4.06	**50.80**
92 Congress 1	**52.34**	19.34	18.61	18.23	16.20	6.21	18.25	21.19	8.56	4.61	7.32	**52.71**
Wilson Plan[a]	23.37	**51.72**	22.93	22.90	13.93	16.72	**49.17**	10.83	8.50	9.29	10.06	4.62
Optimum II—Zero	**51.89**	21.89	21.22	16.13	11.54	7.82	19.46	19.89	7.09	9.10	4.93	**52.83**
Congress 6	**52.18**	19.92	22.36	18.44	17.18	23.60	22.25	21.84	22.65	9.65	4.91	7.60
Congress 10	**53.41**	20.06	19.64	18.93	14.04	7.05	17.15	20.90	8.03	4.94	6.37	**53.34**

Source: Compiled from data from the North Carolina General Assembly, Information Systems Division, 1992.

[a]Scott Kimbrough's plan

Note: Percentages in bold indicate districts that had either a majority or substantial black voting-age population.

plan that made the General Assembly draw this plan that he admitted was idiotic. Representative Art Pope (Republican) had these comments about the precleared congressional plan:

> I think that they are terribly gerrymandered on parts of lines totally apart from what was necessary to create two minority districts. I think the two minority districts could have been created far more compact. I think the reason they were gerrymandered is twofold. It had to do with individual legislators, potential congressional candidates in the two minority districts and second, in order to gerrymander surrounding districts on partisan grounds to minimize any Republican gains.[34]

Though the U.S. Department of Justice precleared Congressional Base Plan #10, there was outrage from Republicans and Democrats alike over the contorted shape of some of the districts. Many felt that the two minority districts disregarded traditional notions of compactness, contiguity, and geographically defined districts. An editorial in the *Raleigh News and Observer* on January 21, 1992, stated, "If a psychiatrist substituted North Carolina's proposed congressional redistricting maps for Rorschach ink blot tests, diagnoses of wackiness would jump dramatically."[35] The *Wall Street Journal*, on February 4, 1992, referred to North Carolina's congressional plan as "political pornography."[36]

CONCLUSION

In reflecting on the congressional redistricting process in North Carolina during 1991 and 1992, several points should be noted. First, the redistricting process centered around partisan and racial gerrymandering. Partisan gerrymandering had an effect on racial gerrymandering. White Democrats had to skillfully craft two majority black districts while protecting incumbent white congresspeople.

Second, the final plan accepted by the U.S. Department of Justice was the product of several factors. One was the climate created by the Justice Department when it decided that all states that fall under the preclearance requirement of the VRA should create minority districts where possible. In addition, because of the increase in black legislators in North Carolina, blacks for the first time in the twentieth century were major players in the redistricting process.

And finally, the Republicans sought to gain congressional seats by pushing for the creation of as many majority black districts as possible.

The Republicans knew that the Democrats depended heavily on black support to win elections. Hence, by concentrating blacks in two or more districts primarily in the cities, the surrounding Republican suburbs have a stronger base and the Democratic base is substantially weakened. This, I believe, was the primary motivation behind the plans submitted by the Republicans.

Representative Tim Hardaway (Democrat) and Representative David Balmer (Republican) had personal motives and partisan motives for the plans that they submitted. Hardaway, who was the author of Optimum II–Zero, created a plan that split Durham County and placed Representative H. M. "Mickey" Michaux (Democrat), a potential rival for one of the newly created minority districts, out of the First District where Hardaway resided and into the Twelfth District. Representative Balmer (Republican) created a myriad of plans that either benefitted the Republicans as a whole or individually increased Balmer's chances of winning a congressional seat. Representative Balmer and Representative Hardaway made unsuccessful bids for U.S. Congress in the 1992 primary elections, losing in the Ninth District Republican primary and in the First District Democratic primary, respectively.

After the 1992 elections, it appeared that the Republicans' strategy of picking up substantial seats in the U.S. Congress as a result of their lobbying for increased majority-minority districts did not pay off. All six of the state's white Democratic incumbents won reelection in 1992. Even Tim Valentine and Stephen Neal won reelection, although both were thought to be extremely vulnerable because of the loss in their districts of so many black voters as a result of redistricting. With two new black Democrats, the Democrats maintained an 8–4 edge over the Republicans.

Redistricting and Democracy

A larger issue that deserves examination is the relationship between redistricting and democracy. Blacks gain descriptive representation with the creation of majority black districts, but is democracy sacrificed in the long run? One goal of Republicans nationally was to gain congressional seats after the 1990s round of redistricting. Blacks now were the majority in North Carolina in two congressional districts. But this accomplishment meant that black influence was severely lessened in the remaining 10 districts. By packing blacks into two districts, their ability to influence the other congressional elections was seriously diminished. One may argue that the white congresspeople elected from those districts will not be as responsive to the concerns of their black constituents as they previously may have been. Without fear of reprisal at the voting booth, they do not have to be. Furthermore, redistricting changed the whole dynamic of safe seats in Congress. Many white Democrats represented safe districts that had been drawn by Democratically controlled state legislatures. By creating majority black districts, which are predominantly Democratic, those districts become less susceptible to partisan competition. However, many of the previously safe Democratic House seats have become more competitive and winnable by Republican candidates. After redistricting in 1991–1992, congressional districts have become increasingly polarized by race and party, and white Democrats have become the major casualty. Ironically, though the 1992 elections seemed to prove the Republicans' strategy ineffective, in 1994, matters were different. The midterm congressional elections in 1994 brought in the "Republican Revolution." The Democrats lost 52 seats in 1994. Critics of race-conscious redistricting have argued that it caused Democrats to lose enough seats to give the Republicans the majority. Not only did the Republicans gain control of the U.S. House of Representatives with the 1994 elections, they also gained control of North Carolina's congressional delegation. In fact, North Carolina's congressional delegation flip-flopped from an 8–4 Democratic majority to an 8–4 Republican majority after the 1994 elections. Therefore, the trade-off between descriptive representation (representatives who are black) and substantive representation (representatives responsive to black needs) becomes relevant here.* The number of blacks in Congress is 39, 38 of whom are Democrats. So when the Republicans gained majority status, black influence diminished considerably. Before the 1994 elections, three black congressmen chaired committees: Ron Dellums (Democrat—California), Armed Services Committee; John Conyers (Democrat—Michigan), Government Operations Committee; and Bill Clay (Democrat—Missouri), Post Office and Civil Service Committee. After 1994, the Republicans regained the majority in the U.S. House of Representatives and the U.S. Senate. The only two black Republicans in the U.S. House or U.S. Senate were Representative Gary Franks and Representative J. C. Watts. Neither had enough seniority to chair a committee. There were no black Republicans in the Senate after the 1994 elections.

Political scientists Paul Gronke and J. Matthew Wilson examined all of the major plans presented to the North Carolina state legislature during the 1990–1991 redistricting process in North Carolina. They estimate

---

*See Carol Swain, *Black Faces, Black Interests*, 1993; David Lublin, *The Paradox of Representation*, 1997, for a discussion of descriptive representation versus substantive representation.

the probability of Democratic and Republican victories in all the plans. They show the strategic motivations behind the drawing of these plans by Democratic and Republican legislators. Using statistical analyses, they demonstrate the partisan bias in each of the plans.[37]

The final plan created contained two majority black districts each with only a 53 percent black voting-age population. I find it interesting to note that no black citizen suggested to either Congressional Redistricting Committee that both these majority black districts lacked an effective black voting majority to ensure black representation. Only the Republican congressional delegation complained to U.S. Assistant Attorney General John Dunne that the black majority district in Base Plan #6 (District 1) might not contain a large enough minority concentration to enable blacks to elect a candidate of their choice. This is particularly interesting in light of past literature and litigation on the "65 percent rule."

A 65 percent black population is said to be required in order to have an effective black voting majority. There are three reasons for this percentage. First, the percentage of the voting-age population that is black tends to be less than that of whites because blacks tend to have lower life expectancy rates, meaning that there are fewer elderly blacks than elderly whites in the same proportion. Moreover, blacks tend to have higher birth rates than whites, which means that there will be a higher percentage of blacks under the age of 18. Thus, the black voting-age population is less than the total population. Second, black voter registration tends to lag behind white voter registration, although the gap closed tremendously from 1980 to 1990. Third, historically, black turnout on election day tends to lag behind white turnout primarily because of socioeconomic reasons. Sixty-five percent has been identified as the rule because when one deducts 5 percent for each of these three factors, 50 percent actually vote.

The 65 percent rule gained legal mooring because of two U.S. Supreme Court cases in the 1970s: *Kirksey v. Board of Supervisors of Hinds County* (1977) and *United Jewish Organizations of Williamsburg v. Carey* (1977). The two separate cases dealt with reapportionment on the state and local levels. Scholars Bernard Grofman, Lisa Handley, and Richard G. Niemi warn that there has been a misreading of these cases and that neither case states that the 65 percent rule is to be adhered to in all cases at all times. Moreover, they argue that the U.S. Justice Department has never adhered to this so-called rule and that there is nothing special about 65 percent. They argue, furthermore, that blacks can win elections to legislative districts that are as low as slightly more than 50 percent black and as high as 65 percent black.[38] Frank Parker, in discussing minority vote dilution in legislative districts, has alleged that short of the 65 percent rule, white legislators have created districts that are 53 percent or 54 percent minority and then have asserted that they have not discriminated because they have created a majority-minority district.[39] However, political scientist Charles Bullock has written that though 65 percent black may be necessary for a black to win election for state or local office, it is not clear that congressional districts must be two-thirds black in population for a black to have a legitimate chance to win.[40] Empirical analysis tends to support Bullock's assertions. Of the 13 newly created majority black districts in 1992, only five were districts that had a 60 percent or higher black population. Six were districts with a black population between 55 percent and 60 percent, and two had a black population between 50 percent and 55 percent. A black candidate for office was elected to Congress from all 13 of the newly created black districts in 1992.

Table 4.2. New Black Congressional Districts, 1992

Representative	District	% Black	% Black VAP
Hilliard (D-AL)	7	67.5	63.5
Meek (D-FL)	17	58.4	54.0
Brown (D-FL)	3	55.0	50.6
Hastings (D-FL)	23	51.6	45.7
McKinney (D-GA)	11	64.1	60.4
Bishop (D-GA)	2	56.6	52.3
Fields (D-LA)	4	66.4	62.6
Wynn (D-MD)	4	58.5	55.8
Clayton (D-NC)	1	57.3	53.4
Watt (D-NC)	12	56.6	53.3
Clyburn (D-SC)	6	62.2	58.3
Johnson (D-TX)	30	50.0	47.1
Scott (D-VA)	3	64.1	61.2

Source: Joint Center for Political and Economic Studies, May 1992.
Note: VAP = voting-age population

The state legislature in North Carolina made its newly acquired congressional seat a Republican-leaning district, creating a 7–5 Democratic majority in the state's congressional delegation. However, the Republicans balked at this plan and asked the U.S. Department of Justice to deny preclearance of it on the grounds that the state of North Carolina could have created more majority-minority districts, which by implication would have meant more Republican-leaning surrounding districts.

In their denial of preclearance of Base Plan #6, the U.S. Department of Justice noted in its rejection letter that North Carolina could have created a second majority-minority district in the southeastern portion of the state. One of Balmer's plans, Balmer 6.2, was the basis of the Republican challenge to Base Plan #6. The Justice Department suggested to North Carolina that it could create a second minority district evidenced by District 12 in Balmer 6.2.

The Democrats, however, crafted a revised plan (Base Plan #10) that created two majority black districts without increasing Republican representation in the remaining districts. The revised congressional plan, approved by the Justice Department, led to an 8–4 Democratic edge over the Republicans.

The Republicans in North Carolina did not resign themselves to accepting the new congressional redistricting plan. They hoped to be more successful in the federal courts by having the enacted plan declared unconstitutional.

NOTES

[1]David Balmer, Letter to Assistant U.S. Attorney General John Dunne, August 5, 1991.

[2]Kathleen Wilde, Letter to Assistant Attorney General John Dunne, September 25, 1991.

[3]Kathleen Wilde, Letter.

[4]Kathleen Wilde, Letter.

[5]Kathleen Wilde, Letter.

[6]Kathleen Wilde, Letter.

[7]Kathleen Wilde, Letter.

[8]Balmer, Letter Sent to Assistant Attorney General John Dunne.

[9]John Dunne, Letter to Tiare B. Smiley, North Carolina Special Deputy Attorney General, October 18, 1991.

[10]Ken Otterbourg, "Districts Debated in Angry Assembly: Plan Is Partisan, Republicans Say" *Winston-Salem Journal*, June 2, 1991: E–1.

[11]"It's Redistricting Time at the N. C. Legislature," *Gastonia Gazette*, June 2, 1991: 2B.

[12]John Dunne, Letter to North Carolina Special Deputy Attorney Tiare Smiley, December 18, 1991.

[13]John Dunne, Letter to North Carolina Special Attorney Tiare Smiley, December 18, 1991.

[14]Interview with Leslie Winner, May 28, 1992, Charlotte, North Carolina.

[15]Interview with Leslie Winner, May 28, 1992, Charlotte, North Carolina.

[16]Interview with Dan Blue, June 2, 1992, Raleigh, North Carolina.

[17]John Dunne, Letter to North Carolina Special Deputy Attorney Tiare Smiley.

[18]Quoted in Van Denton, "G.O.P. Teamed Up For Victory: Redistricting Ruling Debated," *Raleigh News and Observer*, December 25, 1991: 1A.

[19]Ferrel Guillory, "G.O.P. Seeks Change in District Map," *Raleigh News and Observer*, January 9, 1992: B1.

[20]North Carolina General Assembly, Joint Session, House and Senate Redistricting Committees, *Public Hearing on Congressional Redistricting Plans*, January 9, 1992.

[21]North Carolina General Assembly, Public Hearing. January 9, 1992.

[22]V. O. Key, *Southern Politics in State and Nation*, (New York: Alfred Knopf, Inc.) 215.

[23]Interview with Gerry Cohen, May 27, 1992, Raleigh, North Carolina.

[24]Affidavit of Gerry Cohen at 5 and 6, *Pope v. Blue*, 809 F. Supp. 392 (WDNC 1992).

[25]Affidavit of Gerry Cohen at 6.

[26]Charles Mahtesian, "Blacks' Political Hopes Boosted by Newly Redrawn Districts," *Congressional Quarterly Weekly Report*, April 25, 1992, 1090.

[27]Quoted in Ferrel Guillory, "G.O.P. Seeks Change in District Map," *Raleigh News and Observer*, January 9, 1992: B1.

[28]Quoted in Ferrel Guillory B2.

[29]Quoted in Guillory B2.

[30]Van Denton, "Party Loyalty, Black Gains Clash in Redistricting," *Raleigh News and Observer*, January 7, 1992: A1.

[31]Van Denton A2.

[32]Van Denton, "Party Loyalty, Black Gains Clash in Redistricting," *Congressional Quarterly Weekly Report*, January 7, 1992: 2.

[33]Quoted in Van Denton, "U.S. O.K.'s State's New Districts," *Raleigh News and Observer*, February 7, 1992: 1.

[34]Interview with Art Pope, June 2, 1992, Raleigh, North Carolina.

[35]"Reading the Ink Blot." *Raleigh News and Observer*, January 21, 1992: A8.

[36]"Political Pornography II," *Wall Street Journal*, February 4, 1992: A14.

[37]Paul Gronke and Matthew Wilson, "Competing Redistricting Plans as Evidence of Competing Motives." Paper presented at the 1996 Annual Meeting of the Midwest Political Science Association, Chicago, Illinois.

[38]Bernard Grofman, Lisa Handley, and Richard G. Niemi, *Minority Representation and the Quest for Voting Equality* (New York: Cambridge University Press, 1992) 120–121.

[39]Frank Parker, "Racial Gerrymandering and Legislative Reapportionment," *Minority Vote Dilution*, ed. Chandler Davidson (Washington, D.C.: Howard U. Press, 1984) 108.

[40]Charles S. Bullock III. "The Inexact Science of Congressional Redistricting," *PS* 15 (Summer) 1982: 436.

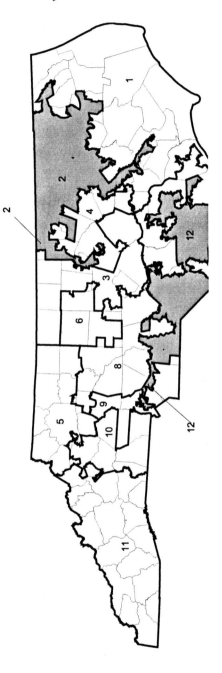

Figure 4.1. Majority Black Districts: Balmer 6.2

Source: North Carolina General Assembly, Information Systems Division, 1999.

Figure 4.2. Majority Black Districts: Justus Plan

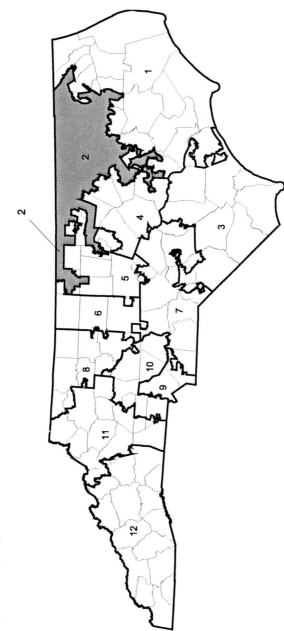

Source: North Carolina General Assembly, Information Systems Division, 1999.

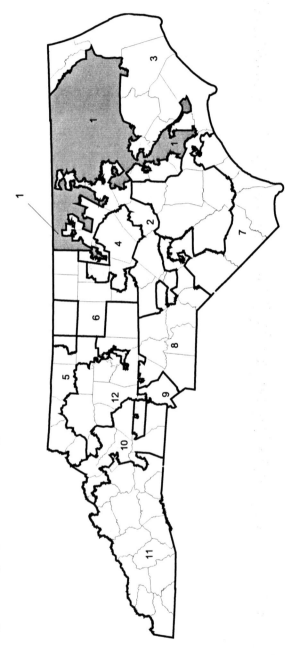

Figure 4.3. Majority Black Districts: Congressional Base Plan #6

Source: North Carolina General Assembly, Information Systems Division, 1999.

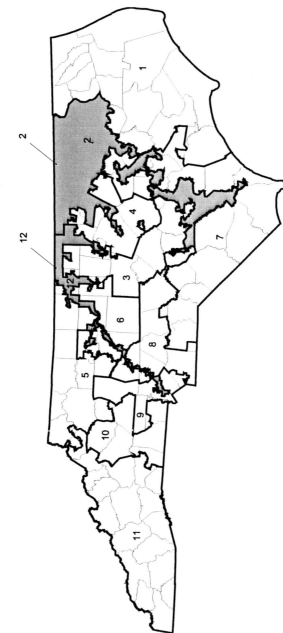

Figure 4.4. Majority Black Districts: Balmer Congress 8.1

Source: North Carolina General Assembly, Information Systems Division, 1999.

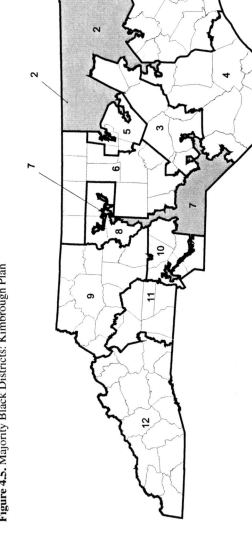

Figure 4.5. Majority Black Districts: Kimbrough Plan

Source: North Carolina General Assembly, Information Systems Division, 1999.

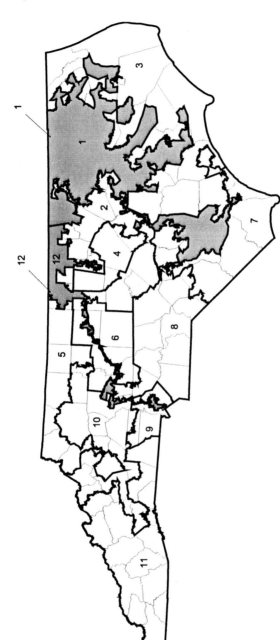

Figure 4.6. Majority Black Districts: 92 Congress 1

Source: North Carolina General Assembly, Information Systems Division, 1999.

Figure 4.7. Majority Black Districts: Optimum II—Zero

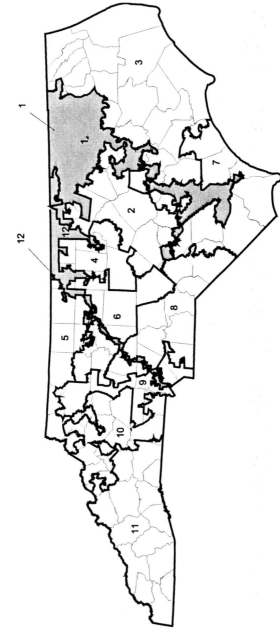

Source: North Carolina General Assembly, Information Systems Division, 1999.

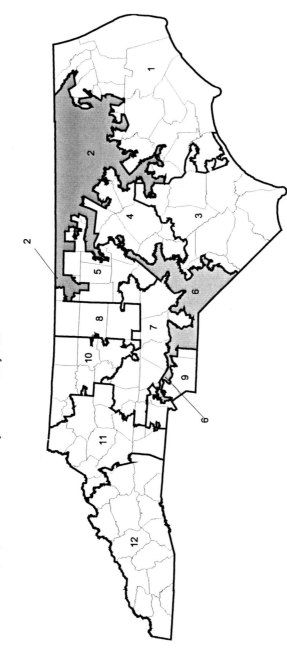

Figure 4.8. Majority Black Districts: Compact 2—Minority Plan

Source: North Carolina General Assembly, Information Systems Division, 1999.

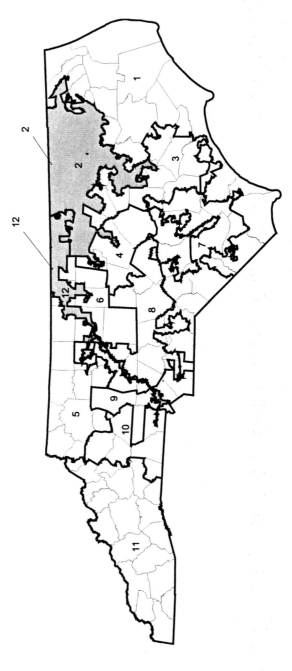

Figure 4.9. Majority Black Districts: Flaherty Plan

Source: North Carolina General Assembly, Information Systems Division, 1999.

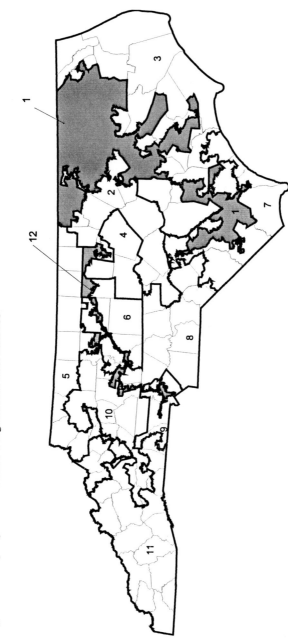

Figure 4.10. Majority Black Districts: Congressional Base Plan #10

Source: North Carolina General Assembly, Information Systems Division, 1999.

PART II

Court Litigation Surrounding Redistricting and Standards of Congressional Redistricting

CHAPTER 5

Legal Issues Surrounding North Carolina's Redistricting Process

Congressional redistricting around the country produced majority black districts after the 1990 census and reapportionment process. This new environment was fostered by U.S. Supreme Court decisions in the 1980s, administrative regulations issued by the U.S. Department of Justice, and the Voting Rights Act of 1982 passed by the U.S. Congress. In this chapter, I review several of the U.S. Supreme Court decisions and regulations in the 1980s that imposed stricter standards for redistricting in the 1990s. Additionally, this chapter focuses on the major legal issues and court battles surrounding North Carolina's two majority black districts. It chronicles these legal disputes all the way to the U.S. Supreme Court.

U.S. SUPREME COURT DECISIONS IN THE 1980s

In the 1980s, the U.S. Supreme Court began tightening its requirements for redistricting. In *Karcher v. Daggett* (1983),[1] the Supreme Court struck down a New Jersey congressional redistricting plan because the population deviation between the most- and least-populated districts was 0.6984, too large according to the Court. The Court stated in its reasoning that no uniform level of population disparity is so small as to be acceptable and that only when states can prove that they are necessary to achieve a legitimate goal will they be allowed. However, the U.S. Supreme Court ruled in *Davis v. Bandemer* (1986)[2] for the first time that partisan gerrymandering that conspicuously gives one party an advantage over another would be subject to legal challenge.

That case involved an Indiana state legislative redistricting plan. The Democrats contended that the Republican-controlled state legislature had drawn legislative districts to maximize Republican voting strength and minimize Democratic voting strength. They accused the Republicans of packing Democrats into districts that already had Democratic majorities and splitting other Democratic districts to ensure Republican advantage.

The high court agreed with the plaintiffs that the partisan gerrymander had violated the Fourteenth Amendment to the U.S. Constitution; however, the Court required more than "intentional" discrimination against an identifiable political group. It stated that the plaintiffs must show "an actual discriminatory effect on that group."[3] The Court opined that here the intent had been proven but a sufficient discriminatory effect had not. Furthermore, the Court declared that

> unconstitutional discrimination occurs only when a redistricting plan will consistently degrade a voter's or a group of voters' influence of the political process as a whole.[4]

Even though the Court ruled that partisan gerrymandering may be subject to legal challenge in *Bandemer*, it is important to remember that the Court did not overturn the Republican plan.

In California, Republican lawmakers challenged a Democratically drawn congressional redistricting map on the ground that it was aggressively partisan. Democratic U.S. Representative Phillip Burton had designed the district to protect Democrats for House elections for the decade. A federal district court ruled that a party seeking to overturn a map must show a general pattern of exclusion from the political process.[5] In this case, *Badham v. Eu* (1989),[6] the Supreme Court in a 6–3 vote refused to hear oral arguments ruling that the map did not constitute an unacceptable partisan gerrymander. Thus, it appears that during the 1980s the high court still firmly believed that the process of redistricting involved political conflict and it was reluctant to strike down even egregious partisan gerrymandering.

VOTING RIGHTS ACT OF 1982 AND ADMINISTRATIVE REGULATIONS ISSUED

Congress revised Section 2 of the Voting Rights Act in 1982 to make it clear that laws that had the effect of discriminating against minority voters were as illegal as those laws that were intended to discriminate. Furthermore, after *Thornburg v. Gingles* (1986) (see Chapter 3), lawmakers nationwide believed this decision required them to create majority-minority districts wherever possible to avoid diluting the minority vote. This signaled a change in existing law because prior to the *Gingles* decision, states only had to satisfy a nonretrogression standard. In other words, states had to make sure that their redistricting plans at least maintained the existing majority-minority districts. Moreover, the U.S. Department of Justice issued regulations in 1987 that paralleled the *Gingles* decision.

Retrogression is actually a form of vote dilution in addition to stacking, packing, and cracking (discussed in Chapter 3). Retrogression as a standard was first established by the U.S. Supreme Court in *Beer v. United States* (1976).[7] Lisa Handley, a voting rights scholar, has defined a redistricting plan as a whole as retrogressive if there are fewer districts in which minorities have a realistic chance to elect candidates of their choice in a new plan than existed under the old plan (assuming that the minority population has not decreased).[8]

BACKGROUND TO REDISTRICTING LAWSUITS IN NORTH CAROLINA IN THE 1990s

The redistricting process in North Carolina was the product of political compromise. The Democratically controlled state legislature had to balance the rights of minority voters as protected by the Voting Rights Act against the concerns of the minority political party. It had the additional task of satisfying the needs of incumbents who wanted to protect their districts. To accomplish this, the legislature created a congressional plan that contained two majority black districts: the First, which meandered from the Virginia border in the Northeast south to the South Carolina border encompassing 28 counties completely or in part; and the Twelfth, which twisted and snarled through central Piedmont North Carolina following Interstate 85 and sprawled through parts of 10 counties from Charlotte to Durham.

The 1991–1992 congressional redistricting process in North Carolina produced a plan by a Democratically controlled legislature that created eight Democratic districts and four Republican districts. For obvious reasons, North Carolina Republicans were unhappy with this arrangement. Republican State Senator N. Leo Daughtry filed *Daughtry v. State Board of Elections* in the U.S. Middle District Court in North

Carolina on November 1, 1991, asking the court to take control of the re-districting process.[9] On July 1, 1992, Judge Richard Erwin in the U.S. Middle District Court dismissed *Daughtry* on the grounds that it was a moot case. But *Daughtry* was only the beginning of a calculated legal strategy on behalf of Republicans in North Carolina to overturn the newly created congressional redistricting plan in North Carolina.

LAWSUITS ARISING OUT OF THE INITIALLY ADOPTED PLAN

Pope v. Blue (1992)

Even before the U.S. Department of Justice had ruled on North Car-olina's revised congressional plan, the Republicans began their legal challenge of the newly drawn districts. On February 2, 1992, North Car-olina state House Representative Art Pope (Republican), filed suit in the U.S. Western District Court in North Carolina. Other plaintiffs included 45 citizens of North Carolina, the North Carolina Republican party, and its chairman, R. Jack Hawke. Defendants named in the suit included Dan Blue (Democrat), Speaker of the state House of Representatives, and other state officials, including Governor James Martin, the secretary of state, and members of the State Board of Elections.

The suit challenged the constitutionality of the congressional plan on the grounds that it lacked compactness and did not adhere to the prin-ciple of communities of interest. The complaint stated:

> The failure of the General Assembly to adopt an equipopulous con-gressional redistricting plan with more compact districts violates the rights of those citizens living in communities of interest to exercise their elective franchise and to participate on an equal basis with those living in communities which have not been fractured by the General Assembly for illegitimate purposes.[10]

Altogether, the plaintiffs' complaint stated five causes of action. Plain-tiffs also sought a temporary restraining order and preliminary injunction to extend the March 2, 1992, deadline for filing notices of candidacy for election to the U.S. House of Representatives until a hearing could take place on the complaint.

The plaintiffs claimed that the congressional redistricting plan en-acted by the state violated their constitutional rights under the Due

Process, Equal Protection, and Privileges and Immunities clauses of the Fourteenth Amendment to the U.S. Constitution. Moreover, plaintiffs alleged the plan violated Article 1, Section 2 of the U.S. Constitution. The complaint stated that according to Article 1, Section 2 of the U.S. Constitution, "Members of the House of Representatives must be chosen 'by the People of the several states' thereby requiring that each person is entitled to an equal, fair and effective vote in a congressional election."[11]

Another cause of action stated by the plaintiffs was that the enacted plan violated the First Amendment to the U.S. Constitution, specifically its protections of freedom of speech and association. According to the complaint, the ratified plan

> violates plaintiffs' First Amendment freedoms by arbitrarily and invidiously discriminating against certain identifiable and cognizable groups of voters and communities of interest solely because of geographic location or partisan affiliation, and by chilling public debate on issues of importance.[12]

The plaintiffs in this case had retained Bernard Grofman to review the proposed redistricting plan with respect to standard criteria of redistricting. Grofman is a specialist on reapportionment and redistricting and has been used as an expert witness in numerous federal voting rights cases. Grofman asserted that the North Carolina congressional plan was seriously flawed, and he supported the claim by the plaintiffs that it violated the Equal Protection Clause of the Fourteenth Amendment with respect to the citizens of North Carolina. According to Grofman, the plan's violations were in at least three categories:

1. The plan violates contiguity.
2. Some districts are so distorted and tortuous that voter confusion is unavoidable, since there is no way to characterize the district boundaries in a way that can readily be communicated to the citizens of the state, thus damaging the realistic possibility of "fair and effective representation."
3. A number of the district lines have been drawn in a capricious and arbitrary manner, creating a "crazy-quilt" pattern that serves rational state purpose, while at the same time violating standard criteria of redistricting.[13]

Opposition to the G.O.P. Arguments. Robert Dorff, a political scientist at North Carolina State University in Raleigh, whose research and teaching interests included electoral representation models, campaigns, and elections, filed a sworn affidavit with the District Court that disagreed with the plaintiffs' assertions. Dorff, a registered Republican, stated that the plaintiffs' contention that the Democrats drew district lines to protect incumbents was probably true. However, noted Dorff, that is plain and simple "current U.S. politics. This advantage holds true for Republicans as well as Democrats."[14] He cites *The Politics of Congressional Elections* by Gary C. Jacobson as supporting evidence of this.*

Moreover, Dorff took issue with the plaintiffs' assertion that contorted districts deny access of constituents to their congresspeople. Dorff stated that "very few districts in the entire United States allow for easy, direct, physical access to a congressman. Geographical dispersion is the norm rather than the exception."[15]

However, Dorff did acknowledge that Grofman's declaration was moored to legal applications and that he, Dorff, was speaking strictly from a political science perspective. Nonetheless, he took issue with Grofman's narrow use of the phrase "communities of interest." Dorff proclaimed:

> Communities of interest, on which political presentation can and should be based, consist of a number of significant dimensions other than geographic contiguity. These include economic, social and cultural interests.[16]

Dan Blue (Democrat) had always maintained that the Twelfth District in Base Plan #10 was an urban district in comparison with the First District, which was largely rural and also majority black. Blue had stated that the Twelfth consisted of the major urban areas of Durham, Greensboro, Winston-Salem, and Charlotte, which were all major cities and more likely to have the same problems associated with urban areas, such as crime, overcrowding, urban decay, and loss of the tax base.

Ironically, computers have added to the confusion in redistricting. The process of redrawing congressional districts used to be relegated to legislators and their staff engaging in painstaking work. Now anyone with the requisite hardware and computer disks full of census and precinct data can create districts on demand. Computer technology has

---

*See Gary C. Jacobson, *The Politics of Congressional Elections* (1992), for discussion of partisan gerrymandering.

teamed up with partisan considerations to make gerrymandering even more egregious. Districts can now be tailored down to the census tract block.

The District Court Moves. On February 28, 1992, the U.S. District Court for the Western District of North Carolina granted the plaintiffs a temporary restraining order delaying the March 2, 1992, deadline for candidates filing for U.S. Congress until March 10, 1992. This was done to allow the court time to hold a hearing on the plaintiffs' complaint.

The defendants subsequently filed a motion with the federal district court to dismiss the claims by the plaintiffs because no constitutional violation had occurred.

On March 9, 1992, a three-judge panel in the U.S. Western District Court in North Carolina held a hearing on the defendants' motion to dismiss. The panel dismissed the plaintiffs' complaint.

The plaintiffs in this case subsequently made an emergency application to Chief Justice William Rehnquist of the U.S. Supreme Court for an injunction and stay of the congressional plan pending an appeal. Rehnquist denied the request.

Shaw v. Barr (1992)

Even before *Pope v. Blue* (1992) had exhausted the appeals process, other North Carolinians were anxious to initiate legal action because of the congressional plan drawn by the state legislature. On March 12, 1992, five white residents of Durham—Ruth Shaw, Melvin Shimm, Robinson O. Everett, Everett's son James Everett, and Dorothy Bullock—filed suit in the U.S. District Court for the Eastern District of North Carolina challenging North Carolina's newly created congressional plan.

Under the 1992 redistricting plan, Shaw and Shimm are part of the Twelfth Congressional District, and the Everetts and Dorothy Bullock, are part of the Second Congressional District. Their suit named as defendants William Barr, Attorney General of the United States, and John Dunne, Assistant U.S. Attorney General and head of the Civil Rights Division. Several North Carolina executive government officials were also named in the suit.

The complaint alleged, among other things, that the congressional redistricting plan implemented by the North Carolina state legislature was unconstitutional and was created because of the coercive requirements imposed by Defendants Barr and Dunne.[17]

The plaintiffs made clear in their complaint that they were not basing their action on the partisan gerrymandering that occurred to create the enacted congressional plan and which was a cause of action on the part of the plaintiffs in *Pope v. Blue* (1992).

Furthermore, the plaintiffs asserted that the Justice Department officials responsible for enforcing the Voting Rights Act coerced the state legislature into creating the enacted congressional plan (the Department of Justice failed to preclear the initial ratified plan by the state legislature) by their unconstitutional interpretation of the Voting Rights Act. The plaintiffs alleged that this action violated the constitutional rights of citizens and voters of North Carolina.

The crux of the plaintiffs' argument was that the Department of Justice's interpretation and implementation of the Voting Rights Act effectively isolates a large number of black persons into two congressional districts separate and apart from the people in North Carolina's other 10 congressional districts.[18] This led to the creation of majority-minority districts to assure the election of minority persons as members of Congress from these districts.[19]

This action, plaintiffs alleged, violates the wording of 42 United States Code Section 1973(b) of the Voting Rights Act. Plaintiffs note that nothing in Section 1973 establishes a right to have members of a protected class elected in numbers equal to their proportion in the population.[20]

Furthermore, the plaintiffs alleged in their complaint that the rejection of the initial plan (Base Plan #6) by the U.S. Department of Justice forced the North Carolina General Assembly to create congressional districts totally unrelated to considerations of compactness, contiguity, and geographic or jurisdictional communities of interest.[21]

The North Carolina congressional primaries were scheduled for May 5, 1992. The plaintiffs in this case had asked the court to issue a preliminary injunction and temporary restraining order to prevent North Carolina officials from taking any action in preparation for primary or general elections for the U.S. House of Representatives.[22]

Both federal and state defendants filed motions to dismiss the lawsuit filed against them. The three-judge district court decided to permit hearing of the motions prior to the May primary.

The hearing was held on April 27, 1992, on the pleading of the plaintiffs and the motions to dismiss that were filed by the defendants. The three-judge U.S. District Court panel dismissed *Shaw v. Barr* (1992) on the grounds that it had no subject matter jurisdiction over the allegations against the U.S. Justice Department officials and that the complaint stated no claim upon which relief could be granted against the defendants. The U.S. District Court delayed issuing its opinion until August 7, 1992, and the plaintiffs immediately appealed to the U.S. Supreme Court.

The federal defendants cited Section 14(b) of the Voting Rights Act as the basis for stating that the federal district court in North Carolina lacked subject matter jurisdiction. Section 14(b) of the Voting Rights Act states that no court other than the District Court for the District of Columbia shall have jurisdiction to issue any restraining order or temporary or permanent injunction against the execution or enforcement of Section 5, or any action of any federal officer or employee.[23]

Moreover, the federal defendants asserted that this provision clearly demonstrated that the U.S. District Court in the Eastern District of North Carolina lacked subject matter jurisdiction to hear the allegations against the U.S. Justice Department officials. To the second charge against the federal defendants challenging the U.S. Attorney General's use of discretionary power delegated to him by Section 5 to determine preclearance decisions, the district court relied on the precedent established in *Morris v. Gressette* (1977). The court restated the defendants' claim that *Morris* has long since established that such discretionary decisions are not subject to judicial review in any court.[24]

Preclearance, a special feature of the 1965 Voting Rights Act, shifts the burden of proof in charges of racial voter discrimination from the alleged victims of voter discrimination to the government. Section 5 of the Voting Rights Act requires that governments that had a history of using literacy tests and in which less than 50 percent of the voting-age population had voted in the 1964 presidential election were deemed "covered" jurisdictions. Therefore, they were required to prove to the U.S. District Court for the District of Columbia (judicial preclearance) or the U.S. Attorney General (administrative preclearance) that any redistricting changes to their current plans do not discriminate against minorities in either purpose or effect. Forty counties in the state of North Carolina fall under this preclearance requirement.[25]

The plaintiffs also had alleged that the congressional plan in North Carolina violates the Equal Protection and Privileges and Immunity clauses of the Fourteenth Amendment. The district court noted that a troubling aspect of that claim was that nowhere did the plaintiffs identify themselves as black voters in whose behalf the challenged districts were created and nowhere do they allege constitutional injury specific to their rights as members of a particular racial classification of voters.[26]

The district court held that the plaintiffs' contention that the race-conscious redistricting plan violated the Fourteenth Amendment to the U.S. Constitution (Equal Protection Clause) and that the Fifteenth Amendment did not "state a legally cognizable claim."[27]

In denying the plaintiffs' claim that any race-conscious redistricting was in and of itself unconstitutional, the district court relied on the precedent set in *United Jewish Organizations of Williamsburg, Inc. v. Carey* (1977).[28] In that case, the U.S. Supreme Court upheld a redistricting plan that divided Hasidic Jewish communities for the purpose of creating a majority black district. Moreover, plaintiffs had asserted that U.S. Attorney General William Barr misinterpreted the Voting Rights Act to require racial quotas in representation. The district court ruled that it had no subject matter jurisdiction over that claim, citing Section 14(b) of the Voting Rights Act, which states that any challenge to the constitutionality of the Voting Rights Act by attacking actions of federal officials who are enforcing Section 5 of the Voting Rights Act can only be heard in the U.S. District Court for the District of Columbia.[29]

The district court concluded that the plaintiffs had raised some interesting questions about the political and social wisdom of the creation of two tortuously configured black majority districts but that ultimately they are political questions (to be settled by the political branches), about which none of the claims of constitutional violation has merit.[30]

The U.S. Supreme Court Hears Shaw v. Barr (1992) on Appeal. The plaintiffs filed their appeal on August 25, 1992 on behalf of Robinson O. Everett of Durham, North Carolina, and others. On September 29, 1992, the U.S. Supreme Court affirmed the dismissal of *Pope v. Blue* (1992) by the three-judge federal district court in North Carolina.

The appellants raised six questions in their direct appeal to the U.S. Supreme Court. Almost all cases that the U.S. Supreme Court hears fall within a discretionary (certiorari) rather than an obligatory (or appeal) category. However, according to Susan Low Bloch and Thomas G. Krattenmaker,

> Appeals, rather than certiorari, to the Supreme Court still lie from decisions of three-judge federal district courts. Many cases involving the Voting Rights Act of 1965 still arise in three-judge district courts.[31]

The Voting Rights Act of 1965 states that "an action pursuant to this subsection shall be heard and determined by a court of three judges in accordance with the provisions of section . . . and any appeal shall lie to the Supreme Court."[32]

On December 7, 1992, the U.S. Supreme Court noted probable jurisdiction in the case. However, jurisdiction was limited to one question:

> Whether a state legislature's intent to comply with the Voting Rights Act and the Attorney General's interpretation thereof precludes a finding that the legislature's congressional redistricting plan was adopted with invidious discriminatory intent where the legislature did not accede to the plan suggested by the Attorney General but instead developed its own.[33]

Shaw v. Reno (1993)

The U.S. Supreme Court set April 4, 1993, as the date that it would hear oral arguments in this case. A headline in a North Carolina newspaper, the *Durham Herald-Sun*, read "Professors Take Case to Court." Of interest was that two legal scholars from Duke University Law School would be squaring off to debate the constitutionality of North Carolina's majority black Twelfth Congressional District. For the appellants, Robinson O. Everett, one of the original plaintiffs, represented himself and the four other Durham residents. For the original defendants (now appellees), Jefferson Powell represented the state of North Carolina. According to the *Durham Herald-Sun*, "Court officials said they're not sure if faculty members from the same school have ever argued against each other there."[34] By the time this case reached the U.S. Supreme Court the Bush administration had left office and the Clinton administration was in office. The plaintiffs' case thus became referred to as *Shaw v. Reno*, the new U.S. Attorney General.

Friend-of-the-court briefs were filed on behalf of both parties to the lawsuit. The Republican National Committee, the Washington Legal Foundation, and the American Jewish Congress all issued briefs in support of the appellants. The U.S. Justice Department, the Democratic National Committee, and the NAACP all filed briefs in support of the state of North Carolina.[35]

On June 28, 1993, at the close of the 1992–1993 term, the U.S. Supreme Court rendered its decision. In a 5–4 ruling, Justice Sandra Day O'Connor wrote, in the opinion for the majority of the Court,

> It is unsettling how closely the North Carolina plan resembles the most egregious racial gerrymanders of the past. . . . A reapportionment plan

linking people who live far apart and who have little in common with one another but the color of their skin bears an uncomfortable resemblance to political apartheid.[36]

The plaintiffs claimed that the district court had violated the Equal Protection Clause of the Fourteenth Amendment because all white voters in the Twelfth District had been merged or submerged with the black voters in the district. Out of a total population in the Twelfth District of 552,386, the total white population stood at 230,888 (41.80 percent), and the total black population in the district at 312,791 (56.63 percent). With respect to registered voters in District 12, 45.90 percent were white and 53.54 percent were black.

Even if the white voters were submerged in the two majority black districts in North Carolina, the U.S. Supreme Court previously had not held this to be a constitutional violation. In *United Jewish Organizations of Williamsburg, Inc. v. Carey* (1977), the U.S. Supreme Court stated that white voters submerged into minority districts suffered no injury because they "will be represented by legislators elected from majority white districts, though they cannot participate in their election."[37]

The lower court applied this reasoning in denying plaintiffs' claim because whites, although in the minority in 2 of the 12 congressional districts in North Carolina, were the majority of voters in the remaining 10 congressional districts. However, the conservative majority in *Shaw* paid little attention to the doctrine of stare decisis, "let the decision stand," and parted with precedent by declaring that white voters in the majority black districts had suffered an injury. *The irony in O'Connor's assertion that white voters were submerged stems from the fact that this is the very problem that black voters face in white districts: Indeed, it is why black districts are needed.*

Justice O'Connor, however, in writing for the Court majority, did state that "this court has never held that race-conscious state decision-making is impermissible in all circumstances."[38] Nevertheless, the Court felt that the appearance of the First and Twelfth Districts in North Carolina "can be viewed only as an effort to segregate the races for purposes of voting, without regard for traditional districting principles and without sufficiently compelling justification."[39]

The Court, albeit parting with precedent, did not overturn it. The ruling reinstated the lawsuit filed on behalf of the five North Carolina voters challenging the creation of two districts in which black voters were in the majority.

The U.S. Supreme Court had stated in *United Jewish Organizations of Williamsburg, Inc., v. Carey* (1977) that "race-conscious plans can be legitimate if they are intended to make up for past discrimination and are adopted to comply with the Voting Rights Act."[40]

The high court did not go so far as to declare the creation of majority-minority districts a violation of the Constitution. Making no rule, it noted that race-conscious redistricting plans could be defended by states if they were their only means of avoiding minority vote dilution.[41] Furthermore, the Court placed the burden of proof on the states that draw race-conscious districts and said states must show that the districts are narrowly tailored to further a compelling state interest. The Court, in essence, without outlawing the racially gerrymandered districts in North Carolina, applied a stricter standard than ever before in declaring them constitutional. The Court found that the district court in North Carolina had erred in dismissing all of the claims made by the plaintiffs (now appellants). Therefore, the U.S. Supreme Court concluded that a plaintiff challenging a reapportionment statute under the Equal Protection Clause may state a claim by alleging that the legislation, though race-neutral on its face, rationally cannot be understood as anything other than an effort to separate voters into different districts on the basis of race.[42]

Because the high court felt that this one claim was sufficient to defeat the state appellees' motion to dismiss, the decision of the district court was reversed and the lawsuit filed by the appellants was reinstated. The case was thus remanded to the U.S. District Court in North Carolina.

A major concern of the U.S. Supreme Court majority in the decision was the creation of oddly shaped districts in which voters seemed to have only one thing in common—the color of their skin. The conservative majority on the Court clearly believed that congressional districts based on race would be unconstitutional unless the state could prove that the districts were drawn to further a compelling governmental interest. Moreover, the Court would apply its most stringent test—strict scrutiny—when determining whether or not districts passed constitutional muster. Justices Byron R. White, Harry A. Blackmun, John Paul Stevens, and David H. Souter all dissented and wrote separate dissenting opinions.*

Reaction to the U.S. Supreme Court's Ruling in Shaw v. Reno (1993). The reaction to the Court's ruling was mixed. Many legal scholars immediately noted the decision was chilling in the sense that it could

*See *Shaw v. Reno*, at 25. The dissenting opinions of Justices White, Blackmun, Stevens, and Souter all dealt with aspects of the Court's abandoning established law by stating that race cannot be taken into account when drawing district boundaries.

jeopardize many of the 26 congressional districts nationwide that were created for either black or Hispanic majorities after the 1990 reapportionment. The late Frank Parker, an attorney with the Lawyers' Committee for Civil Rights Under Law, said that the decision was the most damaging to voting rights in more than a decade. Moreover, Parker asserted that there are many redistricting maps around the country with bizarrely shaped districts. What troubled Parker was that the decision seemed to rest on whether or not the district was compact, for which there is no objective standard.[43]

Elaine Jones, an attorney with the National Association for the Advancement of Colored People Legal Defense and Education Fund, stated those who have not been harmed by the action of the state in drawing districts to enhance black participation now all of a sudden have standing to challenge, and the only districts that are challenged are those that look funny. According to Jones, districts that look funny are all over this country, and most of them are majority white districts.[44]

Others, however, were quite pleased with the decision. The *Wall Street Journal* ran an article by Elizabeth McCaughey, a fellow at the Manhattan Institute, in which she said, "The reasoning the court used to defend racial gerrymandering—virtual representation—violated the principles of American democracy."[45]

Representatives Mel Watt and Eva Clayton, North Carolina's two black congresspeople and whose districts were both majority black, held a news conference in Washington, D.C., on Monday, June 28, 1993, following the U.S. Supreme Court decision. They reaffirmed their confidence that the redistricting plan, which allowed both of them to win congressional seats, would be upheld by the lower federal court.

Representative Watt asserted that the district he represented, the Twelfth, would again be upheld because it had common features other than race. According to Watt, even if the district looked funny on the map, it had common urban problems that made it easier to represent than a traditional district that combined central cities and suburbs. Watt exclaimed, "It is North Carolina's only true urban district."[46]

Watt was responding in part to criticism by the U.S. Supreme Court that his district ignored traditional guidelines in drawing election districts that call for compact districts, embracing whole neighborhoods where voters have a commonality of interests. Watt had maintained all along:

It depends on how you define community. If you define it as a geographic community, then you're right; if you define it as a commu-

nity of interests, then you're wrong. It makes a lot more sense to define
congressional districts in terms of communities of interests than in geographic terms.[47]

Eva Clayton, who represented the state's other majority black district,
the first, agreed with Watt that the U.S. Supreme Court had adopted "an
appearance standard rather than a legal standard in this case."[48] Clayton
remarked that justice is not always pretty. She felt that the U.S. Supreme
Court was more concerned that districts be drawn with a neat shape than
that districts allow for representation of all of the people. Clayton suggested that there was a compelling state interest in creating the Twelfth
District because North Carolina went for 91 years, until 1992, without
electing a black person to Congress—despite a large black population.

The high court stated that the North Carolina state legislature ignored customary guidelines of placing voters in compact districts with
communities of interest. Though customary guidelines may have been
ignored, no federal or state laws were violated by the creation of the
Twelfth District in North Carolina.

In rejecting the practice of racial gerrymandering, Justice O'Connor
wrote for the Court:

> Racial gerrymandering, even for remedial purposes, may Balkanize
> us further from the goal of a political system in which race no longer
> matters.[49]

Contrary to Justice O'Connor's appeal to a future "in which race no
longer matters," it is precisely race that matters and is at issue in these
cases. Racial bloc voting on the part of whites and unfair election practices inspired Section 5 of the Voting Rights Act, which currently requires nine states and parts of eight others to receive preclearance from
the U.S. Justice Department or the District Court for the District of Columbia before those states can make any voting law changes—including
congressional redistricting.

The goal of present-day racial gerrymandering is to create a situation in which more blacks and other minorities can be elected to political
office. The U.S. Supreme Court said that the current means of doing this
may violate the U.S. Constitution because, at least in the Twelfth and
First districts in North Carolina, it denied white voters their right to "fair
and equal" representation.

Congressman Mel Watt took issue with those sentiments when he called Justice O'Connor's opinion "intellectually dishonest." Watt reasoned that the opinion

> suggests that a congressional district which is 53 percent black, as my
> congressional district is, and 47 percent white, is racial apartheid;
> while a congressional district which is 80 percent white and 20 percent
> black is somehow an integrated congressional district . . . It [the decision] talks about black people not being able to represent the interests
> of white constituents, while assuming that white representatives can
> adequately represent the interests of black people.[50]

**Implications of Shaw v. Reno (1993) for Other Majority-Minority
Districts Around the Country.** Many voting rights experts, as well as political and legal scholars, saw the decision in *Shaw v. Reno* (1993) as having implications for congressional districts that had been drawn in the
early 1990s around the country. Many states, particularly those in the Deep
South, had created majority-minority districts for the first time.

Merle Black, a professor of politics at Emory University, believed
the decision in *Shaw v. Reno* (1993) would have a chilling effect on many
of these newly created majority-minority districts. Black suggested:

> The decision could invite scrutiny of several other Southern states where
> 1991 redistricting maps produced districts with string-like looks.[51]

Others felt that the decision left many questions unanswered. Justice
O'Connor, in the majority opinion, had stated that there are "traditional
districting principles such as compactness, contiguity and respect for political subdivisions."[52] However, she further stated that "those are not
constitutionally required criteria and might, in certain circumstances, be
disregarded.[53] Frank Parker of the Lawyers' Committee for Civil Rights
Under Law, noted:

> The decision itself doesn't give clear guidance to states as to what they
> can show to satisfy this constitutional standard, and therefore, states
> are left at sea to try to determine what kinds of justifications will support the creation of new majority-minority districts.[54]

Moreover, asserted Parker:

Potentially, it could affect all 26 newly created majority-black and majority Hispanic congressional districts. The court . . . seems to focus on
race-conscious redistricting and says that's the evil.[55]

Pamela S. Karlan, a voting rights specialist and law professor,
stated:

Don't make ugly districts because you can end up in a lot of litigation.
It doesn't tell you what the outcome of that litigation is going to be, it
just tells you it's going to be costly one way or the other because if you
don't draw districts for minorities that you could draw, they'll file a
lawsuit under section two of the Voting Rights Act which says that you
can't dilute minority voting strength. And if you draw that district and
anybody's even slightly upset about it, you'll face a constitutional law
lawsuit from voters who don't like the district. So it's a sort of you're
damned if you do, damned if you don't.[56]

CONCLUSION

What began as partisan politics in North Carolina erupted into one of the
major U.S. Supreme Court cases of the decade in the area of voting rights
law. The *Shaw v. Reno* (1993) decision signaled a new direction for the
high court. The U.S. Supreme Court had previously considered the practice of gerrymandering to have been political in nature, and it usually de-
ferred to the political branches to resolve any disputes. However, in *Shaw*
the Court staked out an activist role. The strict scrutiny standard places a
tougher burden on states to defend their race-conscious redistricting plans.
The Court said that if a state cannot show a compelling state interest for
creating these districts, then the districts are unconstitutional. *Shaw v. Reno*
(1993) was the Supreme Court's first ruling after the creation of majority-
minority districts throughout the South for the 1992 elections. And the decision was a pivotal one. To proponents of racial redistricting, the decision
was devastating. To opponents, the decision opened the door to renewed
challenges to racial redistricting in other states throughout the South.

NOTES

[1]*Karcher v. Daggett*, 462 U.S. 725 (1983).
[2]*Davis v. Bandemer*, 478 U.S. 109 (1986).

[3]*Davis v. Bandemer* (1986).

[4]*Davis v. Bandemer* (1986).

[5]*Badham v. Eu*, 721 F. 2nd 1170 (NDCA 1983).

[6]*Badham v. Eu*, 488 U.S. 1024 (1989).

[7]*Beer v. United States,* 425 U.S. 130 (1976).

[8]Lisa Handley, "The Quest For Minority Voting Rights: The Evolution of a Vote Dilution Standard and Its Impact on Minority Representation," diss., George Washington University, 1991, 8.

[9]*Daughtry v. State Board of Elections*, Docket No. 2: 91CV00552.

[10]Plaintiffs' Complaint at 30, *Pope v. Blue*, 809 F. Supp. 392 (WDNC 1992).

[11]Plaintiffs' Complaint at 32, *Pope v. Blue*.

[12]Plaintiffs' Complaint at 33, *Pope v. Blue*.

[13]Declaration of Bernard Grofman at 2, *Pope v. Blue*, 809 F. Supp. 392 (WDNC 1992).

[14]Affidavit of Robert Dorff at 2, *Pope v. Blue*, 809 F. Supp. 392 (WDNC 1992).

[15]Affidavit of Robert Dorff at 3, *Pope v. Blue*.

[16]Affidavit of Robert Dorff at 3, *Pope v. Blue*.

[17]Plaintiffs' Complaint at 2, *Shaw v. Barr*, 808 F. Supp. 461 (EDNC 1992).

[18]Plaintiffs' Complaint at 10, *Shaw v. Barr*.

[19]Plaintiffs' Complaint at 10, *Shaw v. Barr*.

[20]Plaintiffs' Complaint at 10, *Shaw v. Barr*.

[21]Plaintiffs' Complaint at 11, *Shaw v. Barr*.

[22]Plaintiffs' Complaint at 16, *Shaw v. Barr*.

[23]*Shaw v. Barr*, at 466.

[24]*Shaw v. Barr*, at 467.

[25]Mack Jones, "The Voting Rights Act As an Intervention Strategy for Social Change: Symbolism or Substance?" *The Voting Rights Act*, ed. Lorn S. Foster (New York: Praeger Publishers, 1985) 67.

[26]*Shaw v. Barr*, at 470.

[27]*Shaw v. Barr*, at 470.

[28]*United Jewish Organizations of Williamsburg, Inc. v. Carey*, 430 U.S. 144 (1977).

[29]*Shaw v. Barr*, at 466.

[30]*Shaw v. Barr*, at 473.

[31]Susan Low Bloch and Thomas G. Krattenmaker, *Supreme Court Politics*, (Anaheim, Calif.: West Publishing Co., 1994) 326.

[32]Barbara Phillips, *How to Use Section 5 of the Voting Rights Act*, 3rd ed. (Washington, D.C.: Joint Center for Political and Economic Studies, 1983) 50.

[33]"Journal of Proceedings,"*United States Law Week* 61 (1992): 3418.

[34]David Folkenflik, "Professors Take Case To Court," *Durham Herald-Sun*, April 19, 1993: A1.

[35]Folkenflik A2.

[36]*Shaw v. Reno*, at 10–13.

[37]*United Jewish Organizations of Williamsburg, Inc. v. Carey*, at 1010, 430 U.S. 144 (1977).

[38]*Shaw v. Reno*, at 10.

[39]*Shaw v. Reno*, at 10.

[40]*United Jewish Organizations of Williamsburg, Inc. v. Carey*, at 1007.

[41]*Shaw v. Reno*, at 11.

[42]*Shaw v. Reno*, at 14.

[43]William Freivogel, "Minority Districts Rejected," *St. Louis Post-Dispatch*, June 29, 1993: 6A.

[44]Peter Applebome, "Ruling On Racial Gerrymandering Could Prompt Similar Challenges," *New York Times*, June 29, 1993: A9.

[45]Elizabeth McCaughey, "Court Deals a Blow to Racial Gerrymandering," *Wall Street Journal*, June 30, 1993: A15.

[46]Quoted in Michael Welch, "Ruling Throws Redistricting Into Question," *USA Today*, June 29, 1993: 2A.

[47]Quoted in Welch 2A.

[48]Quoted in Welch 2A.

[49]*Shaw v. Reno*, at 19.

[50]Kraus, Clifford. "Reaction Muted in Disputed District." *New York Times*, July 4, 1993: I20.

[51]Quoted in Welch 2A.

[52]"All Things Considered," Nina Totenburg Interview with Frank Parker and Pamela S. Karlan, *National Public Radio* Transcript 289, June 1993.

[53]Nina Totenburg Interview, 28.

[54]Nina Totenburg Interview, 28.

[55]Nina Totenburg Interview, 28.

[56]Nina Totenburg Interview, 28.

CHAPTER 6

Subsequent Court Challenges in the South

State legislatures throughout the South created majority black districts for the first time this century for the 1992 elections. In addition to the two majority black districts in North Carolina, many of these black districts came under legal challenge for their awkward shapes. After the Civil War, the South sent a record 22 blacks to Congress, but through black disenfranchisement following the withdrawal of federal troops from the South, black representation in the South and the rest of America was reduced to zero by the end of 1901. Many black politicians are beginning to worry whether recent court challenges striking down many of these majority black districts in the South spell the end of a Second Reconstruction in this nation.

James Clyburn, a black congressman from South Carolina, echoes that sentiment:

> No one felt in 1870, right after the Tilden-Hayes compromise [that evacuated federal troops], there would be no Black people not only in Southern congressional delegations, but in legislatures as well . . . I don't believe we should treat these court decisions lightly.[1]

SOUTHERN STATES THAT HAVE CREATED MAJORITY-MINORITY DISTRICTS FOR THE FIRST TIME THIS CENTURY

South Carolina

The state of South Carolina, which has a black population of 30 percent, had its congressional map drawn by a federal court after the state legislature was unable to reconcile variations in the state House and Senate plans. The oddly shaped majority black district Clyburn represents (the Sixth) has a 62 percent black population and stretches across all or parts of 16 counties. It meanders from Columbia in the central portion of the state to Charleston on the southeastern coast. Clyburn became the first black to represent South Carolina in Congress since 1897 by winning 65 percent of the vote.[2]

Figure 6.1. South Carolina Congressional District Map, 1992

South Carolina

Source: Congressional Quarterly Weekly Report, 1992. By permission, Congressional Quarterly, 1414 22nd Street, NW, Washington, DC 20037.

Florida

In Florida, the congressional redistricting process suffered a fate similar to that of South Carolina. The Republican party filed a lawsuit even before the state legislature had drawn a new plan. A three-judge panel drew the new plan when the legislature gave up. Florida, which has experienced a population explosion over the last two decades, gained four seats in the 1990 reapportionment. Of the four new congressional districts, three were drawn as majority black districts in a state that has a 14 percent black population. Two of the three majority black districts, the Seventeenth and the Twenty-third, were isolated in southern Florida.

Controversy, however, surrounded the newly created Third District, a majority black district in northern Florida that traverses across parts of 14 counties and has been referred to as the "horseshoe" or "wishbone" (see Figure 6.2).[3] The district, with a black population of 55 percent, slithers for 250 miles across 14 counties from Orlando in central Florida and continues north of Jacksonville to the Georgia state line. It is currently represented by black congresswoman Corrine Brown.

Carrie Meek won election in Florida's Seventeenth District in 1992. The district, with a 58 percent black population, has the highest percentage of the state's black residents. Whites make up 37 percent of the population, and residents of Hispanic origin account for 23 percent. The district is located in the southeastern part of Florida and includes parts of North Dade County, parts of Miami, and parts of Carol City. The district meanders from the Broward County line in northern Miami suburbs and southwest along U.S. 1, picking up black neighborhoods along the way. The district includes Liberty City (the scene of a 1980 riot that left 18 dead, and home to Carrie Meek). Alcee Hastings won the 1992 election in the third majority black district in Florida, the Twenty-third. The district, in southeast Florida, traverses over seven counties, but most of the residents live inland from the Atlantic Ocean along a narrow strip of Interstate 95. The district encompasses parts of St. Lucie, Martin, Broward, and Palm Beach counties. Blacks comprise 52 percent of the population, and whites comprise 45 percent. Representative Hastings had been a federal judge until he was impeached by the U.S. House of Representatives on bribery charges in 1988. He was convicted and removed from office by the U.S. Senate in October 1989. Hastings subsequently ran for the U.S. House of Representatives (his conviction did not bar him from being a member of the U.S. Congress). During his congressional campaign, in September 1992 Hastings's conviction was overturned by a federal district judge in

Figure 6.2. Florida Congressional District Map, 1992

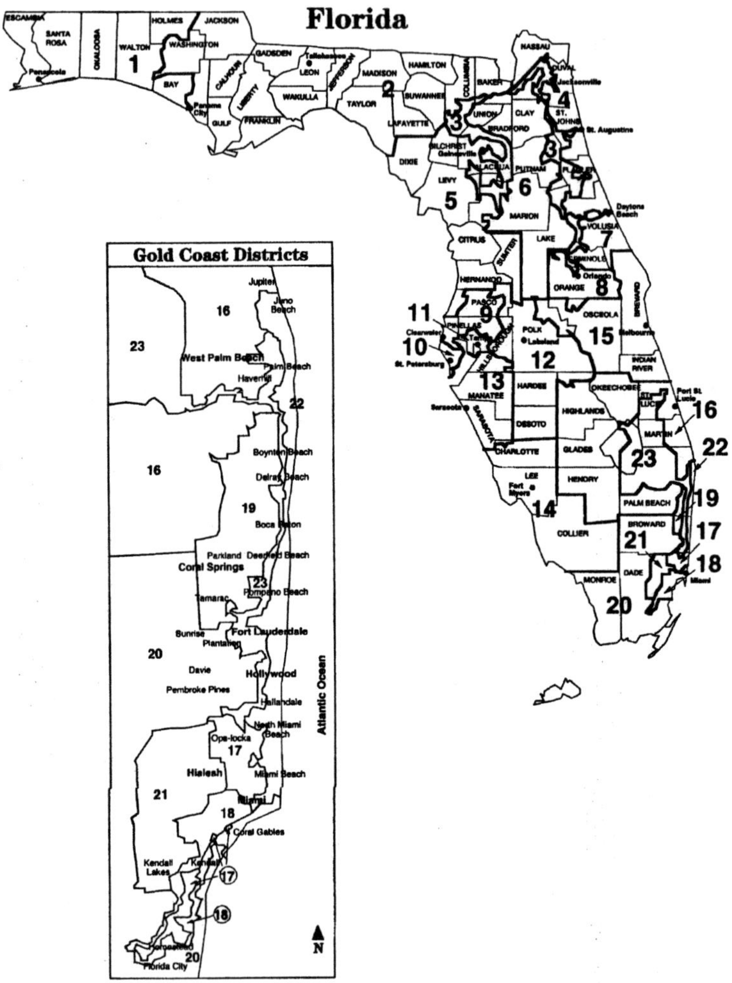

Source: Congressional Quarterly Weekly Report, 1992. By permission, Congressional Quarterly, 1414 22nd Street, NW, Washington, DC 20037.

Washington, D.C. He opted not to return to the bench, preferring to continue his campaign for the open seat in the Twenty-third district. In 1992, all three congresspeople became the first black Americans to win election to Congress in Florida in the twentieth century.

Georgia

Georgia created two new majority black districts in 1992 to comply with the Justice Department mandate. The Fifth District in Georgia, which includes most of Atlanta and Fulton County, was already a majority black district. Georgia gained a congressional seat in the U.S. House

Figure 6.3. Georgia Congressional District Map, 1992

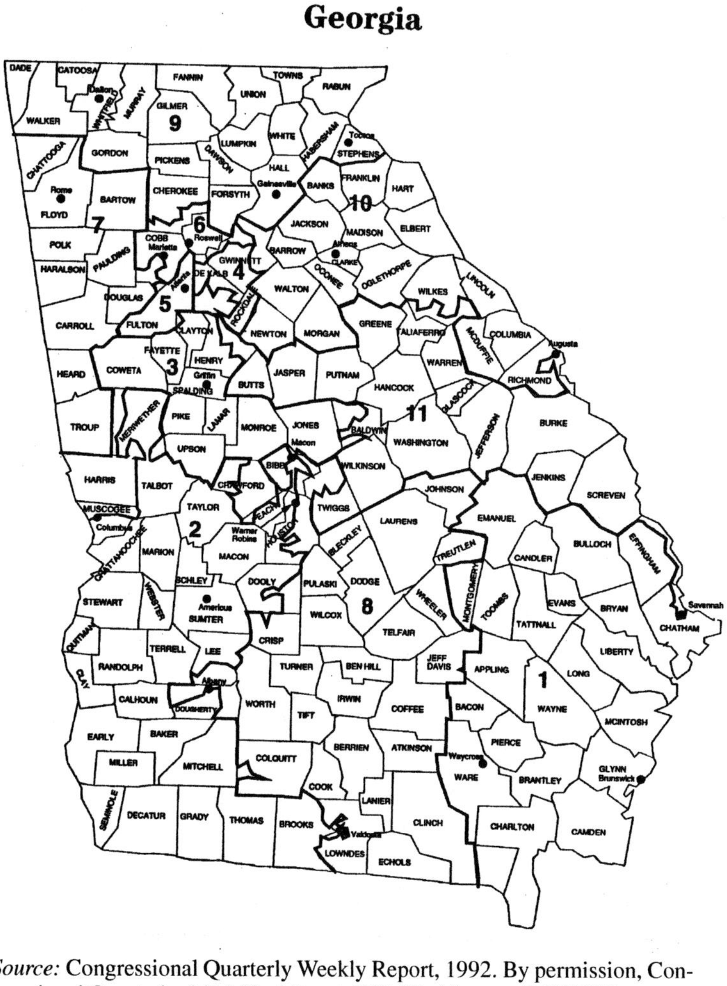

Georgia

Source: Congressional Quarterly Weekly Report, 1992. By permission, Congressional Quarterly, 1414 22nd Street, NW, Washington, DC 20037.

of Representatives in the 1990 reapportionment process due to its substantial population growth in the 1980s, so its delegation rose from 10
members to 11. Republicans supported the creation of more majority-
minority districts in hopes of increasing their numbers in the Georgia
congressional delegation. As was the case in North Carolina, the Republicans reasoned that minority (black and Hispanic) voters would be
taken from incumbent Democratic districts, leaving those districts more
white, conservative, and likely to vote for Republicans. Sanford Bishop
won election in 1992 from one of the newly created majority black districts, the Second District located in southwest Georgia. The district
contains black sections of four urban areas—Macon, Columbus, Al-
bany, and Valdosta—and has a black population of 57 percent. Of the
two newly created majority black districts, the Second and the Eleventh,
it is the Eleventh District that has been singled out for its unusually designed shape.

This district sprawls from Atlanta's southeastern suburbs for 260 miles
east and south until it ends in the coastal port city of Savannah.[4] The district
was formerly represented by black congresswoman Cynthia McKinney
(1992–1996), who won election in 1992 in a district that had a 65 percent
black majority and the largest black concentration of all three majority
black districts, in a state with a black population of 27 percent. McKinney,
troubled by the recent challenge over majority black districts, contended:

> This is Southern White resistance. We began this century with no
> Black representation in Congress, and the prospect is we could end it
> that way.[5]

Louisiana

Louisiana had the unenviable task of creating a second majority black
district to go along with a previously created one. The Department of
Justice mandate came when Louisiana, unlike the other southern states,
actually lost one seat in the U.S. House of Representatives during the
1990 reapportionment process, thus reducing its congressional delegation from eight to seven. Louisiana's initial majority black district, the
Second, was created by federal court order in 1982. In 1981, the state
legislature created a congressional map that had a 45 percent black population. That map was subsequently approved by the U.S. Department of
Justice. Black leaders in Louisiana filed suit in federal court, charging
that the congressional plan "unnecessarily diluted black voting strength,

making it virtually impossible for a black to win a House seat."[6] In the case *Major v. Treen* (1983),[7] a federal district court judge agreed and forced the state legislature to draw new lines. The new map did not take effect until January 1985. At that time, the Second District had a 58 percent black majority but, interestingly enough, continued to elect its white incumbent, Lindy Boggs, until her retirement in 1991.[8]

Because the Second District was based in New Orleans, state legislators had to look elsewhere to locate a majority black population. The final creation was the Fourth District, which was considered by many to be one of the more convoluted congressional districts to come out of nationwide redistricting efforts. The district, which was dubbed the "Z" by a member of Louisiana's nonpartisan House Reapportionment Project, began in Shreveport, in northeast Louisiana, and skirted along the Arkansas border

Figure 6.4. Louisiana Congressional District Map, 1992

Source: Congressional Quarterly Weekly Report, 1992. By permission, Congressional Quarterly, 1414 22nd Street, NW, Washington, DC 20037.

until it reached the Mississippi River on the eastern border. It then traversed south following the Mississippi River and finally slid west into central Louisiana and east into Baton Rouge, the state capital.

The "Z" district zigzagged through all or parts of 28 parishes (counties). Cleo Fields, who won election in 1992 to represent the district, was head of the 1992 state redistricting committee as a state senator. Louisiana has a black population of 31 percent, and its Fourth District was 66 percent black.[9]

Texas

Texas gained three seats in Congress as a result of the 1990 reapportion-

Figure 6.5. Texas Congressional District Map, 1992

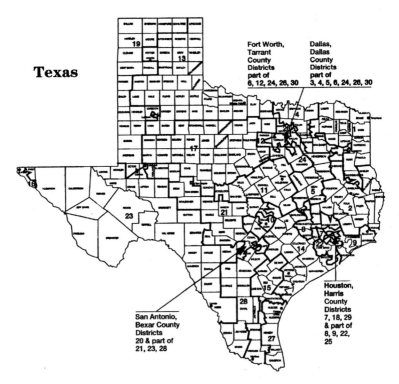

Source: Congressional Quarterly Weekly Report, 1992. By permission, Congressional Quarterly, 1414 22nd Street, Washington, DC 20037.

ment process. Because of considerable gains in its minority (black and Hispanic) community, all three seats were designated majority-minority districts when the legislature drew its new district lines: two majority black districts and one majority Hispanic district. One of the two majority black districts was located in Houston (the Eighteenth) and the other in Dallas (the Thirtieth). The new Hispanic majority district (the Twenty-ninth) was located in Houston (see Figure 6.5).

For the first time since Reconstruction, blacks won elections to the U.S. House of Representatives from Alabama, Florida (three districts), North Carolina (two districts), Virginia, and South Carolina. These five former states of the Confederacy, all with substantial black populations, had previously failed to elect a black to Congress in the twentieth century. In addition, delegations from Louisiana, Texas, and Maryland each increased their number of black American representatives in Congress from one to two, and Georgia (which along with Texas in 1972 sent the South's first blacks to Congress since Reconstruction) increased its black representation in Congress from one to three.[10]

RECENT COURT CHALLENGES TO MAJORITY-MINORITY DISTRICTS AROUND THE COUNTRY

Both supporters and opponents of majority black districts—particularly in the South—were focused on the U.S. Supreme Court when it handed down its ruling in *Shaw v. Reno* (1993). The decision said that congressional districts based solely on race when there were no other common interests are subject to constitutional challenge. This ruling gave the green light to residents in other states throughout the South to proceed with legal challenges where oddly shaped districts had been drawn to create black majority districts. And that is exactly what happened.

Following the *Shaw v. Reno* (1993) decision, a lawsuit was brought in Louisiana challenging its recently drawn redistricting plan, especially the Z-shaped Fourth District. In this case, three white and one black resident of the Fourth challenged the new district. A federal district court declared the plan "the product of unconstitutional racial gerrymandering."[11] The state of Louisiana appealed the decision directly to the U.S. Supreme Court. In Texas, a lawsuit was filed in January 1994 by a group claiming unconstitutional the racial gerrymandering for one black majority district, the Eighteenth, and for one Hispanic majority district, the Twenty-ninth. Both districts are located in Houston.

In Georgia, a lawsuit was filed in January 1994 by a contingent challenging the constitutionality of the majority black Eleventh District on the grounds that it, too, was a violation of the Equal Protection Clause of the Fourteenth Amendment to the U.S. Constitution.

And in Florida, plaintiffs filed a lawsuit in January 1994 challenging the constitutionality of the wishbone-shaped Third District on the grounds that it was created from unconstitutional racial gerrymandering.

Many of the southern states that created majority-minority districts for the first time for the 1992 elections found themselves amidst lawsuits in federal court challenging the creation of majority black or Hispanic districts. Some of these districts were oddly shaped, but they were not the first oddly shaped congressional districts to be drawn in the twentieth century.

Cynthia McKinney, Georgia's Eleventh District representative, pointed out that there are oddly shaped majority white districts around the country. As an example, McKinney points to Tennessee's Fourth Congressional District, which is 96 percent white. She described it as a district "that rambles across 400 miles and looks like the *S* on Superman's chest."[12]

U.S. SUPREME COURT RULINGS ON MAJORITY-MINORITY DISTRICTS THROUGHOUT THE SOUTH

As a result of the 1990s round of redistricting, many states around the South created majority black districts for the first time in the twentieth century. Voters objected to the irregular shapes of many of these districts. Some also objected to the idea of creating special enclaves of black voters for the sole purpose of having a black majority congressional district. Of note, many of the lawsuits were initiated by white candidates who ran for office in these majority black districts but were defeated.

Hays v. Louisiana (1993)

In Louisiana, a three-judge federal panel struck down Louisiana's entire congressional redistricting plan in December 1993.[13] That plan, a product of the Louisiana state legislature, had created two majority black districts out of eight total districts. The federal court specifically objected to the Z-shaped Fourth District represented by black congressman Cleo Fields. That district, which had a 63 percent black voting-age population, was considered by the federal court to violate the standard set by *Shaw v. Reno* (1993) and, therefore, was not a "narrowly tailored" plan to further a "compelling state interest."[14]

The Louisiana legislature went back to the drawing board and adopted a new redistricting plan on April 22, 1994, which was approved by the U.S. Department of Justice. The new plan made the Fourth District more compact and reduced its black voting-age population to 55 percent. The other majority black congressional district, the Second, was left virtually intact. But in July 1994, the same three-judge panel also threw out that districting plan. However, the plan remained in effect for the November 1994 election pending an appeal to the U.S. Supreme Court. The Supreme Court heard an appeal and, in a June 1995 decision, said the plaintiffs who originally brought the challenge lacked standing because they did not live in Fields's Fourth District.[15] The case was sent back to the three-judge panel with the recommendation that it be dismissed but not barring a revised version of the suit. The plaintiffs amended their suit with additional plaintiffs who lived in the Fourth District. On January 5, 1996, the three-judge panel in Louisiana ruled the state's congressional map unconstitutional for the third time since 1993.[16] The federal court appointed a special master who created yet another plan, which reduced the Fourth District's black voting-age population to roughly 27 percent. This plan created seven relatively compact districts in Louisiana and reduced the state to only one majority black district—this in a state with a black population of 31 percent. Congressman Cleo Fields and others appealed to the U.S. Supreme Court. On June 24, 1996, the U.S. Supreme Court refused to hear the case, leaving the court-imposed map in place.[17]

Shaw v. Hunt (1994)

North Carolina's case, now called *Shaw v. Hunt* (1994) (for current governor James Hunt), was remanded to the federal district court in North Carolina. The federal district court for the Eastern District of North Carolina set April 12, 1994, as the date to hear oral arguments in *Shaw v. Hunt* (1994). The state of North Carolina's legal defense was argued by Dayna Cunningham, an attorney for the NAACP Legal Defense and Education Fund. The plaintiffs in this case were represented by Duke University Law Professor Robinson O. Everett. According to David Bositis, senior political analyst at the Joint Center for Political and Economic Studies, the Legal Defense Fund's strategy primarily was to address two issues from Justice O'Connor's written opinion in *Shaw v. Reno* (1993): "First, did the state's reapportionment represent racial gerrymandering, and second, if there were race-conscious redistricting, was the plan narrowly tailored?"[18] An article that appeared in the Durham newspaper, the *Durham Herald-Sun*, said that

Everett argued [on behalf of the plaintiffs] that Watt represents the 55 percent of the 12th District voters who are black. He did not adequately represent the interests of white voters and the business community.[19]

On August 1, 1994, the three-judge federal panel dismissed the lawsuit by the plaintiffs. The court stated that although the districts (majority black) in North Carolina constituted a racial gerrymander,

> We nonetheless conclude that the plan passes constitutional muster under that standard because it is narrowly tailored to further the state's compelling interest in complying with the Voting Rights Act . . . We therefore hold that the plan does not violate the plaintiffs' equal protection rights in the manner alleged, and we give judgment for the defendants accordingly.[20]

It appears that past discrimination was sufficiently compelling for the federal district court to rule that North Carolina did have a compelling governmental interest to create the two majority black districts. Thad Beyle, a political science professor at the University of North Carolina at Chapel Hill, stated, "I think the history of not having any blacks serving in Congress at all was an important factor."[21]

North Carolina had elected only two blacks to Congress since 1901, both of whom were elected in 1992 after the creation of the two majority black districts. Congresswoman Eva Clayton, who represents one of the challenged districts, the First, said she "hoped the decision would reach outside North Carolina."[22]

Congressman Mel Watt, who represents the other majority black district in North Carolina, the Twelfth, took issue with plaintiffs' counsel Everett O. Robinson when Robinson argued that Watt did not represent whites. Watt responded, "That was a racist argument that assumed a minority congressman would not represent the interests of white voters."[23] The effect of the *Shaw v. Reno* (1993) decision on similar redistricting plans around the country has had a devastating effect.

Miller v. Johnson (1995)

Prior to the 1991–1992 redistricting process, Georgia had maintained one majority black district. Population growth since 1980 gave Georgia an additional seat in its congressional delegation after the reapportionment process in 1990. The 1990 census revealed that the black population in

Georgia had increased to 27 percent of the total. During the state legislature's redistricting process, there were calls from the black community for blacks to have a realistic opportunity of electing a candidate of their choice in at least 3 of the 11 congressional districts.

The state legislature drafted a plan that maintained the Atlanta-based black majority Fifth District (by 1980 it was 50 percent black) while adding another majority black district, the Eleventh, which meandered from the outskirts of Atlanta east to Augusta on the South Carolina border and then south to Savannah on the East Coast, covering 260 miles. The district consisted of pockets of black voters in rural areas between these cities and was the largest majority black district in a state where blacks comprised 64 percent of the population.

Georgia's congressional plan was sent to the U.S. Department of Justice for preclearance in 1991 because it, too, is a state required under Section 5 of the Voting Rights Act to receive prior approval before adopting a redistricting plan. The U.S. Justice Department rejected this map on the basis that it diluted minority voting strength in the Second District located in rural southwest Georgia.

The state legislature went back to the drawing board and created a second districting plan that increased the Second District to a 49 percent black population and maintained the majority black Fifth District and majority black Eleventh District. The Justice Department rejected this map as well, so the state legislature increased the black population in the Second District to 57 percent. Georgia now, in effect, had 3 majority black districts out of a total of 11. And the two newly created majority black districts, as well as the Atlanta-based majority black district, all elected black candidates to Congress in 1992.

On January 13, 1994, five white plaintiffs, voters in the new Eleventh District, filed suit in federal court in Atlanta challenging the constitutionality of the Eleventh District. The plaintiffs alleged that the Eleventh District violated the equal protection clause of the Fourteenth Amendment to the U.S. Constitution.

In 1994, in federal district court in Atlanta, a three-judge panel sided with the plaintiffs and rejected Georgia's new congressional redistricting plan by a 2–1 split vote.[24] The State of Georgia appealed directly to the United States Supreme Court because the case involved the Voting Rights Act of 1965. The Supreme Court heard oral arguments on April 19, 1995. On June 29, 1995, it handed down its decision.

In a 5–4 decision, the U.S. Supreme Court struck down the congressional redistricting plan that the Georgia legislature created in 1992 to satisfy the U.S. Justice Department. Specifically, the justices in the majority objected to Georgia's Eleventh District. The majority opinion, delivered by Justice Anthony Kennedy, stated that "the use of race as a 'predominant' factor in drawing district lines should be presumed to be unconstitutional."[25]

After the landmark *Shaw v. Reno* (1993) Supreme Court decision, state officials in Georgia felt reasonably comfortable that they could defend the Eleventh District because it had been drawn to satisfy the U.S. Justice Department and because its shape was not nearly as irregular as the shape of the Twelfth District in North Carolina. Moreover, *Shaw v. Reno* (1993) seemed to turn on the bizarre shape of congressional districts.

But in *Miller v. Johnson* (1995), the majority of the Court appeared to have moved past the shape of a district as the reason for objecting to race-based redistricting. Justice Kennedy made it clear that the Court's holding in *Shaw* was not meant to suggest that a district must be bizarre on its face before it is unconstitutional. "Shape is relevant," asserted Kennedy, "not because bizarreness is a necessary element of the constitutional wrong, but because it may be persuasive evidence that race, and not other districting principles, was the dominant and controlling rationale in drawing district lines."[26]

The Supreme Court decision in *Shaw v. Reno* (1993) had left questions unanswered. Primarily, it failed to resolve what shape majority black districts must conform to in order to be acceptable. But the current majority on the Court has stated clearly that almost no districting based on race would be acceptable.

The high court also took sharp aim at the U.S. Justice Department which, under the Bush administration and continuing under the Clinton administration, had mandated that majority-minority districts be drawn in state congressional districts around the country. The majority opinion proclaimed that the Department of Justice had misinterpreted the Voting Rights Act by requiring the creation of majority-minority districts throughout the land.

Of the four dissenting justices, two—Justice Ruth Bader Ginsburg and Justice David H. Souter—wrote separate opinions.*

The decision in *Miller v. Johnson* (1995) allows federal judges to have far too active a role in the quintessential political task of legislative redistricting. This is clearly judicial activism under the guise of judicial restraint.

---

*See *Miller v. Johnson*, p. 3. Justices Ginsburg and Souter stated that America's long history of racism necessitated race-conscious remedies in some instances.

Although the Court attempted to shore up questions left unanswered in the *Shaw v. Reno* (1993) decision, many questions remained unanswered by this decision. The Court did not say when race could be a factor in redistricting, and it did not say how much weight could be assigned to race in redistricting efforts. Moreover, the majority said that states may satisfy the strict scrutiny test if there is a compelling governmental interest, but it gave no direction to the states as to how this may be accomplished. Georgia's state legislature was sent back to the drawing board to create a districting plan that would pass constitutional muster.

Johnson et al. v. Mortham et al. (1996)

In Florida in April 1996, a three-judge panel ruled Florida's Third Congressional District unconstitutional. They struck down a plan that had been drawn up by a three-judge panel and instructed the state legislature to create a new map. The new map reduced the controversial Third District from a black voting-age population of 50.6 percent to 42.3 percent. The two majority black districts in South Florida were left unchanged.

Shaw II (1996) and *Bush v. Vera* (1996): In June 1996, the Supreme Court nullified four more majority-minority districts. In a Texas case (*Bush v. Vera*)[27] and a North Carolina case (*Shaw v. Hunt*),[28] the Court held that districts that are contorted because of the need to scoop up minority voters likely would be deemed unconstitutional because of their lack of compactness. The Court specifically struck down one majority black district in North Carolina and three majority-minority districts (two majority black and one majority Hispanic) in Texas. The North Carolina case was a reprise of the original *Shaw v. Reno* (1993) that found its way back to the U.S. Supreme Court. In separate opinions, the high court ruled that both North Carolina and Texas relied too heavily on race in drawing the majority-minority districts and that the districts drawn veered too far from traditional districting principles such as compactness. The Court struck down the Twelfth District in North Carolina but dismissed the suit against the First District on the grounds that none of the plaintiffs were residents of the district. The plaintiffs subsequently added residents of the First District and filed another suit. North Carolina's legislature was required to redraw its congressional map as a result of the decision. However, the three-judge district court also ordered the old map to remain in effect for the November 1996 general elections.

Supporters of majority-minority districts in Texas were not so lucky. A three-judge federal district court in Texas ruled in the summer of 1996 that a new map would have to be drawn before the November 1996 elections. It required 13 of Texas's 30 congressional districts to be re-drawn. Primary elections had already been held, so the decision threw the state into political turmoil. The three districts declared unconstitutional in Texas were the Eighteenth in Houston, the Twenty-ninth in Houston, and the Thirtieth in Dallas.

In effect, the U.S. Supreme Court has neutralized race as a factor in the creation of majority-minority districts. Furthermore, it appears to have dismissed the arguments made by the defendants that they created majority-minority districts because of the long history of racial discrimination in their states that had denied minorities a full voice in the political process.

Through these U.S. Supreme Court decisions, lower federal court decisions, and legislative actions, 8 out of the 17 congressional districts in the South with a majority black population have been overturned. Majority black districts have been struck down in Louisiana (one), North Carolina (one), Georgia (two), Florida (one), Virginia (one), and Texas (two). The lone majority black district in South Carolina, the Sixth, was challenged in federal court, but all parties agreed to the challenge's dismissal in 1997.

CONCLUSION

Ironically, after congressional redistricting mandated by the Department of Justice in carrying out the Voting Rights Act of 1965 sent a record number of blacks to Congress, majority black districts have come under court challenge. The U.S. Supreme Court, prior to the decision in *Shaw v. Reno* (1994), had never objected to a congressional district based solely on its shape.

During the days of Jim Crow, southern whites and state and local legislative bodies were not at all concerned about the racial gerrymandering of congressional districts to exclude blacks or to dilute the black vote. Paradoxically, it was the highest court in the land, the U.S. Supreme Court, that was the only branch of government that provided access and justice to black Americans during that time. Now that same branch of government has turned its back on black Americans.

After a single congressional election (1992), black representation increased by 50 percent in the U.S. House of Representatives, when many southern states elected a black to Congress for the first time this century. Recently, the Supreme Court has begun asking states and the U.S. Justice Department to provide reasons for drawing these awkwardly shaped districts that have nothing to do with race. Moreover, the Court appears to have adopted a *visual standard* for the creation of constitutionally acceptable congressional districts.

Of the 435 members of the U.S. House of Representatives, only 39 are black. The black population in America is 12 percent of the total, and black representation in the U.S. House of Representatives is at a historical high of 9 percent. Of the 100 members of the U.S. Senate, not one is an African American. Thus, there are only 39 black members of the U.S. Congress out of a total of 535 members—a mere 7.2 percent.

Supreme Court Justice Sandra Day O'Connor has condemned racial gerrymandering as reinforcing the belief that people should be judged by the color of their skin and has said that racial gerrymandering balkanizes us further from a political system in which race no longer matters.[29] O'Connor has also spoken of the goal of a color-blind society. This argument, although having unquestionable merit, lacks pragmatism. The irony is that the goal of Justice O'Connor and the goal of proponents of majority-minority districts are the same: a color-blind society. It appears that the conflict surrounds not the end, but the means to that end.

Bernard Grofman and Lisa Handley, supporters of racial redistricting, argue that although ideally "we would all rather live in a color-blind world," the realities of residential segregation, racially polarized voting patterns, and the related lack of minority electoral success require the use of color-conscious remedies.[30]

The Voting Rights Act of 1965 was initially passed by Congress to end election practices that excluded blacks from the electoral process. Congress has renewed this act (currently through the year 2007) because patterns of racial bias in the South did not end as quickly as it had envisioned. The remedial efforts of this act have not been accomplished. A conservative Supreme Court completely overlooked the intent of Congress when it passed the original Voting Rights Act and its many renewals.

The creation of majority-minority districts is a practical but temporary solution to a complex problem. Bruce Cain and others have asserted that majority black districts can serve as staging grounds for blacks entering the political arena.[31] By creating majority-minority districts, blacks and other minorities can show the majority that they have the ability and integrity to represent all Americans. Ideally, the need for majority-minority districts should vanish.

Racial lines are falling even in the South, and people are beginning to vote based on the qualifications of the candidates. However, the extent to which patterns of polarized voting still exists should not be ignored. Minority influence in the South would be virtually nonexistent were it not for congressional passage of the Voting Rights Act of 1965 and subsequent renewal and strengthening in 1970, 1975, and 1982. Throughout the 1980s, the U.S. Supreme Court rendered decisions that were designed to provide a legal basis for blacks and other minorities to challenge tactics diluting minority voting strength. These decisions, coupled with a U.S. Justice Department's interpretation of the Voting Rights Act of 1965 and its subsequent amendments requiring the drawing of majority black districts by states where possible, created an environment in which blacks were not to be relegated to a permanent minority voting status. Today, much of that progress, along with majority-minority congressional districts, is being dismantled.

NOTES

[1]Quoted in Kenneth Cooper, "Dismantling Black Political Power," *Emerge*, April 1994: 32.

[2]*CQ's Guide to 1990 Congressional Redistricting* (New York: Congressional Quarterly Inc., 1993) 305.

[3]*CQ's Guide to 1990 Congressional Redistricting*, 86.

[4]*CQ's Guide to 1990 Congressional Redistricting*, 115.

[5]Quoted in Cooper 32.

[6]Rhodes Cook, "Blacks to Gain: Mississippi, Louisiana Redraw District Lines," *Congressional Quarterly Weekly Report*, January 7, 1984: 13.

[7]*Major v. Treen*, 574 F. Supp. 325 (E.D.L.A. 1983).

[8]*CQ's Guide to 1990 Congressional Redistricting*, 125.

[9]*CQ's Guide to 1990 Congressional Redistricting*, 125.

[10]Dewey Clayton, "Making the Case for Majority Black Districts," *The Black Scholar*, Vol. 28, No. 2, Summer 1998: 38–39.

[11]Dave Kaplan, "Drawing and Redrawing the Line," *Congressional Quarterly Weekly Report*, February 19, 1994: 384.

[12]Quoted in Cooper 35.

[13]*Hays v. Louisiana*, 839 F. Supp. 1188 (W.D.La. 1993)

[14]Barbara Spears, "Black-Majority Districts Upheld in North Carolina, Struck in Louisiana," *Voting Rights Review*, Summer 1994: 25.

[15]*U.S. v. Hays*, 115 S.C. 2431 (1995).

[16]*Hays v. Louisiana*, 862 F. Supp. 119 (W.D.La. 1996).

[17]*Hays et al. v. State of Louisiana et al.*, 116 S.C. 2542 (1996), 936 F. Supp. 360 (W.D.La. 1996).

[18]David Bositis, *The Congressional Black Caucus in the 103rd Congress* (Washington, D.C.: Joint Center for Political and Economic Studies, 1994) 60.

[19]Martha Waggoner, "Districts in N. C. Ruled Legal," *Durham Herald-Sun*, August 3, 1994: A5.

[20]Waggoner A5.

[21]Quoted in Guy Coates, "Rulings Differ on Minority Districts," *Durham Herald-Sun*, August 3, 1994: A5.

[22]Quoted in Waggoner A5.

[23]Quoted in Waggoner A5.

[24]Steven A. Holmes, "Voting Rights Experts Say Challenges to Political Maps Could Cause Turmoil," *New York Times*, June 30, 1995: A13.

[25]Linda Greenhouse, "Justices, In 5–4 Vote, Reject Districts Drawn With Race the 'Predominant Factor,' " *New York Times*, June 30, 1995: A13.

[26]*Miller v. Johnson*, (1995), WL 382020 U.S.: 3.

[27]*Bush v. Vera*, No. 94–988, 1996, U.S.

[28]*Shaw v. Hunt*, No. 94–924, 1996, U.S.

[29]*Shaw v. Reno*, at 13, 113 S. Ct. 2816 (1993).

[30]Bernard Grofman and Lisa Handley, "Identifying and Remedying Racial Gerrymandering." *Journal of Law and Politics*, Winter 1992, Vol. VIII, No. 2: 402–404.

[31]Bernard Grofman and Chandler Davidson, "Postscript: What Is the Best Route to a Color-Blind Society?" *Controversies in Minority Voting*, ed. Bernard Grofman and Chandler Davidson (Washington, D.C.: The Brookings Institution, 1992) 315–316.

CHAPTER 7

Standards of Congressional Redistricting

The difficulty that the state legislature in North Carolina faced in attempting to achieve a satisfactory congressional redistricting plan became apparent during the 1991 and 1992 sessions of that body. It approached this task with several well-established standards.

POPULATION EQUALITY, COMPACTNESS, AND CONTIGUITY

In the landmark U.S. Supreme Court case of *Reynolds v. Simms* (1964), the Court issued a series of redistricting guidelines for the states to use:

1. Districts must be as equal in population as is reasonable to achieve.
2. County, city, and other political boundaries should be respected.
3. Districts should be compact.
4. Geographic boundaries (mountains, rivers, etc.) should be respected.
5. Some community of interest should be respected (a district composed mostly of farmers, for example).[1]

According to Bernard Grofman, a specialist in reapportionment, the U.S. Supreme Court's justification for regulating congressional redistricting appears in Article I, Section 2, of the U.S. Constitution, which says that "the House of Representatives shall be composed of members chosen every second year by the People of the several States."[2] Moreover, the

Supreme Court bases its authority for requiring an equal population standard on the states and smaller jurisdictions in the Equal Protection Clause of the Fourteenth Amendment. That amendment reads, in part, "nor shall any State . . . deny to any person within its jurisdiction the equal protection of the laws."[3]

Furthermore, notes Grofman:

> In *Wesberry v. Sanders* (1964), the U.S. Supreme Court asserted that "while it may not be possible to draw congressional districts with mathematical precision, that is no excuse for ignoring our constitution's plain objective of making equal representation for equal numbers of people the fundamental goal for the House of Representatives."[4]

At one time in American history, population equality, contiguity, and compactness were all required at the federal level by congressional statute. Periodically, calls have been made to restore them as mandatory for congressional redistricting.[5]

EQUAL POPULATION

The Supreme Court ruled in *Reynolds v. Simms* (1964) "that districts with unequal populations must meet a 'one-man-one-vote' requirement that districts be substantially equal in population."[6]

The phrase "substantially equal" has had a varied meaning depending on the level of the jurisdiction involved. For congressional redistricting, "all of a state's congressional districts must be equal in population, and no deviations from equal-sized districts are allowed unless they can be justified by state officials."[7]

Because the population equality standard for congressional districts is much higher than that for other jurisdictions, there is no safe range of deviation. The North Carolina House and Senate Redistricting Committees created a list of criteria to follow as they engaged in the redistricting process. Number one on this document sets the ideal congressional district population in North Carolina at 552,386 (see Figure 7.1). The final plan adopted by the North Carolina General Assembly adhered to this guideline. That plan has twelve congressional districts with a population of either 552,386 or 552,387, with a population deviation of one.

Figure 7.1. Redistricting Criteria for Congressional Seats, 1991

The committees responsible for redistricting the twelve congressional seats assigned to North Carolina, assisted by the legislative staff, retained counsel, and the North Carolina Attorney General, shall be guided by the following standards in the development of the congressional districts:

1. In accordance with the requirements of the Article I, Section 2, of the United States Constitution, congressional districts shall be drawn so as to be as nearly equal in population as practicable—the ideal district population being 552,386.
2. In accordance with the Voting Rights Act of 1965, as amended, and the 14th and 15th Amendments to the United States Constitution, the voting rights of racial minorities shall not be abridged or denied in the formation of congressional districts.
3. All congressional districts shall be single member districts, as required by 2 U.S.C. Section 2c, and shall consist of contiguous territory.
4. It is desirable to retain the integrity of precincts. For the purpose of this criterion, precincts shall mean only the voting tabulating districts as demarcated in the General Assembly's automated redistricting system database as of May 1, 1991. This criterion does not apply to counties where voting tabulating districts are not demarcated in the General Assembly's automated redistricting system database on that date.
5. Census blocks shall not be divided except to the extent that they were divided in the automated redistricting system database for precinct boundaries or to show previous districts.

Source: North Carolina General Assembly Joint House and Senate Redistricting Comm., 1991.

RESPECT FOR POLITICAL BOUNDARIES

The second guideline, which states that county, city, and political boundaries should be respected, has been relaxed over the years. Because many states, including North Carolina, must comply with the Voting Rights Act, or because they may find it necessary to divide a county to achieve population equality, respect for political boundaries is not adhered to as stringently as it has been in the past. In North Carolina, in particular, in the enacted legislative plan 44 counties were split into two or more congressional districts, and seven counties were split into three or more congressional districts. Bernard Grofman, who wrote a declaration on behalf of the plaintiffs in *Pope v. Blue* (1992), complained of North Carolina's disregard for this standard:

> In like manner, even though there may be legitimate explanations for some of its peculiar features, it appears fair to characterize North Carolina's proposed congressional plan, on balance, as a crazy-quilt without rational basis except as incumbency protection . . . Such massive violations of political subunit boundaries cannot be justified in terms of population equalization considerations, nor any other legitimate state purpose.[8]

North Carolina's state constitution is silent on dividing counties for congressional redistricting. However, the *Redistricting Criteria Guide* adopted by the House and Senate Congressional Redistricting Committees states that: "It is desirable to retain the integrity of precincts."[9] North Carolina's final enacted congressional plan divided counties, precincts, census tracts, and census blocks.

CONTIGUITY AND COMPACTNESS

An element of compactness is the concept of contiguity. Bernard Grofman has defined contiguity as follows:

> [I]f every part of the district is reachable from every other part of the district without crossing the district boundary, i.e., the district is not divided into two or more discrete pieces.[10]

What is meant conventionally by contiguity is that all parts of a district must be connected at some point on dry land. However, this is not always the case. According to political scientists David Butler and Bruce Cain:

> [S]ome kinds of noncontiguity are unavoidable. An off-shore island, for instance, has to be attached to mainland districts by water unless it has, by itself, close to the ideal population for a district.[11]

Contiguity is usually one of the less controversial elements of compactness. However, Grofman, in his declaration in support of plaintiffs in *Pope v. Blue* (1992), felt that the final enacted congressional plan in North Carolina contained some discontiguous districts. He asserted that:

[I]t appears that either Congressional District 12 splits Congressional District 6 into two discontiguous pieces or Congressional District 6 splits Congressional District 12 into two discontiguous pieces or both. From the map, Congressional District 12 appears to pass through one side of District 6 and emerge from out the other side. If that does not result in District 6 being bisected into discontiguous pieces, the state of North Carolina would appear to be exercising skills superior to those of the late Houdini's famous "sawing a woman in half" trick.[12]

In the *Redistricting Criteria Guide* drafted by the North Carolina House and Senate Redistricting Committees, the third criterion clearly states that:

All congressional districts shall be single member districts, as required by 2 U.S.C. Section 2.c., and shall consist of contiguous territory.[13]

According to North Carolina's legislature, as long as a district contains territory that touches other territory in that district at a point, it is generally considered to be contiguous.[14] Thus, it appears that, the allegations of discontiguity by Bernard Grofman notwithstanding, the North Carolina state legislature considered all 12 districts it had created to be contiguous.

COMPACTNESS

The most controversial of the redistricting guidelines is the requirement that districts should be compact. North Carolina's Congressional Base Plan #10 (the enacted plan) gained national if not international notoriety due to what many observers termed the lack of compactness in the Twelfth District. The debate over oddly shaped congressional districts was not limited to North Carolina; many southern states' congressional plans drew similar responses as to a lack of compactness. Even some members of the North Carolina state legislature's redistricting committees and staff attorneys for those committees acknowledged that some of the districts in the enacted congressional plan were not compact.

Dennis Winner, chair of the North Carolina Senate Redistricting Committee, stated that the Voting Rights Act and *Gingles*, the case that interprets it, requires the creation of minority districts when it can be done in a reasonably compact way. Winner thought that because North Carolina's population was so rural and dispersed, it was impossible to create a reasonably compact minority district. Additionally, Winner said that when the minority districts are made uncompact, the districts around them are going to be contorted.[15]

The word "compactness" is generally used in the geographic sense. It is principally used in redistricting as an argument and/or a standard against gerrymandering. Ernest Reock, author of the Reock test for compactness, states:

> If specific standards of compactness must be met, many efforts to establish gerrymandered districts may be placed at a disadvantage. Without some requirement of compactness, the boundaries of a district may twist and wind their way across the map in fantastic fashion in order to absorb scattered pockets of partisan support.[16]

Law professors Daniel Polsby and Robert Popper, in an article entitled "The Third Criterion: Compactness as a Procedural Safeguard Against Partisan Gerrymandering," credit Bernard Grofman as having pointed out that potential remedies for gerrymandering come in two forms: political and formal. A remedy is political when a redistricting plan must meet the approval of a bipartisan panel. The other form of remedy that Grofman mentions is a formal one. Polsby and Popper propose that compactness be a formal remedy for gerrymandering:

> In addition to adhering to criteria which mandate that representational districts be composed of contiguous territories and have equal populations, we suggest that those who define district boundaries must also be required to respect a third criterion, the constraint of compactness. Without the ability to distend district lines so as to include or exclude blocks of voters whose political loyalties are known, it is not practically possible to gerrymander.[17]

But Grofman has written that reliance on such formal criteria as compactness or equal population as devices to prevent gerrymandering is wrong. He asserts that:

> With respect to compactness, the usefulness of requiring that districts be compact has been vastly overrated. With the exception of its potential usefulness as an [indicia] of possible gerrymandering, I do not believe there is anything desirable per se about districts that look like squares or circles. If we look at census tracts, or townships, or

neighborhoods, or other obvious political building blocks, it is rare indeed to find regular geometric figures or even figures that can be aggregated into neat geometric patterns, especially while satisfying equal population constraints.[18]

Law Professor Pamela S. Karlan takes a close look at the issue of geographic compactness in an article entitled "Maps and Misreadings: The Role of Geographic Compactness in Racial Vote Dilution Litigation." Karlan examines the three-part test that the Supreme Court enunciated in *Thornburg v. Gingles* (1986).[19] The Court ruled that a minority legislative district should be drawn if three basic conditions were met: minority geographic compactness, minority political cohesiveness, and the level of bloc voting by whites. In her discussion, Karlan cites a case from Baldwin County, Alabama, that addressed significant issues pertaining to geographic compactness. The case, *Dillard v. Baldwin County Board of Education* (1988),[20] was a vote dilution case in which black plaintiffs challenged the use of at-large elections by the Board of Education. Baldwin County had a 13.86 percent black population, which was concentrated in neighborhoods along the county's border. The black plaintiffs proposed a seven-district plan with one majority black district.

The county argued in this case that the plaintiffs' plan failed to meet the first prong of the *Gingles* test "because it is too elongated and curvaceous and thus fails to meet the requirement of compactness."[21] In ruling in favor of the plaintiffs, the federal appellate court stated that by compactness, *Gingles* "does not mean that a proposed district must meet, or attempt to achieve, some aesthetic absolute, such as symmetry or attractiveness."[22]

Compactness has been used as a legal standard referring to regularity in shape and size of an election district. Some political scholars such as Bruce Cain and David Butler have argued that an aspect of compactness is "that districts should have relatively geometrical shapes, without many branches, dips, or jagged edges."[23] Moreover, they posit that it is possible to defend the concept of compactness for its instrumental value and not just its value as a constraining criterion, i.e., as an antigerrymandering device. They argue that

[c]ontorted and sprawling districts make it harder for representatives to do their jobs. If the districts cover too much territory, or if they cross rugged terrain with no natural access, parts of the districts may be cut off from the rest of the seat. Representatives may even feel deterred

from visiting the remote sections of the seats as frequently as they should. Even when the geographical features of the district are not a factor, a seat that zigs and zags through may have less of a sense of common identity than one that encompasses a compact area, making constituents more confused and ignorant than they would otherwise be about their representatives.[24]

Law professor Richard Pildes and political scientist Richard Niemi examined several federal court cases prior to the *Shaw v. Reno* (1993) decision that dealt with the compactness requirement. They found that the federal courts have been inconsistent in their rulings as to what constitutes a compact district. They cite *Dillard* as one extreme ruling by the courts where it appeared that the government's interest in increasing minority representation outweighed the creation of contorted districts. At the opposite extreme, they noted *Bryant v. Lawrence County* (1993).[25] In this federal court case out of Mississippi, the court rejected a proposed district as an odd contortion because it "reaches down to get a pocket of white voters in the south-east-central part of the county and then curves around to the west and then back to the northeast corner of the county."[26] Moreover, according to Niemi and Pildes, only 25 states require that districts be compact. And all but two of those (Iowa and Colorado) define compactness in qualitative terms. They clearly see this lack of quantitative standards of measuring districts as contributing to the inconsistencies on the part of the courts.

Other literature concerning geographical compactness examines the element of shape (Reock, 1961; Taylor, 1973; Grofman, 1985; Niemi et al., 1990; Horn et al., 1993; Pildes and Niemi, 1993). Indeed, legal challenges around the South to many of the congressional redistricting plans created as a result of the 1991–1992 round of redistricting were based on the creation of irregularly shaped districts.

The most commonly measured characteristic of shape is compactness. Because compactness has been used as a standard for judging legislative districts, some method of measuring it has been required. A circle is the most compact shape in the sense that it has the smallest possible perimeter relative to the area contained within it. Therefore, a simple measure of compactness compares the ratio of perimeter to area. The larger the perimeter relative to the area, the less compact the district.

Compactness remains a guideline for redistricting, but not a requirement. Although some states have a constitutional or statutory requirement that congressional districts be compact, neither the U.S. Constitution nor the North Carolina state constitution explicitly require it. The subject of compactness and ways of measuring it will be revisited in Chapter 8.

COMMUNITIES OF INTEREST

Another redistricting guideline that is related to compactness is whether a district maintains a community of interest. There is no agreement on how to define a community of interest. According to David Butler and Bruce Cain:

> Usually communities are defined in terms of local government bound-aries—city and county borders—but those do not always coincide with other kinds of communities, such as ethnic and racial neighborhoods, topographical features, media markets, socioeconomic homogeneity, and the like. There is wide scope for argument about how a particular "natural community" should be defined, and no one has yet offered clear answers to the general problem.[27]

The Twelfth Congressional District in North Carolina consists of parts of 10 counties. It is a majority black district that snakes for 160 miles along Interstate 85, beginning west of Charlotte, then heading north through Winston-Salem, and then east through Greensboro to Durham. It has been criticized, among other reasons, for lacking a community of interest and for consisting of many different communities of interest. Some have argued that voters in this district have nothing in common but skin color or language patterns. However, the state of North Carolina argued before the U.S. Supreme Court in *Shaw v. Reno* (1993) that the district had a common urban identity.

Gerry Cohen, director of bill drafting for the North Carolina General Assembly, stated that communities of interest were considered in the creation of the final plan. He noted that the term compactness was subject to interpretation. Defending this district as part of Congressional Base Plan #10, the state legislature argued that its plan demonstrated political compactness and socioeconomic compactness, if not geographic compactness. Both political compactness and socioeconomic compactness approximate a standard for commonality of interests. Thus, Cohen asserted:

> [B]lacks in Durham, Charlotte, Greensboro, High Point, Salisbury . . . in those urban areas had far more in common than black voters or vot-ers in general under Balmer's plan from Charlotte to Wilmington. They argue that the district although it looks on a map less contiguous . . . in

terms of political cohesiveness and socioeconomic [factors] in fact, people have much more commonality of interest in the Twelfth.[28]

Cohen even possessed data supporting that assertion. He produced a chart that showed that 76.16 percent of the population in District 12 of the enacted plan resided in cities with a population of 20,000 or more. The chart also showed that conversely, 76.94 percent of the population in District 1 lived in cities with fewer than 20,000 people. According to Cohen, the two districts

> were set up as mirror images of each other. One set up basically—and this was conscious—one . . . essentially minority district was set up by the legislature, to be dominated by rural black interests and the other by urban black interests. That even a lot of black legislators would say that there's crosscutting things, being black is obviously a unifying factor among blacks but being in an urban and rural area cuts against, I mean there's a different interest at the same time.[29]

Mel Watt, the congressman who represents the Twelfth District in North Carolina, refers to it as the premier urban district in the state. Watt routinely brushed off criticism that the district did not encompass a single community.

Moreover, law professor Lani Guinier, in her discussion of cumulative voting in her book *The Tyranny of the Majority* (1994), addresses the concept of community. Indeed, according to Guinier, under a modified at-large system such as cumulative voting, "All voters have the potential to form voluntary constituencies based on their own assessment of their interests."[30] Guinier, in essence, is proposing a nonracial means to a racial end. Black voters and other groups who share common interests should be able to elect a winning candidate, assuming they vote cohesively. Government professor Michael Jones Correa has explored how the term "community" has alternative meanings to the traditional territorial one, particularly among Latin Americans in New York.[31] Butler and Cain add this about communities of interest:

> There are places where ethnic grouping, occupational patterns, housing types, physical frontiers like hills and rivers, or simply local traditions do seem to identify a precise geographic area as a distinct community, but sometimes such lines are blurred or are not recognized by the inhabitants concerned. In such cases, any boundary must be arbitrary.[32]

Butler and Cain state that there is disagreement over how a "natural community" should be defined, which communities of interest are legitimate and which are not. Moreover, they assert that the need to preserve the boundaries of local governmental units and communities of interest is grounded in legislative representation theory. They note that the major tenets of this theory are that "representatives should be delegates and not trustees (at least to some significant degree)."[33] Furthermore, these elected officials "should represent the interests of groups and communities . . . and not just the median preference of a disaggregated set of individual voters."[34] Of course, this view is in contrast with the view articulated by the English philosopher Edmund Burke, who believed that representatives were sent by their constituents to vote their conscience in their role as a trustee. They are, indeed, required to consider the views of their constituents, but they are not required to vote according to those views.[35] This is an important distinction with respect to communities of interest, state Butler and Cain, because

> if the representative is meant to be a Burkean representative who is not obliged to focus on parochial district concerns, then seats do not need to be designed (and in fact should not be designed) to respect communities of interest of any kind. To do so would only place undue constituency pressures upon the representative. Thus, a communities of interest approach necessarily implies a delegate theory of representation.[36]

Several observations will help put these arguments in perspective. Empirical studies of Congress (see Fenno, *Home Style*, 1978) show that few congresspeople view themselves as "delegates," mainly because their constituencies are so diverse that there is no coherent set of policy preferences or commonality of interests shared by all. So an Equal Protection issue arises: *Why should majority black districts be held to a standard that does not apply to majority white districts?*

Furthermore, in the United States, blacks have shared a history of oppression and a continuing experience of racism and discrimination that does situate them in a common relation to the majority. Thus, the issue is not skin color or language use, but a shared culture created in response to and in resistance against white domination. The black church, black literature, jazz, rap, the dozens, soul food, and extended family patterns are all part of this common culture. One can make a forceful argument that because of these shared experiences, a community of interest certainly exists among blacks in America.

ALTERNATIVE PLANS PRESENTED TO THE
GENERAL ASSEMBLY

The final enacted plan of the North Carolina state legislature was not the only plan containing two majority black districts that was considered for adoption (see Chapter 4). Several plans had been submitted to the state legislature before and after the U.S. Department of Justice rejected the state's initial submission in late 1991 (which had created only one majority black district). For purposes of my analysis, I have chosen six of these plans that contained at least two majority-minority districts to be examined along with the original enacted plan (Congressional Base Plan #6) and the final enacted plan (Congressional Base Plan #10).

Several of these alternative plans submitted to the state legislature, including the final enacted plan, used the Interstate 85 corridor for the creation of an urban majority black district. Gerry Cohen, head of legislative drafting for the state legislature, offered the following explanation:

> An urban black district in the Piedmont could be connected from Gastonia to Durham along the I–85 corridor because that highway was often located in black neighborhoods. For example, in Guilford County, I–85 is bulldozed through six Greensboro precincts, two of which are more than 99 percent black and two others which are nearly 50 percent black. In Mecklenburg County, I–85 goes through 13 Charlotte city precincts, five of which are 98 percent or more black, and another six of which are majority black.[37]

North Carolina's spatial patterns of residential housing predictably reflect the country as a whole. However, as noted in the *Statistical Abstract of North Carolina*, the migratory trend for blacks in the Piedmont Urban Crescent area of North Carolina, which includes Charlotte, Winston-Salem, Greensboro, Durham, and Raleigh, tends to be just the opposite of that for whites:

> Probably the most important conclusion to be drawn . . . is that of the immense strength of the rural-urban relocation of black people. Extraordinary because it is happening precisely at the time when more and more people in general are shifting their domicile from urban to suburban and exurban locations, and especially so in the Piedmont.[38]

Moreover, according to the *Statistical Abstract*:

> Whereas the black population is shifting its weight generally from a rural to an urban location, within the cities the distinction between

black and non-black concentrations can be even more clearly drawn. A sharp spatial separation between the races is one of the most readily defined contrasts in the cities.[39]

The final plan accepted by the U.S. Department of Justice (Congressional Base Plan #10) contained two majority black districts, one of which, District 12, was the Interstate 85 corridor district.

Cohen said that another factor that contributed to the sprawling nature of the two majority black districts in the adopted plan was that Raleigh, the capital city, which has a sizable black population, was not included in either black district in the enacted plan. Cohen asserted that Raleigh (Wake County) and Chapel Hill (Orange County)

> have the lowest percentage of racial bloc voting. The black area in Raleigh was not put in either of the districts largely because legislative leaders felt by having a district that was Raleigh and Chapel Hill and Cary [just outside of Raleigh], that given the voting patterns in Wake and Orange and Chatham [adjacent to Orange County] counties that a black could be elected from this district . . . I guess it's clear that the voting patterns in those three counties are such that, well, certainly blacks would not control anything, they only make up twenty percent of the vote, it's clear that blacks have and can get elected.[40]

Furthermore, according to Cohen, there was a reluctance on the part of the black leadership in the state legislature to put Raleigh in either of the majority black districts in the enacted plan, even though the districts would have been more compact. The black leadership felt strongly that combining the black community in Raleigh with the white communities of Chapel Hill, Cary, and Raleigh would give a black candidate a realistic chance at a third seat. Studies in North Carolina had shown that this district had the least amount of racially polarized voting in the state.[41]

NOTES

[1]Carmine Scavo, "Redistricting Will Be Tough Task," *Greenville Daily Reflector*, March 31, 1991: E3.

[2]Article 1, Section 2, United States Constitution.

[3]United States Constitution, Fourteenth Amendment.

[4]Bernard Grofman, "Criteria for Districting: A Social Science Perspective," *U.C.L.A. Law Review*, Vol. 33, October 1985: 81.

[5]Ernest C. Reock Jr., "Measuring Compactness as a Requirement of Legislative Apportionment," *Midwest Journal of Political Science*, February 5, 1961: 70.

[6]Grofman 80.

[7]Frank Parker, "Changing Standards in Voting Rights Law," *Redistricting in the 1990s: A Guide for Minority Groups*, ed. William P. O'Hare (Washington, D.C.: Population Reference Bureau, Inc., 1989) 57.

[8]Declaration of Bernard Grofman at 5, *Pope v. Blue*, 809 F. Supp. 392 (W.D.N.C. 1992).

[9]Affidavit of Gerry Cohen at Attachment E, *Pope v. Blue*, 809 F. Supp. 392 (W.D.N.C. 1992).

[10]Grofman 84.

[11]David Butler and Bruce Cain, *Congressional Redistricting: Comparative and Theoretical Perspectives* (New York: Macmillan Publishers, 1992) 61.

[12]Declaration of Bernard Grofman at 2, *Pope v. Blue*, 809 F. Supp. 392 (W.D.N.C. 1992).

[13]Affidavit of Gerry Cohen at Attachment E, *Pope v. Blue*, 809 F. Supp. 392 (W.D.N.C. 1992).

[14]*Redistricting 1991: Legislator's Guide to N. C. Congressional Redistricting* (Raleigh: Research Division, N. C. General Assembly, 1991) 12.

[15]Interview with Dennis Winner, May 27, 1992, Raleigh, North Carolina.

[16]Ernest C. Reock Jr., 71.

[17]Daniel Polsby and Robert Popper, "The Third Criterion: Compactness as a Procedural Safeguard Against Partisan Gerrymandering," *Yale Law and Policy Review*, Vol. 9, 1991: 302.

[18]Bernard Grofman, "Criteria for Districting: A Social Science Perspective," *U.C.L.A. Law Review*, Vol. 33, October 1985: 89–90.

[19]Pam Karlan, "Maps and Misreadings: The Role of Geographic Compactness in Racial Vote Dilution Litigation," *Harvard Civil Rights-Civil Liberties Law Review*, Vol. 24, Winter 1989: 200–201.

[20]*Dillard v. Baldwin County Board of Education*, 686 F. Supp. 1459 (M.D. Ala. 1988).

[21]Pam Karlan, "Maps and Misreadings," 211.

[22]Karlan 211.

[23]David Butler and Bruce Cain, *Congressional Redistricting: Comparative and Theoretical Perspectives*, (New York: Macmillan Publishers, 1992) 61.

[24]Butler and Cain 61.

[25]*Bryant v. Lawrence County*, 814 F. Supp. 1346, 1350 (S.D. Miss. 1993).

[26]Richard Pildes and Richard Niemi, "Expressive Harms, 'Bizarre Districts,' and Voting Rights: Evaluating Election-District Appearances After *Shaw v. Reno*," *Michigan Law Review* Vol. 92, December 1993: 532.

[27]Butler and Cain 70.

[28]Interview with Gerry Cohen, May 27, 1992, Raleigh, North Carolina.

[29]Interview with Gerry Cohen.

[30]Lani Guinier, *The Tyranny of the Majority: Fundamental Fairness in Representative Democracy* (New York: The Free Press, 1994) 127.

[31]Michael Jones Correa, "Defining Community: Latin American Immigrants and the Politics in Queens," Paper Presented at the 1993 Workshop on Race, Ethnicity, Representation, and Governance, Center for American Political Studies, Harvard University, Cambridge, Massachusetts.

[32]David Butler and Bruce Cain, *Congressional Redistricting*, 70.

[33]Butler and Cain 72.

[34]Butler and Cain 71.

[35]Kenneth Janda et al., *The Challenge of Democracy* 4th ed. (Boston: Houghton Mifflin Co., 1995) 409.

[36]David Butler and Bruce Cain, *Congressional Redistricting*, 71.

[37]Interview with Gerry Cohen, May 27, 1992, Raleigh, North Carolina.

[38]*Statistical Abstract of North Carolina Counties* 6th ed. (Raleigh: N. C. State Data Center, 1991) 66.

[39]*Statistical Abstract* 66.

[40]Interview with Gerry Cohen, May 27, 1992, Raleigh, North Carolina.

[41]Interview with Gerry Cohen, May 27, 1992.

CHAPTER 8

Calculating Compactness in North Carolina Plans

Critics of North Carolina's enacted plan attacked the convoluted shape of the newly created majority black Twelfth District. They alleged that North Carolina could have created a second majority black district to satisfy the U.S. Justice Department mandate without resorting to what they considered such bizarre map-making.

A number of recent studies have examined some of the critical issues concerning congressional redistricting in the 1990s. One work has analyzed the major redistricting plans considered by the North Carolina legislature in terms of the distribution of African Americans, the normal Democratic vote, and the expected probability of a Democratic win in each district.[1] Still other works assess various measures for examining the compactness of districting plans and then apply some of those to districts around the nation, comparing different districts in different states to one another based on these different measures.[2]

The final plan selected by the North Carolina state legislature created two majority-minority districts. Much of the criticism of this plan centered around allegations that the two majority-minority districts deviated from traditional districting guidelines of compactness and contiguity. However, there were alternative plans creating two or more majority-minority districts that were presented to the state legislature, but they were rejected by the Democratic majority. I have identified several different quantitative measures of compactness to test this claim. Unlike previous works, my study compares the two majority-minority districts of the enacted plan with the majority-minority districts of the alternative plans in terms of compactness. My objective is to determine whether any of the proposed plans created majority-minority districts that were more compact than the majority-minority districts of the enacted plan.

North Carolina's 22 percent black population is dispersed throughout the state in both urban and rural areas. Nonetheless, a large percentage of blacks resides in the rural Coastal Plains and Tidewater counties of the northeastern part of the state. All of the plans examined created a majority-minority district with a substantial portion of the population coming from this region. Therefore, all the alternative plans examined, except Congressional Base Plan #6, had essentially a rural district and an urban district. For this reason, my analysis compares the rural majority-minority district in Congressional Base Plan #10 (the enacted plan) with the rural majority-minority districts in the major alternative plans. I also have compared the urban majority-minority district in Congressional Base Plan #10 with the urban majority-minority districts in the alternative plans.

MEASURES OF COMPACTNESS

Political scientist Peter Taylor suggests that politicians, political commentators, and political scientists are fascinated by the shapes of electoral districts.[3] Shape in its most general form is only a classificatory concept. Taylor notes that shape generally allows only a nominal and as such imprecise level of measurement. Many areal shapes are compared to the shapes of familiar objects, such as the comparison of Italy to a boot. However, Taylor notes:

> But if we compare areal shapes to geometric shapes whose basic properties are known, we can produce shape measures at a ratio level. This is one of the basic approaches of political scientists who compare electoral district properties with an ideal circle. When we do this we are in fact making our shape concept more specific, and we usually call these measurements measures of compactness.[4]

There are numerous measures of compactness but no universal agreement on a single best measure insofar as all measures have advantages and disadvantages.

Compactness is usually considered in geographical terms. Much of the literature on compactness centers on identifying the best standards of measure. Several techniques have been devised to measure compactness, among them the determination of the ratio of a congressional district's length to its width, and the number of sides of a district. Though no measures of compactness have become a standard, several measures are considered fairly viable by scholars in the field. Richard Niemi et al. note that a figure is compact if it is closely or firmly packed together.[5]

They identify dispersion, perimeter, and possibly population as three components for any satisfactory measure of compactness. They generally agree that the perimeter length of a figure taken by itself is not a good measure because a fixed perimeter length can yield numerous shapes that differ widely in their spread. Additionally, they caution that dispersion measures alone are inadequate because they are insensitive to perimeter irregularities that may indicate gerrymandering. Niemi notes that a "nearly circular district . . . though almost ideal in its dispersion— would raise considerable suspicion . . . if its boundary were a jagged border of small but inexplicable twists and turns."[6] Population, according to Pildes and Niemi, focuses not just on the shape of a district but on "the distribution of population between a district and its surrounding territory."[7] Niemi et al. argue that measuring compactness has become problematic not because it is difficult to define but because of the multidimensional nature of compactness.[8]

A taxonomy of compactness measures has been developed by various scholars in the field (e.g., Manninen, 1973; Niemi et al., 1990; Horn et al., 1993). Each of their classifications builds on the previous measures identified. Because no single test is flawless, I have identified five to be used to examine the majority-minority districts in the eight plans being analyzed.* The five measures are as follows:

polygon area—area only test

polygon perimeter—perimeter only test

Grofman Test—area/perimeter quotients test

Schwartzberg Test—area/perimeter quotients test

Reock Test—dispersion test

According to Niemi et al., it is not land but the distribution of voters that is important in determining whether a district is compact. Thus, a district is not compact if it is shaped like a square but the population is concentrated within a thin line running diagonally across it. Conversely,

*These measures were identified by staff members of the North Carolina General Assembly Legislative Services Office, Automated Systems Division.

a district is compact if the population lives within a perfect square but the district has the appearance of a tortured camel.[9]

Pildes and Niemi, who compared congressional districts around the country after the 1990 round of redistricting, did not use population measures in assessing compactness of districts. They noted that the *Shaw v. Reno* (1993) Supreme Court decision did not give states clear guidelines for measuring what a bizarre district is. However, they stated that much of the language in the opinion "invokes many synonyms for widely dispersed districts and for those whose borders are severely distorted."[10] The decision made references to how North Carolina's Twelfth Congressional District traversed in snakelike fashion for 160 miles and was no longer at points than the I–85 corridor. Furthermore, the *Shaw* decision alluded to "the concentration of a 'dispersed' minority population and to individuals 'widely separated by geographical and political boundaries.'"[11] These statements led Pildes and Niemi to conclude that the Supreme Court was not concerned with how the district boundaries twisted and turned, but how spread out the districts were, both geographically and with respect to such matters as rural versus urban. They concluded that dispersion and perimeter measures were most appropriate for measuring shape in the more usual sense. In my study, I also do not include any population measures of compactness.

Polygon area is the sum of the area of all units assigned to a district. The smaller the area, the more compact the district.[12] This measure has been criticized on the grounds that size is not relevant for assessing the compactness of a district.[13]

Polygon perimeter is the distance around the district's boundary line(s). The shorter the perimeter, the more compact the district. This measure has been described as lacking because long perimeters do not necessarily imply uncompact districts.[14]

The Grofman Test takes the perimeter of a district and divides it by the square root of the area of the district to yield an area/perimeter ratio. This test was devised by using a circle as a standard of comparison. For the Grofman Test:

$$C = \frac{P}{\sqrt{A}}$$

where C = Compactness,
      P = Perimeter,
      A = Area,
as applied to a circle, assuming the radius = 1, using 3.14 for pi,

$$C = \frac{2\pi r}{\sqrt{\pi r^2}}$$

$$C = \frac{2(3.14)\ (1)}{\sqrt{(3.14)\ (1)^2}} = 3.54$$

According to the Grofman Test, this is the number to use as a standard of comparison when assessing compactness of legislative districts. In principle, the ratios may vary between 3.545, which is the most compact, and infinity. The Grofman Test is a good measure, according to Horn et al. (1993), because it corrects for the dimension problem of area by taking the square root of the area. The Schwartzberg Test uses the perimeter of a district and compares it to the perimeter of a circle of an equal area to that of the district. For the Schwartzberg Test:

$$C = \frac{P}{2}\sqrt{\pi A}$$

where C = Compactness,
            P = Perimeter,
            A = Area,
            as applied to a circle,

$$A = \pi r^2$$
$$P = 2\pi r$$
$$r = \frac{P}{2}\ \pi$$

This equation yields a ratio of zero to one. As the ratio gets closer to one, the district is more compact. The Schwartzberg Test also uses a circle as its standard. This is because the ratio of the perimeter to the area is smallest for a circle. Both the Grofman Test and the Schwartzberg Test have been cited as good measures of perimeter, but poor measures of dispersion.[15]

The Reock Test determines the area of the smallest circle containing the district. The area of the district is divided by the area of the smallest circle containing the district to produce a ratio between zero (0) and one (1). For the Reock test:

$$R = A(D)/A(C)$$

where R = Ratio,
         A = Area,
         D = District,
         C = Circle.

The closer the ratio is to one, the more compact the district. This is a relatively sound and simple measure to use. The circle provides an ideal example of compactness: It is the most compact plane figure because it maximizes the area enclosed within a given perimeter. Therefore, the degree of compactness of a district may be measured by the relationship of the district area and the area of the smallest possible circumscribing circle. The Reock Test is considered a good measure of dispersion.[16]

Even the best measurements for compactness have relative strengths and weaknesses. Consequently, I have attempted to use more than one measure to examine the districts in the various plans.

RESULTS OF CALCULATIONS

Comparison of Urban Districts

Polygon Area Test. Table 8.1 shows the urban districts using the polygon area test on all plans. Upon analysis of these various plans, District 12 in Congressional Base Plan #10, (Con 10, the enacted plan) has an area of 852 square miles. It has the smallest area of all the urban districts and, according to the polygon area test of compactness, it is the most compact district. Balmer 6.2, which the Republicans offered to the U.S. Department of Justice as an alternative to Con 10, had an urban District 12 with a polygon area of 5,251 square miles—the least compact according to this measure.

Polygon Perimeter Test. The second measure of compactness that I used for my analysis is polygon perimeter. Table 8.2 shows the perimeter of each of the urban districts in the congressional plans. District 6 of Compact 2 plan had the shortest, and the most compact, perimeter at 813 miles. District 7 of the Wilson plan had a perimeter of 919 and was the second shortest perimeter of the districts. District 12 of the enacted plan (Con 10) had the third shortest perimeter of 929 miles. Balmer 6.2 had the longest perimeter, at 1,394 miles.

Grofman Test. The third measure of compactness that I used was the Grofman Test, in which the perimeter is divided by the square root of the area to yield a perimeter/revised area ratio. Table 8.3 shows the

Table 8.1. Polygon Area Test: Comparison of Polygon Area of the Urban Districts of the Alternative Plans with the Enacted Plan in North Carolina

Plan	District	Polygon Area (sq. mi.)	Rank
Con 10	**12**	**852**	**1**
Balmer 6.2	12	5,251	6
Wilson	7	2,441	5
92 Con 1	12	1,583	3
Balmer 8.1	12	1,358	2
Compact 2	6	1,984	5
Flaherty	12	1,657	4

Note: Con 6 does not appear in the above plan or in any urban plans because it contained only one majority black district, which was a rural district.

Note: Most compact district appears in bold.

Table 8.2. Polygon Perimeter Test: Comparison of the Urban Districts of the Alternative Plans with the Enacted Plan in North Carolina

Plan	District	Polygon Perimeter (mi.)	Rank
Con 10	12	929	3
Balmer 6.2	12	1,394	7
Wilson	7	919	2
92 Con 1	12	1,012	6
Balmer 8.1	12	949	4
Compact 2	**6**	**813**	**1**
Flaherty	12	1,000	5

Note: Most compact district appears in bold.

results of this test on the seven urban districts. Using 3.545 as the standard of comparison for the most compact district, District 6 of Compact 2 yielded a ratio equal to 18.257. District 12 of Con 10 yielded the least compact district among all the plans with a ratio equal to 31.831. None of the plans yielded a ratio anywhere near the ideal 3.545.

Table 8.3. Comparison of Urban District of the Enacted Plan with the Urban Districts of the Alternative Plans (Grofman Test)

Plan Name	Number of District	Area of District (sq. m.)	Perimeter of District (m.)	Grofman Ratio	Rank
Con 10	12	2,205,857,555	1,495,018	31.83154289	7
Balmer 6.2	12	13,598,731,953	2,242,695	19.23184757	3
Wilson	7	6,322,935,999	1,479,304	18.60364479	2
92 Con 1	12	4,100,031,481	1,628,172	25.42767700	5
Balmer 8.1	12	3,515,839,396	1,528,278	25.77435745	6
Compact 2	**6**	**5,137,288,022**	**1,308,616**	**18.25766644**	**1**
Flaherty	12	4,290,754,669	1,609,667	24.57362343	4

Note: Most compact district appears in bold.

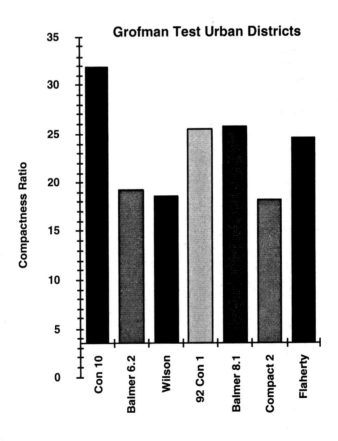

Table 8.4. Comparison of Urban District of the Enacted Plan with the Urban Districts of the Alternative Plans (Schwartzberg Test)

Plan Name	Number of District	Area of District (sq. m.)	Perimeter of District (m.)	Circle Perimeter (m.)	Schwarzberg Ratio	Rank
Con 10	12	2,205,857,555	1,495,018	166492.0423	0.111364574	7
Balmer 6.2	12	13,598,731,953	2,242,695	413384.2780	0.184324787	3
Wilson	7	6,322,935,999	1,479,304	281879.9213	0.190549016	2
92 Con 1	12	4,100,031,481	1,628,172	226985.6198	0.139411327	5
Balmer 8.1	12	3,515,839,396	1,528,278	210193.4907	0.137536162	6
Compact 2	**6**	**5,137,288,022**	**1,308,616**	**254080.7169**	**0.194159873**	**1**
Flaherty	12	4,290,754,669	1,609,667	232205.0125	0.144256553	4

Note: Most compact district appears in bold.

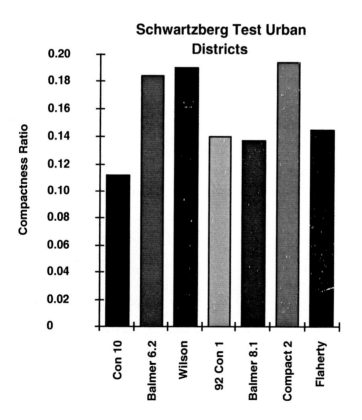

Table 8.5. Comparison of Urban District of the Enacted Plan with the Urban Districts of the Alternative Plans (Reock Test)

Plan Name	Number of District	Area of Circle (sq. m.)	Area of District (sq. m.)	Reock Ratio	Rank
Con 10	12	47,480,120,384	2,205,857,555	0.0464586	7
Balmer 6.2	12	93,115,307,327	13,598,731,953	0.1460419	2
Wilson	**7**	**35,855,098,186**	**6,322,935,999**	**0.1763469**	**1**
92 Con 1	12	62,454,267,446	4,100,031,481	0.0656485	5
Balmer 8.1	12	53,337,515,004	3,515,839,396	0.0659168	4
Compact 2	6	40,207,840,774	5,137,288,022	0.1277683	3
Flaherty	12	75,266,691,348	4,290,754,669	0.0570074	6

Note: Most compact district appears in bold.

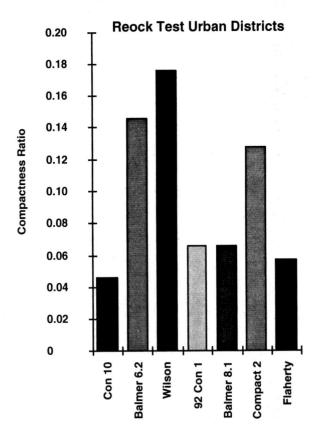

Schwartzberg Test. The fourth measure of compactness that I used was the Schwartzberg Test, in which the perimeter of a district is divided by the perimeter of a circle of an area equal to the area of the district. Table 8.4 shows the results of this test as performed on the urban districts of all of the congressional plans. Based on the Schwartzberg Test, all of the districts yielded a ratio within a relatively small range. District 6 of Compact 2 was the most compact of all the plans with a ratio of .194, but District 7 of Wilson (.190) was only slightly less compact. The least compact district was District 12 of Con 10, with a ratio of .111.

Reock Test. The fifth measure of compactness that I calculated for each district in the various plans was the Reock Test. In this case, the area of the district is divided by the area of the smallest circle containing the district to produce a ratio between zero (0) and one (1). The closer the ratio to one, the more compact the district. Table 8.5 shows the results of the Reock Test after it was performed on the seven urban districts. All of the districts were relatively uncompact. However, District 7 of the Wilson plan was the most compact of those examined. It had a Reock ratio of .176. District 12 of Balmer 6.2 was the second most compact, with a Reock ratio of .146. District 12 of Con 10 was the least compact district of all seven urban districts, with a Reock ratio of .046.

Comparison of Rural Districts

Polygon Area Test. I have examined the rural districts in the alternative plans utilizing the polygon area test. The area of each of the districts is shown in Table 8.6. District 1 of Con 6, the majority black district of the first plan enacted by the legislature, had an area of 8,125 square miles. This district, which was initially approved by the U.S. Department of Justice, was enlarged, and the area for District 1 in Con 10 was increased to 8,647 square miles, making it the second largest area of all the rural districts in the alternative plans. It is only smaller than Con 1, in which District 1 has an area of 8,904 and is the least compact district. District 2 under Balmer 6.2 had the smallest area and thus is the most compact district according to this measure, with an area of 5,336 square miles.

Polygon Perimeter Test. The polygon perimeter test was performed on the more rural of the majority black/minority districts of the alternative plan. The results of the test are shown in Table 8.7. In terms of polygon perimeter, District 1 of Con 10 has the next to longest perimeter at

Table 8.6. Polygon Area Test: Comparison of Polygon Area of the Rural Districts of the Alternative Plans with the Enacted Plan in North Carolina

Plan	District	Polygon Area (sq. m.)	Rank
Con 10	1	8,647	7
Balmer 6.2	**2**	**5,336**	**1**
Wilson	2	5,941	3
92 Con 1	1	8,904	8
Balmer 8.1	2	5,968	4
Compact 2	2	6,306	5
Flaherty	2	5,467	2
Con 6	1	8,125	6

Note: Most compact district appears in bold.

Table 8.7. Polygon Perimeter Test: Comparison of the Rural Districts of the Alternative Plans with the Rural District of the Enacted Plan in North Carolina

Plan	District	Polygon Perimeter (m.)	Rank
Con 10	1	2,025	7
Balmer 6.2	2	911	2
Wilson	**2**	**733**	**1**
92 Con 1	1	2,280	8
Balmer 8.1	2	1,487	6
Compact 2	2	1,408	5
Flaherty	2	1,137	3
Con 6	1	1,379	4

Note: Most compact district appears in bold.

2,025 miles, which is second least compact only to District 1 in Con 1, which had the longest perimeter and was the least compact district at 2,280 miles. The most compact district is District 2 of the Wilson Plan, with a perimeter of only 733 miles.

Table 8.8. Comparison of Rural District of the Enacted Plan with the Rural Districts of the Alternative Plans (Grofman Test)

Plan Name	Number of District	Area of District (sq. m.)	Perimeter of District (m.)	Grofman Ratio	Rank
Con 10	1	22,381,812,118	3,259,088	21.78454353	7
Balmer 6.2	2	13,820,784,198	1,466,405	12.47347870	2
Wilson	**2**	**15,388,124,913**	**1,179,444**	**9.50789712**	**1**
Con 1	1	23,061,250,922	3,669,055	24.16088239	8
Balmer 8.1	2	15,456,453,930	2,392,911	19.24737972	6
Compact 2	2	16,331,515,319	2,265,386	17.72674392	5
Flaherty	2	14,158,883,413	1,829,171	15.37233374	6
Con 6	1	21,042,727,986	2,218,910	15.29638010	3

Note: Most compact district appears in bold.

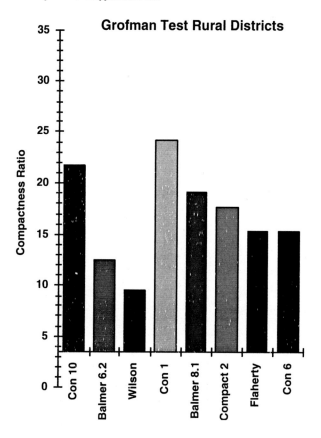

Table 8.9. Comparison of Rural District of the Enacted Plan with the Rural Districts of the Alternative Plans (Schwartzberg Test)

Plan Name	Number of District	Area of District (sq. m.)	Perimeter of District (m.)	Circle Perimeter (m.)	Schwartzberg Ratio	Rank
Con 10	1	22,381,812,118	3,259,088	530337.5421	0.16272575	7
Balmer 6.2	2	13,820,784,198	1,466,405	416745.6655	0.28419547	2
Wilson	**2**	**15,388,124,913**	**1,179,444**	**439741.6485**	**0.37283809**	**1**
Con 1	1	23,061,250,922	3,669,055	538327.0206	0.14672089	8
Balmer 8.1	2	15,456,453,930	2,392,911	440716.8756	0.18417604	6
Compact 2	2	16,331,515,319	2,265,386	453020.6406	0.19997503	5
Flaherty	2	14,158,883,413	1,829,171	421812.3114	0.23060299	4
Con 6	1	21,042,727,986	2,218,910	514228.0576	0.23174804	3

Note: Most compact district appears in bold.

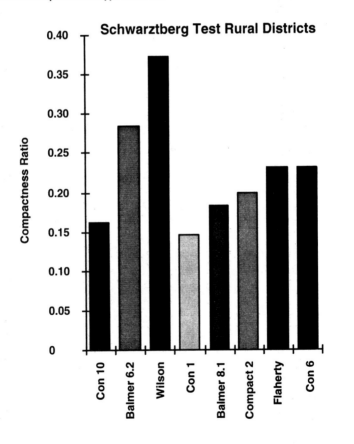

Table 8.10. Comparison of Rural District of the Enacted Plan with the Rural Districts of the Alternative Plans (Reock Test)

Plan Name	Number of District	Area of Circle (sq. m.)	Area of District (sq. m.)	Reock Ratio	Rank
Con 10	1	88,372,271,045	22,381,812,118	0.2532674	5
Balmer 6.2	2	92,115,307,327	13,598,731,953	0.1460419	8
Wilson	**2**	**41,553,918,549**	**15,388,124,913**	**0.3703171**	**1**
92 Con 1	1	77,406,877,838	23,061,250,922	0.2979225	3
Balmer 8.1	2	63,114,686,341	15,456,453,930	0.2448947	6
Compact 2	2	70,967,658,244	16,331,515,319	0.2301262	7
Flaherty	2	50,565,797,443	14,158,883,413	0.2800091	4
Con 6	1	62,225,770,513	21,042,727,986	0.3381674	2

Note: Most compact district appears in bold.

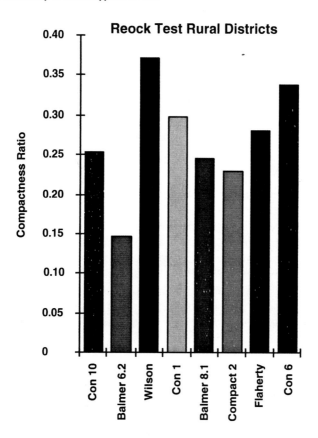

Grofman Test. Examining the rural districts of all the plans via the Grofman Test (by dividing the perimeter by the square root of the area), the results are given in Table 8.8.

When examining the rural districts using 3.545 as our standard of comparison, District 2 of the Wilson plan was the most compact district, yielding a ratio of 9.507. The least compact district was District 1 of Con 1, which was 24.160. District 2 of Balmer 6.2 was the second most compact district, with a ratio of 12.473. It does appear that based on the Grofman Test, Wilson District 7 (urban) and Wilson District 2 (rural) were the most compact of all the plans.

Schwartzberg Test. Table 8.9 shows the results of the Schwartzberg Test, which was performed on the rural districts of all of the plans. Using the Schwartzberg Test, District 2 of the Wilson plan is the most compact, at 0.372. District 2 of Balmer 6.2 is the second most compact district, yielding a ratio of 0.284. District 1 of Con 1 is the least compact, with a ratio of 0.146.

Reock Test. The results of the examination of the rural districts in the alternative plans using the Reock test appear in Table 8.10. All of the districts are relatively uncompact. District 2 of the Wilson plan is the most compact, with a Reock ratio of 0.370. Balmer 6.2 is the least compact with a Reock ratio of only 0.146.

CONCLUSION

The results of my analysis of the eight different redistricting plans are unexpected. Although five different tests of compactness were used, one plan was clearly the most compact for the rural districts and another was clearly the most compact for the urban districts. Moreover, of the five different tests of compactness used to examine the seven different plans with an urban majority-minority district, District 6 of Compact 2 was the most compact for three of the tests (see Table 8.11). Furthermore, District 2 of the Wilson plan was the most compact for four of the five tests used to examine the majority-minority districts for the eight urban plans (see Table 8.11).

The enacted plan (Con 10) is flawed. District 1 (rural) and District 12 (urban) lack compactness. The drawing of both of these districts was based primarily on political considerations. Con 10 was the most compact district for only the Polygon Area Test for the urban districts.

Table 8.11. Matrix of the Most Compact Urban and Rural Districts Under All Five Tests of Compactness

Compactness Test	Most Compact (Urban)	Most Compact (Rural)
Polygon Area	Base Plan 10 District 12	Balmer 6.2 District 2
Polygon Perimeter	Compact 2 District 6	Wilson District 2
Grofman Test	Compact 2 District 6	Wilson District 2
Schwartzberg Test	Compact 2 District 6	Wilson District 2
Reock Test	Wilson District 7	Wilson District 2

An alternative, the Wilson Plan, was clearly a better plan submitted to the state legislature. Not only was it the most compact rural district examined for four out of five of the tests, it was the most compact plan for its urban district in one of the five tests, and it was the second most compact of the urban districts for three out of the remaining four tests. However, the Wilson Plan fell short on the basis of other criteria considered by the state legislature, such as a higher percentage of black registered voters in the two majority black districts and protection of incumbent congresspeople.

All of the plans fared poorly in terms of being close to an ideal standard of compactness for any of the various tests. All of the districts in the enacted plan appear to be substantially less compact than the districting plan for North Carolina in the 1980s. Furthermore, the districts in the enacted plan appear to be no less compact than other districts drawn around the country where race was not a factor at all. The Democratically controlled state legislature in North Carolina had before it a plan that was more compact than Con 10: *The Wilson plan was clearly more compact and created two majority black districts as well.*

Once the redistricting process was completed after the 1990 census, people across the South protested. They believed that the U.S. Justice Department mandate to create majority-minority districts had forced southern states into drawing maps with oddly shaped congressional districts. In

North Carolina, this was not really the case. The North Carolina state legislature could have drawn a congressional map with two reasonably compact majority black districts, but it chose to do otherwise; so there is a common misperception on the part of the general public on this issue.

The state legislature in North Carolina did, in fact, use compactness as a criterion for the drawing of congressional districts. However, the Democratically controlled legislature found it impossible to protect white incumbent Democrats and create two majority-minority districts without resorting to irregularly shaped district lines. Thus, the issue of compactness lost out to political considerations.

NOTES

[1]Paul Gronke and J. Matthew Wilson, "Competing Redistricting Plans as Evidence of Political Motives: The North Carolina Case," Paper Presented at the 1996 Annual Meeting of the Midwest Political Science Association, Chicago, Illinois.

[2]Richard H. Pildes and Richard G. Niemi, "Expressive Harms, 'Bizarre Districts,' and Voting-Rights: Evaluating Election-District Appearances After *Shaw v. Reno*," *Michigan Law Review*, Vol. 92, December 1993.

[3]Peter J. Taylor, "A New Shape Measure for Evaluating Electoral District Patterns," *American Political Science Review*, Vol. 67, September 1973: 947.

[4]Peter J. Taylor, "A New Shape Measure for Evaluating Electoral District Patterns," 947.

[5]Richard G. Niemi et al. "Measuring Compactness and the Role of a Compactness Standard in a Test for Partisan and Racial Gerrymandering." *Journal of Politics*, Vol. 52, November 1990: 1158.

[6]Richard G. Niemi et al., 1158.

[7]Richard H. Pildes and Richard G. Niemi, 556.

[8]Richard G. Niemi et al., 1159.

[9]Niemi et al., 1159.

[10]Richard H. Pildes and Richard G. Niemi, 557.

[11]Richard H. Pildes and Richard G. Niemi, 557.

[12]David L. Horn, et al. "Practical Application of District Compactness," *Political Geography*, March 1993, 107.

[13]Niemi et al., 1160.

[14]Horn et al., 107.

[15]Horn et al., 109.

[16]Horn et al., 108.

CHAPTER 9

Conclusion: The Case for
Majority Black Districts
Remains Compelling

*In 1965, Congress passed the Voting Rights Act
to provide minorities opportunities to fully
participate in the political process; participation that had been denied for so long. One hun-
dred years after the Civil War, states across the
country were still using poll taxes, literacy tests,
and gerrymandering to undermine the political
voice of black minority communities. In state
legislatures, lines were drawn to split black
communities among districts to prevent their
political strength, and to prevent the election of
candidates of their choice.*
—CONGRESSMAN CLEO FIELDS,
D-LOUISIANA, 1995

Black representation in American politics is under threat today. The
Supreme Court has now opened the floodgates to challenges to majority-
minority districts drawn throughout the South. Of the 17 congressional
districts located in the South with a majority black population (by the
1992 elections), 8 have been overturned by the federal courts or through
legislative intervention. A conservative U.S. Supreme Court has been
dismantling the achievements that minorities have made in electoral politics over the last 30 years.

The Voting Rights Act of 1965, coupled with the Fifteenth Amendment
to the U.S. Constitution, opened the door to black electoral participation in

167

America. The U.S. Supreme Court appears to have turned the Voting Rights Act on its head and with it, the intent of Congress.

The Supreme Court's rulings and critics' claims about majority black districts are based on a variety of errors. Though Supreme Court Justice Sandra Day O'Connor and other critics call the creation of majority black districts the equivalent of political apartheid, this is an erroneous view. David Bositis, a research analyst at the Joint Center for Political and Economic Studies, has demonstrated that African Americans continue to be represented by white elected officials.

> After the swearing in of the 103rd Congress [1993–1994], 17 out of a total of 125 southern representatives, or 13.6 percent, were black. The seventeen districts they represent contain 42.1 percent of the region's black electorate. The 60 districts represented by white Democrats contain 38.0 percent of the [southern] black electorate, with an average black voting age population in each district of 13.9 percent. Finally the 48 districts represented by white Republicans contain 19.9 percent of the southern black electorate and have a black voting age population in each district averaging 9.5 percent.[1]

Moreover, Bositis warns that

> one should not be misled about where matters stand on the distribution of voters. Despite the changes, black voters continue to be represented more often by white representatives than black: 57.9 percent versus 42.1 percent.[2]

Critics of majority black districts showcase the few successes of black candidates in majority white districts as all the more reason that racially polarized voting no longer exists and, by implication, there is no need for majority black districts. Carol Swain and Abigail Thernstrom are two of the staunchest critics of majority black districts being drawn as a strategy to increase black representation. Swain readily showcases blacks who have been elected to Congress from districts that are not majority black: Andrew Young (1972, Atlanta, Georgia), Harold Ford (1974, Memphis, Tennessee), Katie Hall (1982, Gary, Indiana), Alan Wheat (1982, Kansas City, Missouri), and Gary Franks (1990, Connecticut).[3] Swain elaborates on how remarkable such a list is because it goes beyond the traditional liberal white constituencies in Massachusetts and California that one might expect to elect black candidates.[4]

Carol Swain writes:

> In spite of such positive changes, however, the Voting Rights Act has also brought several unintended consequences that have impeded progress toward a color-blind society. One of these has been an overemphasis on the creation of majority-black political units, which despite evidence to the contrary, many assume are needed to elect black politicians.[5]

Abigail Thernstrom has also been a vocal opponent of majority black districts. In their most recent book, she and her husband Stephan Thernstrom argue that

> the number of black legislators in Congress and elsewhere will remain limited if African-American candidates are not willing to wade into the biracial waters—to run in majority white constituencies and put together biracial coalitions. In 1996 a number of black incumbents ran in majority white districts newly drawn as a consequence of Supreme Court decisions, but prior to that election, few black candidates were ready to do so.[6]

Using North Carolina as a case study, the empirical evidence simply does not support the claims of critics such as Swain and the Thernstroms. Swain points to a handful of successes spanning over two decades and scattered throughout the country.

The Thernstroms claim that blacks had not won in majority-white districts because prior to 1996, there was a dearth of candidates:

> Black candidates cannot win elections in which they do not run. And social scientists who calculate the odds of winning in a majority-white constituency cannot assess contests in which there has been no black candidate in the race. The scholarly literature on voting rights is littered with such statements as "The state's history demonstrates no evidence for the election of African Americans to the state legislature or the U.S. House of Representatives other than in majority-minority districts." But the authors of such statements (often quoted by the civil rights community) are reviewing a history in which potential black candidates, even in recent years, have stayed on the political sidelines.[7]

Recent history in North Carolina, however, clearly shows that blacks were not bystanders on the political sidelines; black candidates were in fact actively seeking congressional office in the South. Eva Clayton, the current congresswoman representing the First District, while a law student in 1968 ran unsuccessfully against white incumbent congressman L. H. Fountain in the Second District Democratic primary. In the Fourth District, David W. Stith, president of the Southeastern Business College in Durham, made a bid for the U.S. Congress. He challenged the incumbent Democrat, Representative Nick Galifianakis, and Charles Holloman, the white business manager of the state's Department of Community Colleges, in the Democratic primary that very same year. Stith lost to the incumbent.

In 1972, L. H. Fountain, a staunch conservative on racial and social issues, was challenged in his 10th term by Howard Lee, the mayor of Chapel Hill. Howard Lee was director of human development at Duke University. In 1969, he had become the first black mayor of a predominantly white southern city. The Second District's black population had been enhanced to 40.1 percent of the district, and it was believed that a black could finally mount a serious challenge. Lee lost to Fountain, however, in the Democratic primary.

In 1981, the state legislature's redistricting plan attempted to protect the incumbent Fountain by drawing the Second District in a way to exclude Durham, Raleigh, and Chapel Hill, known for their liberal, black, and Republican voters. According to Tom Eamon, a political scientist, the U.S. Department of Justice struck down this plan on December 8, 1981, under the Voting Rights Act on the grounds that "racial considerations had caused the legislature to create an unusually shaped district to protect Fountain from black voters in Durham County."[8] The state legislature held a special session in February 1982 and created a new plan that the Department of Justice accepted. The new Second District now incorporated Durham County with nine rural counties that were already part of the Second District. This changed the Second drastically. Moreover, asserted Eamon, "With almost 30 percent of the district's voters now from Durham County, the 69-year-old Fountain announced his retirement."[9] H. M. (Mickey) Michaux, a black attorney and former state legislator from Durham, ran against I. T. (Tim) Valentine, a conservative attorney and former state legislator from eastern North Carolina, for the open seat. Also running in that Democratic primary was James Ramsey, a conservative former state House Speaker from Roxboro in Person County. No candidate won a clear majority in the primary, however: Michaux led with 44 percent of the vote, Valentine came in second with 33 percent, and Ramsey finished third with 22 percent. Valentine immediately called

for a runoff, and in that election Valentine defeated Michaux 54 percent
to 46 percent in one of the most racially divisive contests in the country
in 1982.*

In 1984, incumbent congressman Tim Valentine was challenged for
his seat in the Second District by state Representative Kenneth B.
Spaulding, a black attorney from Durham. Spaulding was a descendant
of George Henry White, the last black member of Congress from North
Carolina (1897–1901). And in the Fourth District, Howard Lee ran
against white incumbent, Democrat Ike Andrews. It was the second time
in the modern era that a black candidate had run for Congress in North
Carolina from more than one district in the same election. The white incumbent defeated the black challenger in both primaries: Tim Valentine
defeated Kenneth Spaulding, and Ike Andrews defeated Howard Lee.
Spaulding subsequently mounted another challenge against Valentine
but lost again in 1986 in the Second District in North Carolina. So, by the
time that North Carolina created two majority black districts and elected
its first black to Congress this century, there had been numerous unsuccessful attempts by blacks over the previous 30 years to win election to
Congress.

Majority white districts throughout the South were not electing
blacks, although electable black candidates were seeking office. Kenneth
Spaulding, who had served as a state legislator from North Carolina before running unsuccessfully for Congress in 1984 and 1986 in the Second District, remarked:

> It wasn't because good Black candidates didn't run. It was that good
> qualified Black candidates couldn't run and win based on the districts
> that were drawn.[10]

The Voting Rights Act as amended in 1982, coupled with the U.S.
Supreme Court decision in *Thornburg v. Gingles* (1986), sent a strong
message to southern states to create majority black districts for the 1992
elections. Previous efforts by blacks to win election to Congress from the
South had been only marginally successful. Spaulding was right: This
was not because qualified black candidates were not seeking office to
Congress. It was because qualified blacks were unable to win elections in
majority white districts due to racial bloc voting on the part of whites.

*Social science literature has documented how runoff elections have been a tac-
tic used in the South to disadvantage blacks (see Chandler Davidson, 1984).

INCUMBENCY EFFECT AND RACIALLY POLARIZED VOTING

As opponents of majority-minority districts, the Thernstroms have argued that such artificial constructions are unnecessary because black representatives can be elected by white voters and by multiracial coalitions. They cite as evidence the recent successes of Corinne Brown (Florida), Sanford Bishop (Georgia), and Cynthia McKinney (Georgia), black candidates who won in 1996 after their majority black districts had been dismantled and redrawn into districts that were predominantly white. Referring to the Georgia races in particular, and the subsequent appeals by black voters for restoration of at least one of the majority black districts, the Thernstroms claim:

> In winning handily in majority-white constituencies in that Deep South state, Cynthia McKinney and Sanford Bishop had made history in insisting that they were still in need of electoral arrangements that protected black candidates from white competition, McKinney and Bishop were (in effect) asking the Court to ignore those significant victories. They had remained reluctant swimmers in the biracial waters that just a month earlier had proven so hospitable to them.[11]

Predictions of black electoral success in majority white districts neglect the tremendous advantages bestowed upon incumbents. Many political observers were not sure how black congressional candidates would fare in those states where the majority black districts had been dismantled. Incumbent black members of Congress had more victories than defeats competing against whites in majority white districts in the general election in 1996. In the four affected states that held congressional elections using the new maps for the November 5, 1996 general elections (Texas, Florida, Georgia, and Louisiana), none of the incumbent minority members was defeated. Moreover, four blacks won election in majority white districts. Three of those victories occurred in the Deep South (Bishop, Georgia—2; McKinney, Georgia—4; Brown, Florida—3) and one occurred in the Midwest (Carson, Indiana—10). Julia Carson of Indiana's Tenth Congressional District won the election for an open seat in a district that has only a 27 percent black voting-age population. However, Indiana does not fall under the provisions of Section 5 of the Voting Rights Act, which applies to states with a history of racial discrimination; it was not one of the 11 states of the Confederacy; and it has previously elected a black to statewide office.

These electoral victories in the South, however, do not portray the complete picture. Once Louisiana's congressional map was redrawn as a result of a federal court order, Cleo Fields, the black incumbent from the Fourth District, declined to seek reelection in 1996. His majority black district had been dismantled, and the white Republican incumbent in the Fifth District decided to run in the new majority white Fourth District. That left the conservative Fifth District without an incumbent and altogether unlikely to elect a black representative.

Georgia Congresswoman Cynthia McKinney, who won reelection on November 5, 1996, with 58 percent of the vote in a majority white district, the Fourth, addressed the importance of majority black districts in her victory speech, stating:

> To the pundits who will try to draw conclusions from our victory, and misuse it as a justification to dismantle all minority districts, I say: "Think again." I am here today specifically because the people of the old 11th District [her former constituency] lifted me on their shoulders. Without the opportunity to represent them or develop a track record, a candidate such as myself might never have had the resources and name recognition necessary to win in the district.[12]

McKinney clearly attributes much of her victory to name recognition among white and black voters and the significant advantages of incumbency. Gary C. Jacobson noted in *The Politics of Congressional Elections* (1992) that incumbency is the single best predictor of winning election to Congress. Since 1950, roughly 90 percent of all incumbents have been reelected to the U.S. House of Representatives. Incumbents generally raise more money than challengers, have greater name recognition, secure projects for their home district (pork), provide casework through staff for their constituents, and have use of the franking privilege (free mailings) and other perquisites. All told, incumbents have a powerful arsenal in their bid for reelection. It was the majority black Eleventh District, with a 65 percent black majority, that enabled McKinney to first win election to Congress in 1992.

David Bositis warns against reading too much into the victories of Bishop, McKinney, and Brown. According to Bositis, all three faced weak opponents who did not raise enough money to mount a serious challenge.[13] Furthermore, the actual number of black nominees who sought office for the U.S. Congress from majority white districts dropped from 27 percent in 1990 to 22 percent in 1996.[14]

Majority black congressional districts were created to increase the representation of black Americans in the U.S. House of Representatives. Twenty-six blacks were elected to the 102nd Congress (1990–1992). Eighteen of the 26 blacks (69.2 percent) were from districts that had a 50 percent or higher black population. Five represented districts where no racial group was a majority (19.2 percent), and only three represented majority white districts (11.5 percent). Thus, even before the creation of 13 new majority black districts in 1992, the majority of congressional districts throughout the United States from which blacks were being elected were majority black.

Of the 16 new black members elected to the U.S. House of Representatives in 1992, 12 were elected from southern states. Prior to the 1992 congressional elections, six southern states had no black representation in Congress. But after 1992, only one southern state, Arkansas, had failed ever to elect a black to Congress. And of 16 new black members elected to Congress in 1992, 13 were elected from newly created majority black districts.

THE MYTH OF CONTIGUITY AND COMPACTNESS

Another myth that has been promulgated by the U.S. Supreme Court and others concerns the prevalence of contiguity and compactness in congressional districts. Critics have charged that the newly created majority black districts violate traditional notions of compactness and contiguity and thus deviate drastically from the shapes of conventional districts. In fact, irregularly shaped congressional districts have long been a part of the American political landscape. An examination of congressional district maps around the country reveals a number of oddly shaped majority white districts. For example, Louisiana's Eighth Congressional District from 1971 to 1973 rambled across the entire state from the Texas border on the west all the way east to New Orleans, covering 300 miles. After the 1980 U.S. Census, California Congressman Phillip Burton created a bizarrely shaped district (District 18) that meandered from western central California to the Nevada border on the east and was divided by two other congressional districts. The district was clearly the result of partisan politics (see Chapter 5) and drawn to protect the Democratic incumbents. The Fourth District in Tennessee is a majority white district that snakes for 290 miles and is rarely more than 20 miles wide; it reaches south from the Virginia border almost to the Mississippi border. Although the U.S. Supreme Court ruled in *Shaw v. Reno* (1993) that the

Table 9.1. Congressional Districts Represented by Blacks, 1991

Representative	District	Principal City	% BVAP[a]
Mfume (D-MD)	7	Baltimore	73.0
Gray (D-PA)	2	Philadelphia	80.0
Collins (D-IL)	7	Chicago	67.0
Savage (D-IL)	2	Chicago	70.0
Hayes (D-IL)	1	Chicago	92.0
Conyers (D-MI)	1	Detroit	71.0
Collins (D-MI)	13	Detroit	71.0
Stokes (D-O)	21	Cleveland	62.0
Lewis (D-GA)	5	Atlanta	65.0
Clay (D-MO)	1	St. Louis	52.0
Wheat (D-MO)	5	Kansas City	23.0
Dellums (D-CA)	8	Oakland	27.0
Dixon (D-CA)	28	Los Angeles	39.0
Waters (D-CA	29	Los Angeles	50.0
Dymally (D-CA)	31	Compton	34.0
Washington (D-TX)	18	Houston	41.0
Franks (R-CT)	5	Waterbury	4.0
Flake (D-NY)	6	Queens	50.0
Towns (D-NY)	11	New York	47.0
Rangel (D-NY)	16	New York	49.0
Owens (D-NY)	12	Brooklyn	80.0
Ford (D-TN)	9	Memphis	57.0
Jefferson (D-LA)	2	New Orleans	59.0
Espy (D-MS)	2	Greenville	58.0
Payne (D-NJ)	10	Newark	58.0
Norton (D-DC)		Washington, DC	65.8

Source: CQ Weekly Report and *The Congressional Black Caucus in the 103rd Congress* by David Bositis.

Note: Norton is a nonvoting delegate.

[a]BVAP = black voting-age population.

majority black Twelfth District in North Carolina failed the standard of compactness, it is a standard that the U.S. Supreme Court has clearly ignored in the past.

Behind the high-minded discussions of "race-blind" redistricting, there lurks an intensive partisan battle. Though this process of redistricting has always been highly partisan, race has been added to the redistricting equation, especially for the southern states. Traditionally, the majority party in the state legislature created districting plans that attempted to advantage its party at the expense of the opposition party and protect its congressional incumbents. However, after the U.S. Justice Department mandated majority black districts, Democrats (who held the majority in all

Figure 9.1. California Congressional District Map, 1982

Source: Congressional Quarterly Weekly Report, 1982. By permission, Congressional Quarterly, 1414 22nd Street, NW, Washington, DC 20037.

Figure 9.2. Tennessee Congressional District Map, 1992

Tennessee

Source: Congressional Quarterly Weekly Report, 1992. By permission, Congressional Quarterly, 1414 22nd Street, NW, Washington, DC 20037.

of the southern state legislatures in 1990) had to both craft districts that protected Democratic incumbents *and* create districts that had a majority of black voters (who overwhelmingly tend to vote Democratic). As was clearly the case in North Carolina, some of the awkwardly shaped minority districts that were created around the South for the 1992 elections were a result of these political shenanigans.

Less than 10 years after blacks finally achieved a significant presence in the U.S. Congress, the country's most representative governmental body, the U.S. Supreme Court appears determined to put an end to this Second Reconstruction. Moreover, the high court is now using the Fourteenth Amendment to the U.S. Constitution, a law that was designed to give, and has effectively given, minorities rights in this country, as a tool to undermine some of those very rights.

States now confront a dilemma. On the one hand, if states dismantle majority black districts, they open themselves up to a challenge of vote dilution by minorities, which is a violation of Section 2 of the Voting Rights Act. On the other hand, if states fail to dismantle the majority black districts, whites will file lawsuits claiming that the states' activities constitute a violation of the Equal Protection Clause of the Fourteenth Amendment to the U.S. Constitution.

THE UNFINISHED BUSINESS OF RACIAL EQUALITY

It has been just three and one-half decades since passage of the Voting Rights Act of 1965. Since that time, blacks and other minorities have made an enormous amount of progress in all aspects of the political process, including gaining representation in the nation's most representative governing body. In 1969 the Congressional Black Caucus had only 10 members. It was not until 1983 that 20 blacks served in Congress. Today there are 39 blacks in Congress. But there are ominous signs on the horizon. Political and economic forces are at work that are determined to dismantle the creation of majority black districts.

Population size and the strategic location of people can play a large role in determining political power in America. More than 50 percent of the country's black population lives in the South, 15 percent live in the Northeast, 20 percent in the North-central area, and 8 percent in the West. One would think that black political strength would be greatest in the South. But prior to 1992, in the 11 states that had comprised the Confederacy, only 5 of the 116 congressional districts, or 4.3 percent, elected black congresspeople. However, this setup changed after the 1990 census. Blacks, with the assistance of the Voting Rights Act and the U.S. Department of Justice's insistence that state legislators draw congressional districts in a more equitable manner, saw the creation of majority black districts throughout the South. As a result, in 1992 the number of black congresspeople from the South increased from 5 to 17.

The current discourse about a color-blind society is a distraction from the reality that racial equality in America remains an illusive goal. Majority black districts in the South were created because race had been consistently used in the past to exclude blacks from the political process. Gerrymandering to include blacks and other minorities was a crucial step toward overcoming the historical exclusion of minorities. When the mistakes and distortions are cleared away, the case for majority black districts remains compelling: The prospects for inclusive democracy in the United States are at stake.

NOTES

[1]David Bositis, *The Congressional Black Caucus in the 103rd Congress* (Washington, D.C.: Joint Center for Political and Economic Studies, 1994) 57.

[2]Bositis, 58.

[3]Carol Swain, *Black Faces, Black Interests: The Representation of African Americans in Congress* (Cambridge: Harvard University Press, 1993) 199.

[4]Swain, 99.

[5]Carol Swain, "Some Consequences of the Voting Rights Act," *Controversies in Minority Voting*, ed. Bernard Grofman and Chandler Davidson (Washington, D.C.: Brookings Institution, 1992) 294.

[6]Stephan Thernstrom and Abigail Thernstrom, *America in Black and White: One Nation, Indivisible* (New York: Simon and Schuster, 1997) 485.

[7]Stephan Thernstrom and Abigail Thernstrom, 485.

[8]Thomas F. Eamon, "From Pool Hall to Parish House in North Carolina," *Strategies for the Mobilization of Black Voters*, ed. Thomas E. Cavanaugh (Washington, D.C.: Joint Center for Political Studies, 1987) 104.

[9]Eamon, 107.

[10]Quoted in Kenneth Cooper, "Dismantling Black Political Power," *Emerge*, April 1993: 37.

[11]Stephan Thernstrom and Abigail Thernstrom, 485–486.

[12]Quoted in Askia Muhammad, "Smaller Black Caucus Returns to Congress," *The Final Call*, February 27, 1997, available online at <http://www.noi.org/finalcall/national/blackcaucus.html>

[13]David Bositis, "The Future of Majority-Minority Districts and Black and Hispanic Legislative Representation," Paper presented at the Joint Center for Political and Economic Studies Conference on a New Framework for Redistricting, January 8, 1997, Washington, D.C.

[14]Bositis, "The Future of Majority-Minority Districts," 4.

BIBLIOGRAPHY

BOOKS

Anderson, E. (1981). *Race and politics in North Carolina: 1872–1901*. Baton Rouge: Louisiana State University Press.

Bloch, S. L., & Krattenmaker, T. G. (1994). *Supreme Court politics*. Anaheim, CA: West.

Bositis, D. (1994). *The Congressional Black Caucus in the 103rd Congress*. Washington, D.C.: Joint Center for Political and Economic Studies.

Butler, D., & Cain, B. (1992). *Congressional redistricting: Comparative and theoretical perspectives*. New York: Macmillan.

Cain, B. (1992). Voting rights and democratic theory. Toward a color-blind society? In B. Grofman & C. Davidson (Eds.), *Controversies in minority voting* (p. 268). Washington, D.C.: Brookings Institution.

Carter, S. (1994). Foreword. In C. L. Guinier (Ed.), *The tyranny of the majority*. New York: Free Press.

Christopher, M. (1971). *America's black congressmen*. New York: Cromwell.

Clay, W. L. (1992). *Just permanent interests: Black Americans in Congress, 1870–1991*. New York: Amistad.

CQ's Guide to 1990 Congressional Redistricting. (1993). New York: Congressional Inc.

Davidson, C. (Ed.) (1984). *Minority vote dilution*. Washington, D.C.: Howard University Press.

Davis, G. A., & Donaldson, O. F. (1975). *Blacks in the United States: A geographic perspective*. Boston: Houghton Mifflin.

Eamon, T. F. (1987). From pool hall to parish house in North Carolina. In T. E. Cavanaugh (Ed.), *Strategies for the mobilization of black voters* (pp. 101–136). Washington, D.C.: Joint Center for Political Studies.

Fenno, R. F. (1978). *Home style: House members in their districts.* Boston: Little, Brown.

Franklin, J. H. (Ed.) (1980). *From slavery to freedom: A history of Negro Americans* (5th ed.). New York: Knopf.

Grofman, B. (1992). Expert witness testimony and the evolution of voting rights case law. In B. Grofman & C. Davidson (Eds.), *Controversies in minority voting* (pp. 197–229). Washington, D.C.: Brookings Institution.

Grofman, B., & Davidson, C. (Eds.) (1992). Postscript: What is the best route to a color-blind society? *Controversies in minority voting* (pp. 300–317). Washington, D.C.: Brookings Institution.

Grofman, B., Handley, L., & Niemi, R. G. (1992). *Minority representation and the quest for voting equality.* New York: Cambridge University Press.

Guinier, C. L. (1992). Voting rights and democratic theory: Where do we go from here? In B. Grofman & C. Davidson (Eds.), *Controversies in minority voting.* Washington, D.C.: Brookings Institution.

Guinier, C. L. (1994). *The tyranny of the majority: Fundamental fairness in representative democracy.* New York: Free Press.

Hacker, A. (1992). *Two nations: Black and white, separate, hostile, unequal.* New York: Macmillan.

Jacobson, G. C. (1992). *The politics of congressional elections.* New York: HarperCollins.

Janda, K., Berry, J. M., & Goldman, J. (1995). *The challenge of democracy* (4th ed.). Boston: Houghton Mifflin.

Jones, M. (1985). The Voting Rights Act as an intervention strategy for social change: Symbolism or substance? In L. S. Foster (Ed.), *The Voting Rights Act* (pp. 63–84). New York: Praeger.

Key, V. O. (1949). *Southern politics in state and nation.* New York: Alfred Knopf.

Kousser, J. M. (1992). The Voting Rights Act and the two Reconstructions. In B. Grofman & C. Davidson (Eds.), *Controversies in minority voting* (pp. 135–176). Washington, D.C.: Brookings Institution.

Lowi, T. J. (1969). *The end of liberalism: Ideology, policy, and the crisis of public authority.* New York: Norton.

Lublin, D. (1997). *The paradox of representation.* Princeton, NJ: Princeton University Press.

1991–1992 redistricting and reapportionment community education handbook. (1991). (2nd ed.). Washington, D.C.: National Coalition on Black Voter Participation.

O'Hare, W. P., et al. (1991). *African Americans in the 1990s*. Washington, D.C.: Population Reference Bureau.

Parker, F. (1984). Racial gerrymandering and legislative reapportionment. In C. Davidson (Ed.), *Minority vote dilution* (pp. 85–117). Washington, D.C.: Howard University Press.

Parker, F. (1989). Changing standards in voting rights law. In W. P. O'Hare (Ed.), *Redistricting in the 1990s: A guide for minority groups* (pp. 55–66). Washington, D.C.: Population Reference Bureau.

Phillips, B. (1983). *How to use Section 5 of the Voting Rights Act* (3rd ed.). Washington, D.C.: Joint Center for Political and Economic Studies.

Pitkin, H. F. (1967). *The concept of representation*. Berkeley: University of California Press.

Redistricting 1991: Legislator's guide to North Carolina congressional redistricting. (1991). Raleigh: North Carolina General Assembly, Research Division, 12.

Smith, J. O., Rice, M., & Jones, W., Jr. (1991). *Blacks and American government*. Dubuque, IA: Kendall Hunt.

Swain, C. (1992). Some consequences of the Voting Rights Act. In B. Grofman & C. Davidson (Eds.), *Controversies in minority voting* (pp. 294–296). Washington, D.C.: Brookings Institution.

Swain, C. (1993). *Black faces, black interests: The representation of African Americans in Congress*. Cambridge, MA: Harvard University Press.

Thernstrom, A. (1987). *Whose votes count?: Affirmative action and minority voting rights*. Cambridge, MA: Harvard University Press.

Thernstrom, S., & Thernstrom, A. (1997). *America in black and white: One nation, indivisible*. New York: Simon and Schuster.

West, C. (1993). *Race matters*. Boston: Beacon.

Woodward, C. V. (1966). *The strange career of Jim Crow* (3rd ed.). New York: Oxford University Press.

ARTICLES

Bragdon, P. (1990, June 2). Democrats' ties to minorities may be tested by new lines. *Congressional Quarterly Weekly Report*, 1739–1742.

Bullock, C. S., III (1982, Summer). The inexact science of congressional redistricting. *PS* (15), 431–438.

Clayton, D. (1998). Making the case for majority black districts. *Black Scholar*, 28(2), 36–46.

Cook, R. (1984, January 7). Blacks to gain: Mississippi, Louisiana redraw district lines. *Congressional Quarterly Weekly Report*, 13.

Cooper, K. (1994, April). Dismantling black political power. *Emerge*, 30–37.

Davidson, J. (1997, October). Caged cargo. *Emerge*, 36–46.

Donovan, B. (1991, December 21). Redistricting: Political dance played out through legal wrangling. *Congressional Quarterly Weekly Report.*

Grofman, B. (1985, October). Criteria for redistricting: A social science perspective. *UCLA Law Review*, 33, 77–183.

Grofman, B., & Handley, L. (1992). Identifying and remedying gerrymandering. *Journal of Law and Politics*, (8)2, 345–404.

Horn, D. L., et al. (1993, March). Practical application of district compactness. *Political Geography*, 12(2), pp. 103–120.

Kaplan, D. (1994, February 19). Drawing and redrawing the line. *Congressional Quarterly Weekly Report,* 384–385.

Karlan, P. (1989, Winter). Maps and misreadings: The role of geographic compactness in racial vote dilution litigation. *Harvard Civil Rights-Civil Liberties Law Review*, 24, 173–248.

Mahtesian, C. (1990, April 25). Blacks' political hopes boosted by newly redrawn districts. *Congressional Quarterly Weekly Report*, 1087–1089.

Mahtesian, C. (1992, February 29). N. C. Republicans settle complaint. *Congressional Quarterly Weekly Report*, 487.

Niemi, R. G., Grofman, B., Carlucci, C., & Hofeller, T. (1990, November). Measuring compactness and the role of a compactness standard in a test for partisan and racial gerrymandering. *Journal of Politics*, 52(4), 1155–1181.

Pildes, R. H., & Niemi, R. G. (1993, December). Expressive harms, "bizarre districts," and voting rights: Evaluating election-district appearances after *Shaw v. Reno*. *Michigan Law Review*, 92, 483–587.

Polsby, D., & Popper, R. (1991). The third criterion: Compactness as a procedural safeguard against partisan gerrymandering. *Yale Law and Policy Review*, 9, 483–587.

Reock, E. C., Jr. (1961, February 5). Measuring compactness as a requirement of legislative apportionment. *Midwest Journal of Political Science*, 70–74.

Spears, E. (1994, Summer). Black-majority districts upheld in North Carolina, struck in Louisiana. *Voting Rights Review*, 1–35.

Swain, C. (1995, Fall). The future of black representation. *American Prospect*, 78–83.

Taylor, P. J. (1973, September). A new shape measure for evaluating electoral district patterns. *American Political Science Review*, 67(3), 947–950.

NEWSPAPER ARTICLES

Applebome, P. (1993, June 29). Ruling on racial gerrymandering could prompt similar challenges. *The New York Times*, p. A9.

Coates, G. (1994, August 3). Rulings differ on minority districts. *Durham Herald-Sun*, p. A5.

Davis, M. (1991, July 15). Republicans attack state redistricting. *Wilmington Morning Star*, p. B3.

Denton, V. (1991, December 25). G.O.P. teamed up for victory: Redistricting ruling debated. *Raleigh News and Observer*, p. 1A.

Denton, V. (1992, January 7). Party loyalty, black gains clash in redistricting. *Raleigh News and Observer*, p. A1.

Denton, V. (1991, May 30). Redistricting plan defended, derided. *Raleigh News and Observer*, p. 1.

Denton, V. (1992, February 7). U.S. O.K.'s state's new districts. *Raleigh News and Observer*, p. 1.

Duncan, P. (1990, August 13). Race-based congressional districts? *The Washington Times*, p. D3.

Edsall, T. B. (1990, July 7). GOP goal: Gain ground by fostering "majority-minority" districts. *The Washington Post*, p. A6.

Effron, S. (1991, June 11). U.S. House members write letter opposing N. C. redistricting plan. *Greensboro News and Record*, p. 1.

Fletcher, M. (1998, March 1). Kerner prophecy on race relations came true, report says. *Washington Post* online edition. <http://www.washingtonpost. com>.

Folkenflik, D. (1993, April 19). Professors take case to court. *Durham Herald-Sun*, p. A1.

Freivogel, W. (1993, June 29). Minority districts rejected. *St. Louis Post-Dispatch*, p. 6A.

Greenhouse, L. (1995, June 30). Justices, in 5–4 vote, reject districts drawn with race the "predominant factor." *The New York Times*, p. A13.

Guillory, F. (1992, January 9). G.O.P. seeks change in district map. *Raleigh News and Observer*, p. B1.

Guinier, C. L. (1994, February 27). Who's afraid of Lani Guinier? *New York Times Magazine*, p. 54.

Holmes, S. A. (1995, June 30). Voting rights experts say challenges to political maps could cause turmoil. *The New York Times*, p. A13.

Hoskinson, C. (1991, June 14). Congressional redistricting plans draw jeers. *Greenville Daily Reflector*, p. A2.

Hoskinson, C. (1991, June 16). Republicans see political gains in redistricting. *Greenville Daily Reflector*, p. B1.

It's redistricting time at the N. C. legislature. (1991, June 2). *Gastonia Gazette*, p. E1.

Kome, H. (1991, July 7). Computers allow public access into redistricting. *Hendersonville Times-News*, p. C1.

Kraus, C. (1993, July 4). Reaction muted in disputed district. *The New York Times*, p. I20.

Leavitt, P., El Nasser, H., & Davis, R. (1994, August 2). Judges uphold N. C.'s black-majority districts. *USA Today*, p. 3A.

McCaughey, E. (1993, June 30). Court deals a blow to racial gerrymandering. *The Wall Street Journal*, p. A15.

O'Brien, K. (1990, September 3). New district could boost blacks' chance. *Charlotte Observer*, p. B1.

O'Brien, K. (1990, September 3). New seat could aid black voice. *Charlotte Observer*, p. 1.

Otterbourg, K. (1991, June 2). Districts debated in angry assembly. *Winston-Salem Journal*, p. E1.

Pear, R. (1991, July 21). Under the voting law, citizens' rights get more than lip service. *New York Times*, p. E4.

Political pornography II. (1992, February 4). *The Wall Street Journal*, p. A14.

Reading the ink blot. (1992, January 21). *Raleigh News and Observer*, p. A8.

Scanlon, L. (1997, June 11). Jobs, money, education divide Americans. *Louisville Courier-Journal*, p. A15.

Scavo, C. (1991, March 31). Redistricting will be tough task. *Greenville Daily Reflector*, p. E3.

Waggoner, M. (1994, August 3). Districts in N. C. ruled legal. *Durham Herald-Sun*, p. A5.

Welch, M. (1993, June 29). Ruling throws redistricting into question. *USA Today*, p. 2A.

COURT CASES AND OTHER GOVERNMENT DOCUMENTS

Affidavit of G. Cohen. Pope v. Blue. 809 F. Supp. 392 (W.D.N.C. 1992).

Affidavit of R. Dorff. Pope v. Blue. 809 F. Supp. 392 (W.D.N.C. 1992).

Article I, Section 2, paragraph 3, United States Constitution.

Badham v. Eu, 488 U.S. 1024 (1989).

Baker v. Carr, 369 U.S. 186 (1962).

Ballenger, C., Coble, H., McMillan, J. A., & Taylor, C. (1991, June 5). Letter to Dennis J. Winner.

Balmer, D. (1991, August 5). Letter to Assistant U.S. Attorney General John Dunne.

Beer v. United States 425 U.S. 130 (1976).

Brown v. Board of Education, 347 U.S. 483 (1954).

Bryant v. Lawrence County, 814 F. Supp. 1346, 1350 (S.D. Miss. 1993).

Bush v. Vera, No. 94–988, 1996 U.S.

City of Mobile v. Bolden, 446 U.S. 55 (1980).

Cohen, G. (1991, October 14). Memorandum submitted to the U.S. Department of Justice.

Colegrove v. Green, 328 U.S. 549 (1946).

Daughtry v. State Board of Elections, Docket No. 2:91 CV00552.

Davis v. Bandemer, 478 U.S. 109 (1986).

Declaration of B. Grofman, Pope v. Blue. 809 F. Supp. 392 (W.D.N.C. 1992).

Dillard v. Baldwin County Board of Education, 686 F. Supp. 1459 (M.D. Ala. 1988).

Dunne, J. (1991, October 18). Letter to North Carolina Special Deputy Attorney General Tiare B. Smiley.

Dunne, J. (1991, December 18). Letter to North Carolina Special Deputy Attorney General Tiare B. Smiley.

Ellisen, V. (1991, June 13). Transcript of Congressional Redistricting Public Hearing.

Hays v. Louisiana, 839 F. Supp. 1188 (W.D.La. 1993).

Hays v. Louisiana, 862 F. Supp. 119 (W.D.La. 1996).

Hays, et al., v. State of Louisiana, et al. 116 S.C. 2542 (1996), 936 F. Supp. 360 (W.D.La. 1996).

Johnson v. DeGrandy, 62 U.S.L.W. 4755 (1994).

Johnson et al. v. Mortham, et al., 94–40025 (N.D.Fla. 1996).

Journal of Proceedings, *The United States Law Week*, 61 (1992). 3418.

Karcher v. Daggett, 462 U.S. 725 (1983).

Major v. Treen, 574 F. Supp. 325 (E.D.La. 1983).

Miller v. Johnson, 1995 WL 382020 (U.S.).

North Carolina Department of Justice (1991). Section 5 submission for North Carolina congressional redistricting. Chapter 601. Raleigh: North Carolina Government Printing Office, C28D.

North Carolina General Assembly, Joint Session, House and Senate Redistricting Committees (January 9, 1992). *Public hearing on congressional redistricting plans.*

Plaintiffs' complaint, Shaw v. Barr, 808 F. Supp. 461 (E.D.N.C. 1992).

Plaintiffs' complaint, Pope v. Blue, 809 F. Supp. 392 (W.D.N.C. 1992).

Plessy v. Ferguson, 163 U.S. 537 (1896).

Pope v. Blue, 809 F. Supp. 392 (W.D.N.C. 1992).

Redistricting 1991: Legislator's guide to North Carolina legislative and congressional redistricting (1991). Raleigh: North Carolina General Assembly Research Division.

Shaw v. Barr, 808 F. Supp. 461 (E.D.N.C. 1992).

Shaw v. Hunt, No. 94–924, 1996 U.S.

Shaw v. Reno, 113 S. Ct. 2816 (1993).

Statistical Abstracts of North Carolina Counties (6th ed.) (1991). Raleigh: North
    Carolina State Data Center.
Thornburg v. Gingles, 478 U.S. 30 (1986).
United Jewish Organizations of Williamsburg, Inc. v. Carey, 430 U.S. 144 (1977).
U.S. Cong. Rec. (1994, March 22). 1965 Voting Rights Act under attack. 103rd
    Con., 2nd Sess., H1876.
U.S. Constitution, Fourteenth Amendment.
U.S. Department of Commerce, Bureau of the Census (1990). 1990 Census Pop-
    ulation for the United States is 249,632,692; Reapportionment will shift 19
    seats in the U.S. House of Representatives. *U.S. Department of Commerce
    News* (press release). Washington, D.C.: U.S. Government Printing Office.
United States v. Hays, 115 S.C. 2431 (1995).
Wesberry v. Sanders, 376 U.S. 1 (1964).

INTERVIEWS

Balmer, David. Personal interview by author. Tape recording, Raleigh, North
    Carolina. June 2, 1992.
Blue, Dan. Personal interview by author. Tape recording, Raleigh, North Carolina.
    June 2, 1992.
Cohen, Gerry. Personal interview by author. Tape recording, Raleigh, North
    Carolina. May 27, 1992.
Coleman, Carolyn. Personal interview by author. Tape recording, Raleigh, North
    Carolina. May 27, 1992.
Fitch, Toby. Personal interview by author. Tape recording, Raleigh, North Carolina.
    June 3, 1992.
Pope, Art. Personal interview by author. Tape recording, Raleigh, North Carolina.
    June 2, 1992.
Winner, Dennis. Personal interview by author. Tape recording, Raleigh, Carolina.
    May 27, 1992.
Winner, Leslie. Personal interview by author. Tape recording, Charlotte, North
    Carolina. May 28, 1992.

OTHER SOURCES

All Things Considered. (June 1993). Nina Totenburg interview with Frank
    Parker and Pam Karlan. *National Public Radio*, Transcript 289.
Bositis, D. (1997, January 8). *The future of majority-minority districts and black
    and Hispanic legislative representation.* Paper presented at the Joint Center
    for Political and Economic Studies Conference on a New Framework for
    Redistricting, Washington D.C.

Clayton, D. M. (1995). *The politics of congressional redistricting: A North Carolina case study.* Unpublished doctoral dissertation, University of Missouri, Columbia.

Correa, M. (1993). *Defining community: Latin American immigrants and the politics in Queens.* Paper presented at the Workshop on Race, Ethnicity, Representation, and Governance: Harvard University, Center for American Political Studies, Cambridge, MA.

Gronke, P., & Wilson, M. (1996). *Competing redistricting plans as evidence of political motives.* Paper presented at the annual meeting of the Midwest Political Science Association, Chicago, IL.

Handley, L. (1991). The quest for minority voting rights: The evolution of a vote dilution standard and its impact on minority representation. Doctoral dissertation, George Washington University, Washington, D.C.

Mannihen, D. L. (1973). *The role of compactness in the process of redistricting.* Unpublished master's thesis. Seattle: University of Washington Press, Department of Geography.

Muhammad, A. (1997, February 25). Smaller black caucus returns to Congress. *The Final Call.* Available: <http://www.noi.org/finalcall/national/blackcaucus.html>.

Stolberg, S. G. (1998, September 19). U.S. life expectancy hits new high. *National Center for Policy*, online, <http://www.public.policy.org>.

United States Department of Commerce, Bureau of the Census (1998). *Total money income in 1996 of persons 25 years old and over, by educational attainment, sex, region, and race—Continued (persons as of March 1997).* <http://www.census.gov/population/socdemo/race/black/tabs97/tab09B.txt>.

Wilde, K. (1991, September 25). Letter to Assistant United States Attorney General John Dunne.

Index

ACLU, *see* American Civil Liberties Union
Acquired Immune Deficiency Syndrome (AIDS), 12
Administrative preclearance, 101
African Americans:
  ACLU and, 49, 57–58, 59, 61, 62, 67, 70
  AIDS and, 12
  Abraham Lincoln and, 14
  Alabama and, 3, 15, 76, 121, 139
  Anthony Kennedy and, 126
  apartheid and, 4, 19, 104, 108, 168
  Arizona and, 35
  Arkansas and, 16, 33, 119, 174
  Badham v. Eu and, 94
  Baker v. Carr and, 36
  Beer v. United States and, 95
  Bill Clinton and, 22, 26, 103, 126
  birth rate of, 75
  Brown v. Board of Education and, 19, 20
  Bryant v. Lawrence County and, 140
  Bush v. Vera and 127
  California and, 35, 74, 94, 168, 174, 176
  citizenship rights of, 2, 15

City of Mobile v. Bolden and, 37–38
Civil Rights Act and, 2, 19, 20, 49
Civil War and, 2, 5, 15, 22, 24, 34, 113, 167
Colegrove v. Green and, 36
Colorado and, 140
"communities of interest" and, 6, 70, 72, 96, 98, 100, 106, 107, 108, 133, 141–143
Compact 2-Minority Plan and, 68, 71, 87
compactness and, 39, 127, 134, 136, 137–141, 145, 149–166, 74,176
computers and, 45–46, 48, 52, 53, 68, 98–99
Confederate States of America and, 34, 172, 178
Congressional Black Caucus and, 5, 11, 20–21, 22, 178
Connecticut and, 22, 168
Constitutional Convention and, 14
contiguity and, 6, 106, 107, 108, 136–137, 138, 141, 149, 174
Continental Congress and, 14
"cracking" and, 38, 95
crime rates and, 12–13

African Americans (*continued*):
cumulative voting and, 28, 142–143
Daughtry v. State Board of Elections and, 61, 95–96
Davis v. Bandemer and, 39, 93–94
Declaration of Independence and, 14
democracy and, 6, 7, 11, 13, 26, 27, 28, 73, 106, 178
Democratic Party and, 16, 19, 20, 21, 22, 33–34, 40–43, 45–49, 51, 52, 53, 58, 60, 62, 63, 65, 66, 67, 68, 69, 70, 72, 73, 74, 75, 76, 77, 94, 95, 96, 98, 103, 118, 149, 165, 166, 167, 170, 171, 174, 175, 176–177
descriptive representation and, 23–29, 73, 74
Dillard v. Baldwin County Board of Education, 139, 140
"discouraged workers" and, 25
education levels of, 12, 13
electoral history of, 11
Emancipation Proclamation and, 14
employment and, 12, 13, 24–25
federal court decisions and, 39, 43, 60, 61, 62, 63, 77, 94, 95–96, 97, 98, 99, 100, 101, 102, 103, 104, 105, 107, 114, 115–116, 118–119, 121, 122–123, 124–127, 128, 139, 140, 167
Fifteenth Amendment and, 2, 15, 17, 135, 167
First Amendment and, 97
Florida and, 3, 35, 76, 115–116, 121, 122, 127–128, 172
Fourteenth Amendment and, 2, 15, 36, 94, 96–97, 101, 102, 104, 134, 135, 177
George Bush and, 24, 40, 41, 60, 103, 126
Georgia and, 6, 15, 21, 35, 36, 76, 115, 117–118, 121–122, 124–127, 128, 168, 172, 173

gerrymandering and, xi, 2, 7, 18, 37–39, 45, 60, 70, 72, 93, 94, 98, 100, 103, 105, 106, 107, 109, 121, 122, 123, 128, 129, 138, 139, 151, 167, 178
grandfather clauses and, 2, 18
Great Depression and, 19
"great migration" and, 24
Great Society and, 20
Grofman Test and, 151, 152–153, 154–156, 161, 164, 165
Harry Truman and, 19
Hays v. Louisiana and, 122–123
Hayes-Tilden Compromise and, 2, 17, 113
health care and, 12, 13
Helms-Gantt Senate race and, 48, 51, 52
Hispanics and, 105, 108, 115, 118, 120-121, 122, 127
incarceration rates of, 13
Illinois and, 35
Indiana and, 22, 94, 168, 172
Interstate 85 Corridor Plan and, 65–66, 68, 70, 144, 145
Iowa and, 35, 140
Jayhawkers and, 17
"Jim Crow" laws and, 19, 128
Johnson et al. v. Mortham et al., 127–128
Kansas and, 35
Kentucky and, 35
Kirksey v. Board of Superiors of Hinds County , 75
Ku Klux Klan and, 17
Lani Guinier and, 26–28, 142
Lawyers' Committee for Civil Rights and, 106
life expectancy of, 12, 75
literacy tests and, 2, 18, 101, 167
Louisiana and, 15, 35, 76, 118–120, 121, 122–123, 128, 167, 172, 173, 174
Major v. Treen and, 118–119

majority districts and, xi, 1, 2, 3–4,
5, 6–7, 19, 22, 23, 33, 38, 42,
46, 47–48, 53, 61–62, 63, 64,
65, 66, 67, 68, 69, 70, 72,
73–74, 75, 76, 77, 80, 81, 82,
83, 84, 85, 86, 87, 88, 89, 93,
95, 102, 103, 104, 106, 107,
113, 114, 115, 117, 118, 119,
121–130, 139, 141, 142, 143,
144, 145, 149, 155n, 156n,
157n, 158n, 159, 160n, 163n,
165, 166, 171, 172, 173, 174,
176–178
majority-minority districts and, 6,
11, 22, 33, 44, 47, 61, 62, 73,
95, 100, 105, 114–130,
149–151, 164, 165–167
Maryland and, 2, 76, 121
Massachusetts and, 21, 35, 38, 168
Michigan and, 35, 74
in Midwest, 22–23, 24, 35
migration of, 21, 22–23, 24, 35, 144
Miller v. Johnson and, 6, 124–127
minority districts and, 38, 39, 48,
57, 58, 59, 60, 62, 63, 64–65,
67, 68, 70, 72, 73, 76, 77, 102,
104, 108, 109, 138, 139, 159,
177
Mississippi and, 15, 174
Missouri and, 22, 74, 168
Montana and, 35
NAACP and, 52, 53, 58, 61, 62,
65, 67, 69, 70, 103, 105, 123
National Urban League and, 24
Native Americans and, 14, 47, 50,
51, 59, 60, 62, 68, 69
net worth of, 12
Nevada and, 174
New Deal and, 19
New Jersey and, 35, 93
New York and, 19, 21, 35
North Carolina and, 2, 3, 5–6, 16,
17, 18, 28, 34–53, 57–89, 93–109,
118, 121,123–128, 133–145,
149–166, 169–171, 174, 176

in Northeast, 22–23, 24, 35, 178
Ohio and, 35
Optimum II–Zero Plan and, 66, 73,
86
"packing" and, 38, 95
Pennsylvania and, 35
Plessy v. Ferguson and, 18
political experience and, 4
poll taxes and, 2, 18, 167
polygon area test and, 151, 152,
154–155, 159–160, 164, 165
polygon perimeter test and, 151,
152, 154, 155, 159–160, 165
Pope v. Blue and, 96–99, 100, 102,
136–137
population of, 18–19, 75,
128–129, 178
preclearance and, 101
"race-based districting" and, 1, 4,
5, 25–28, 126
"race-blind redistricting" and, 6,
176
reapportionment, 23, 34–37,
97–104, 113–130
Reconstruction and, 2, 5, 11, 15,
16, 17, 18, 20, 113, 121, 177
Reconstruction Act and, 15–16
redistricting and, 1, 3, 5, 23, 34–36,
38, 39–40, 51, 52, 57–77, 93, 94,
95–109, 113–130, 133–145,
149–166, 176, 177
Reock Test and, 151, 153–154,
158, 159, 164, 165
representation theory and, 23–29,
73, 74
Republican Party and, 16, 19, 20,
21, 22, 33–34, 41–42, 46–49,
51–52, 60–61, 62, 63, 64, 66,
67, 68, 69, 70, 72, 73, 74–75,
76, 77, 94, 95, 96, 97–98, 103,
115, 118, 154, 167, 170, 171,
174, 175, 176–177
retrogression and, 94, 95
Reynolds v. Simms and, 133–134
Richard Nixon and, 21

African Americans (*continued*):
Ronald Reagan and, 44, 60
Sandra Day O'Connor and, 103, 104, 107, 108–109, 123, 129, 168
Schwartzberg Test and, 151, 153, 157, 159, 162, 164, 165
segregation and, xi, 4, 19, 20, 23, 24, 25, 104, 129
Shaw v. Barr and, 99–103
Shaw v. Hunt and, 123–124
Shaw v. Reno and, 3–4, 6, 103–109, 121, 122, 123, 124, 126, 127, 128, 140, 141, 152
single-parent families and, 11–12
Sixty-five Percent Rule and, 75–76
slavery and, 2, 13–14
South and, 1, 2, 3, 4, 5, 6–7, 15, 16, 17, 18–19, 20, 21, 33–35, 38, 42, 108, 109, 113–130, 137, 140, 165, 167–174, 178
South Carolina and, 3, 15, 64, 65, 76, 95, 114, 115, 121, 125, 128
"stacking" and, 38, 95
substantive representation and, 24–29, 73, 74
suburbs and, 21, 24–25, 36, 68, 73, 98, 106, 115, 125, 137, 142, 144, 150, 152, 159–164, 165
Tennessee and, 16, 33, 36, 122, 168, 174, 177
Texas and, 16, 21, 35, 76, 120–121, 127–128, 172, 174
Thirteenth Amendment and, 2, 14–15
Thornburg v. Gingles and, 43–44, 62, 95, 137, 139
Three-fifths Compromise and, 14
United Jewish Organizations of Williamsburg v. Carey and, 75, 102, 104–105
United States Armed Services and, 19
United States Bureau of Labor Statistics and, 25

United States Census and, 2, 3, 34, 35, 40, 45, 48, 52, 99, 124, 135, 136, 138, 165, 174, 178
United States Congress and, xi–xii, 2, 3, 4, 5, 6, 16–19, 20–22, 25–26, 33, 34, 35, 36, 37–38, 39, 41–42, 73, 74–75, 76, 77, 93, 94, 96, 97, 99, 100, 113, 115–121, 128–129, 133–145, 149–166, 167, 168, 169, 170, 171, 172, 177, 178
United States Constitution and, 2, 6, 13–15, 17, 34, 36–37, 39, 94, 96–97, 99, 101, 102, 104, 105, 107, 108, 121, 122, 125, 126, 127, 134, 135, 140–141, 167, 177
United States Department of Justice and, 2, 3, 5, 33, 34, 40, 43, 44, 48, 52, 53, 54, 57, 59–60, 61, 62–63, 64, 65, 66, 69, 70, 72, 75, 76, 77, 93, 95, 96, 99, 100, 101, 102, 103, 107, 117, 118, 123, 125, 126, 128, 130, 144–145, 149, 154, 159, 165–166, 170, 176, 178
United States Department of Labor and, 12
United States District Courts, *see* federal courts
United States House of Representatives and, 14, 16, 17, 20, 21, 22, 34–36, 41, 93, 94, 96, 97, 99, 100, 115, 117–118, 121, 128–129, 133–145, 169, 173, 174
United States Senate and, 16, 17, 21, 22, 74–75, 115, 129
United States Supreme Court and, 3–4, 6, 17, 18, 19, 20, 23, 26–28, 36–39, 43–44, 61, 62, 75–76, 93, 94, 95, 96, 99, 101, 102, 103–109, 119, 121–125, 126–130, 133–134, 136–137, 140, 141, 152, 167, 168, 169, 171, 174, 176, 177

urban areas and, 21, 23, 24–25, 36,
64, 98, 106,118, 141, 142, 144,
150, 152, 154, 155, 156, 157,
158, 159, 165
Virginia and, 3, 15, 35, 64, 65, 76,
95, 121, 128, 174
Voting Rights Act and, 2, 4, 5, 6–7,
19, 37–38, 41–44, 54, 57,
58–59, 61, 62, 70, 72, 93,
94–95, 100, 101, 102, 103, 104,
105, 107, 109, 125, 126,
129–130, 135, 137, 167–168,
169, 170, 172, 171, 177, 178
Washington and, 35
Wesberry v. Sanders and, 36, 134
and West, 22–23, 24, 35, 178
West Virginia and, 35
Whites and, xi, 3, 4, 11–13, 17, 18,
19, 24, 25, 26, 33, 34, 42, 43,
44, 48, 53, 58, 64–65, 67, 69,
72, 73, 74, 75, 76, 99–103, 104,
105, 106, 107, 108, 115, 118,
119, 121, 122, 124, 128, 139,
140, 143, 145, 168, 169, 170,
171, 172, 173, 174, 177
Wilson Test and, 154, 155, 156,
157, 158, 159, 160, 161, 162,
163, 164, 165
World War I and, 19
World War II and, 19
"zero tolerance" and, 12–13
Alabama, State of, 3, 15, 76, 121,
139
*America in Black and White: One
Nation, Indivisible* (1997), 4
America's Black Congressman
(1971), 18
American Civil Liberties Union
(ACLU), 49, 57–58, 59, 61, 62,
67, 70
American Indians, *see* Native
Americans
American Jewish Conference, 103
Anderson, Eric, 16–17
Andrews, Ike, 171
Apartheid, 4, 19, 104, 108, 168

Arkansas, State of, 16, 33, 119, 174
Arizona, State of, 35

Badham v. Eu (1989), 94
Baker v. Carr (1962), 36
Ballenger, Representative Cass, 37, 48
Balmer Congress 6.2, 47, 57, 59, 60,
70, 71, 77, 80, 154, 155, 156,
157, 158, 159, 160, 161, 162,
163, 164, 165
Balmer Congress 7.8, 50, 57, 59, 71
Balmer Congress 8.1, 59, 63–64, 65,
66, 71, 83, 155, 156, 157, 158,
160, 161, 162, 163
Balmer Congress 9.1, 63
Balmer Congress 10.1, 63
Balmer Congress Block Level, 50, 57
Balmer Congress Final Version, 63
Balmer, Representative David,
47–48, 50, 51, 52, 57, 59, 63,
66, 70, 73, 141, 154, 155
Barr, U.S. Attorney General William,
99, 102
Beer v. United States (1976), 95
Beyle, Professor Thad, 124
Bishop, Representative Sanford, 118,
172, 173
Black Faces, Black Interests (1995),
4, 74n
Black Americans, *see* African
Americans
Black, Professor Merle, 108
Blackmun, Justice Harry, 105
Blacks and American Government
(1991), 24
*Blacks in the United States: A Geo-
graphic Perspective* (1975), 22
Bloch, Susan Low, 102
Blue, State Representative Dan, 43,
47, 50, 61, 62, 96, 98
Boggs, Representative Lindy, 119
Bolick, Clint, 26–27
Bositis, David, 123, 168, 173, 175
Brooke, Senator Edward, 21
Brown, Representative Corrine, 115,
172, 173

Brown v. Board of Education (1954), 19, 20
Bryant v. Lawrence County (1993), 140
Bullock, Charles, 76–77
Bullock, Dorothy, 99
Burke, Edmund, 143
Burton, U.S. Representative Phillip, 94, 174
Bush, President George, 24, 40, 41, 60, 103, 126
Bush v. Vera (1996), 127
Butler, David, 136, 139, 141, 142–143

Cain, Bruce, 26, 129, 136, 139, 141, 142–143
California, State of, 35, 74, 94, 168, 174, 176
Carson, Congressman Julia, 22, 172
Carter, Professor Stephen, 27
Certiorari, 102
Cheatham, Congressman Henry P., 17
Chisholm, Congresswoman Shirley, 20
Christopher, Maurine, 18
City of Mobile v. Bolden (1980), 37–38
Civil Rights Act (1964), 2, 19, 20, 49
Civil War, 2, 5, 15, 22, 24, 34, 113, 167
Clay, Congressman William, 16, 20, 21, 74
Clayton, Representative Eva, 28–29, 37, 106–107, 124, 170
Clement, Councilman Howard III, 67–68
Cleveland, City of, 21
Clinton, President Bill, 22, 26, 103, 126
Clinton's Quota Queen (1993), 27
Clyburn, Representative James, 113–114
Coble, Representative Howard, 48
Cohen, Gerry, 44–45, 52, 59, 66, 141, 142, 145

Colegrove v. Green (1946), 36
Coleman, Carolyn, 53
Colorado, State of, 140
"Communities of interest," 6, 98, 106–107, 133, 141–143
Compact 2-Minority Plan, 68, 71, 87, 155, 156, 157, 158, 159, 160, 161, 162, 163, 165
"Compactness," 6, 39, 70, 72, 96, 100, 106, 107, 108, 127, 134, 136, 137–141, 145, 149–166, 174, 176
    Grofman test and, 151, 152–153, 154–156, 161, 164, 165
    polygon area test and, 151, 152, 154–155, 159–160, 164, 165
    polygon perimeter test and, 151, 152, 154, 155, 159–160, 165
    Reock test and, 151, 153–154, 158, 159–164, 165
    Schwartzberg test and, 151, 153, 157, 159, 162, 164, 165
    Wilson test and, 154, 155, 156, 157, 158, 159, 160, 161, 162, 163, 164, 165
Computers, 45–46, 48, 52, 53, 68, 98–99
Computers Allow Public Access Into Redistricting (1991), 45
Confederate Congress, 34
Confederate States of America, 34, 172, 178
Congressional Base Plan #1, 46, 47, 48, 49
Congressional Base Plan #2, 47, 48, 49
Congressional Base Plan #3, 50
Congressional Base Plan #4, 50
Congressional Base Plan #5, 50
Congressional Base Plan #6, 50, 51, 52, 57, 58, 59, 60, 65, 69, 71, 75, 77, 82, 100, 144, 150, 159, 160, 161, 162, 163
Congressional Base Plan #7, 68, 69–70

Congressional Base Plan #8, 68, 70
Congressional Base Plan #9, 69–70
Congressional Base Plan #10, 69–70,
     71, 72, 77, 89, 98, 137, 141, 144,
     145, 150, 154, 155, 156, 157,
     158, 159, 160, 161, 162, 163,
     164, 165
Congressional Black Caucus, 11, 20,
     178
   formation of, 20
   membership of, 20–21
   Richard Nixon and, 21
Connecticut, State of, 22, 168
Constitutional Convention (1787), 14
Contiguity, 6, 106, 107, 108,
     136–137, 138, 141, 149, 174
Continental Congress (1776), 14
Conyers, Congressman John, Jr., 20,
     74
Correa, Professor Michael Jones, 142
"Cracking," 38, 95
Cumulative voting, 28, 142–143
Cunningham, Dayna, 123

Daughtry v. State Board of Elections
     (1991), 61, 95–96
Daughtry, State Senator N. Leo, 61,
     95–96
Davis, George, 22
Davis v. Bandemer (1986), 39, 93–94
Dawson, Congressman William, 20
Declaration of Independence, 14
Dellums, Congressman Ron, 74
Democracy, 6, 7, 11, 13, 26, 27, 28,
     73, 106, 178
Democratic National Committee
     (DNC), 103
Democratic Party, 1, 3, 4, 5, 6, 16, 19,
     20, 21, 22, 33–34, 37, 40, 41,
     42, 43, 45, 46, 47, 49, 51, 52,
     53, 58, 60, 62, 63, 65, 66, 67,
     68, 69, 70, 72, 73, 74, 75, 76,
     77, 94, 95, 96, 98, 118, 149,
     165, 166, 167, 170, 171, 174,
     175, 176–177

DePriest, Congressman Oscar, 19
Descriptive representation, 23–29,
     73, 74
Diggs, Congressman Charles C.,
     20–21
*Dillard v. Baldwin County Board of
     Education* (1988), 139, 140
*District Debated in Angry Assembly:
     Plan is Partisan, Republicans
     Say,* 60
Dole, Senator Robert, 27
Dorff, Professor Robert, 97–98
Duke University, 103, 123, 170
Duncan, Phil, 44
Dunne, Assistant U.S. Attorney
     General John, 41, 44, 48, 57, 59,
     61, 75, 99
Durham Herald-Sun, 103, 123–124

Eamon, Professor Tom, 170
Edsall, Thomas, 42
Emancipation Proclamation (1863),
     14
Erwin, Judge Richard, 96
Everett, James, 99
Everett, Robinson O., 99, 102, 103,
     123–124

Federal courts, 39, 43, 173
   Badham v. Eu and, 94
   Bryant v. Lawrence County and,
     140
   *Daughtry v. State Board of Elec-
     tions* and, 61, 95–96
   *Dillard v. Baldwin County Board
     of Education* and, 139
   Hays v. Louisiana and, 122–123
   Johnson et al. v. Mortham et al.
     and, 127–138
   Major v. Treen and, 118–119
   Miller v. Johnson and, 124–127
   North Carolina and, 60–61, 63, 77,
     123–124
   Pope v. Blue and, 96–99, 100,
     102

Federal courts (*continued*):
  redistricting and, 94, 107, 114,
    115–116, 118, 121, 122, 128,
    139, 140, 167
  Shaw v. Barr and, 99–102, 103, 104
  Shaw v. Hunt and, 123–124
  Shaw v. Reno and, 103, 104, 105
  Thornburg v. Gingles and, 62, 95
  U.S. Department of Justice and, 63
Fields, Representative Cleo, 120,
    122–123, 167, 173
Fifteenth Amendment, 2, 15, 17, 102,
    135, 167
First Amendment, 97
Fitch, Representative Toby, 52–53,
    61, 62, 67
Flaherty, Representative David, 69,
    71, 88, 155, 156, 157, 158, 160,
    161, 162, 163
Florida, State of, 3, 35, 76, 115–116,
    121, 122, 127–128, 172
Ford, Congressman Harold, 168
Fountain, Congressman L. H., 170
Fourteenth Amendment, 2, 15, 36,
    94, 96–97, 101, 102, 104, 122,
    125, 134, 135, 177
Franklin, John Hope, 15
Franks, Representative Gary, 22,
    74–75, 168
From Slavery to Freedom (1980), 15

Galifianakis, Representative Nick,
    170
Georgia, State of, 6, 15, 21, 35, 36,
    76, 115, 117–118, 121–122,
    124–127, 128, 168, 172, 173
Gerry, Governor Eldridge, 38–39
Gerrymandering, xi, 2, 7, 18, 129,
    138, 139, 178
  history of, 38–39
  in North Carolina, 45, 60, 70, 72,
    93, 94, 98, 100, 103, 105, 106,
    107, 109, 123–124, 138, 139, 151
  redistricting and, 38–39

in South, 2, 121, 122, 123, 124,
    128
United States Supreme Court and,
    39
Voting Rights Act and, 37, 38, 167
Ginsberg, Ben, 41
Ginsburg, Justice Ruth Bader, 126
GOP, *see* Republican Party
Grandfather clauses, 2, 18
Great Depression, 19
"Great migration" (1915), 24
Great Society, 20
Grofman, Bernard, 75–76, 97, 129,
    133, 136, 137, 138–139, 140,
    151, 152–153, 154–155, 156,
    161, 164, 165
Grofman Test, 151, 152–156, 161,
    164, 165
Gronke, Professor Paul, 75
Guilkeson, Bill, 65–66
Guinier, Professor Lani, 26–28, 142

Hacker, Professor Andrew, 13
Hall, Congressman Katie, 168
Handley, Lisa, 75–76, 95, 129
Hardaway, Representative Thomas,
    65–66, 73
Hastings, Representative Alcee,
    115–116
Hawke, Republican Party Chairman
    R. Jack, Jr., 63, 70, 96
Hawkins, Congressman Augustus, 20
Hays v. Louisiana (1993), 122–123
Hayes, President Rutherford B., 17
Hayes-Tilden Compromise (1876), 2,
    17, 113
Hefner, Congressman W. G., 37
Helms–Gantt Senate Race (1990),
    48, 51, 52
Hispanics, 105, 108, 115, 118,
    120–121, 122, 127
Hitler, Adolf, 19
Holloman, Representative Charles,
    170

Horn, David, 140, 151, 153
Hunt, Governor James, 123–124
Hunt, Representative Sam, 49
Hunter, Bob, 48
Hyde, Senator Herbert, 72
Hyman, Congressman John A., 17

Illinois, State of, 35
Indiana, State of, 22, 94, 168, 172
Interstate 85 Corridor Plan, 65–66, 68, 70, 144, 145
Iowa, State of, 35, 140

Jacobson, Gary C., 98, 173
Jayhawkers, 17
"Jim Crow" laws, 19, 128
Johnson et al. v. Mortham et al. (1996), 127–128
Jones, Elaine, 106
Jones, Linwood, 43
Jones, Representative Walter B., Jr., 69
Jones, Professor Woodrow, Jr., 24
Jordan, Congressman Barbara, 21
Judicial preclearance, 101
Just Permanent Interests (1992), 20
Justus, Representative Larry, 47, 50, 51, 68, 69, 71, 81

Kansas, State of, 35
Karcher v. Daggett (1983), 83
Karlan, Representative Pamela, 109, 139
Kennedy, Justice Anthony, 126
Kentucky, Commonwealth of, 35
Key, V. O., 16, 65
Kimbrough, Scott, 64–65, 71, 83
Kirksey v. Board of Supervisors of Hinds County (1977), 75
Kome, Hunter, 45
Krattenmaker, Thomas G., 102
Ku Klux Klan, 17

Lancaster, Congressman Martin, 37
Lawyers' Committee for Civil Rights, 106
Lee, Mayor Howard, 170, 171
Lincoln, President Abraham, 14
Literacy tests, 2, 18, 101, 167
Louisiana, State of, 15, 35, 76, 118–120, 121, 122–123, 128, 167, 172, 173, 174
Lovett, Willie, 49
Lublin, David, 74n
Lumbee Indians, 47

Major v. Treen (1983), 118–119
Majority districts (African American), xi, 1, 2, 3–4, 5, 6–7, 19, 22, 23, 33, 38, 42, 53, 76, 93, 143, 174, 176, 177, 178
    in North Carolina, 3, 4, 6, 46, 47–48, 49, 52, 53, 61–62, 63, 64, 65, 66, 67, 68, 69, 70, 72, 73, 74, 75, 77, 80, 81, 82, 83, 84, 85, 86, 87, 88, 89, 93, 95, 104, 106, 107, 113, 123–124, 141, 142, 144–145, 149, 155n, 156n, 157n, 158n, 159, 160n, 163n, 165, 166, 171
    in South, xi, 1, 2, 3, 4, 6, 33, 113, 114, 115, 117, 118, 119, 121–130, 139, 171, 172, 173, 174, 176–177, 178
    U.S. Supreme Court and, 6, 102, 103, 104, 122, 123, 128–130, 168
Majority districts (white), 3, 4, 22, 104, 122, 168, 169, 171, 172, 173, 174
Majority-minority districts, 11, 22, 33, 44, 95
    in North Carolina, 6, 61, 62, 73, 100
    in South, 33
    Supreme Court and, 105
Martin, Governor James G., 63, 96
Maryland, State of, 2, 76, 121

Massachusetts, Commonwealth of,
     21, 35, 38, 168
McCaughey, Elizabeth, 106
McKinney, Representative Cynthia,
     118, 122, 172, 173
McMillan, Congressman Alex, 37, 48
Meek, Representative Carrie, 115
Merrit, Tom, 66
Michaux, Representative H. M.
     "Mickey," 40, 65, 73, 170–171
Michigan, State of, 35, 74
Midwest:
     migration from, 35
     migration to, 22–23, 24
     U.S. House seats from, 35
Migration, 22-23, 24, 144
     great (1915), 24
     from Midwest, 35
     to Midwest, 22–23, 24
     from Northeast, 35
     to Northeast, 21, 22–23, 24
     from South, 22–23, 24
     to South, 35
     to West, 22–23, 24, 35
Miller v. Johnson (1995), 6, 124–127
Minority districts, 38, 48, 49, 57, 76,
     108, 172
     in North Carolina, 57, 58, 59, 60,
        62, 63, 64–65, 67, 68, 70, 72, 73,
        77, 102, 149–151, 164, 165–166
     in South, 114–130, 165–166, 167
     U.S. Supreme Court and, 104, 108,
        109, 126, 127–128, 167
Mississippi, State of, 15, 140, 174
Missouri, State of, 22, 74, 168
Montana, State of, 35
Morris v. Gressette (1977), 101

NAACP, *see* National Association for
     the Advancement of Colored
     People
National Association for the Ad-
     vancement of Colored People
     (NAACP), 24, 49, 52, 53, 58,

61, 62, 65, 67, 69, 70, 103, 105,
     123
National Urban League, 24
Native Americans, 14, 47, 50, 51, 59,
     60, 62, 68, 69
Neal, Congressman Stephen, 37, 73
Nevada, State of, 174
New Deal, 19
New Jersey, State of, 35, 93
New York, State of, 19, 21, 35
Newkirk, Glenn, 45–46
Niemi, Richard, 75–76, 140, 151, 152
92 Congress 1, 68, 71, 85, 155, 156,
     157, 160, 161, 162, 163, 164
Nix, Congressman Robert, 20
Nixon, President Richard M., 21
North Carolina, State of, 2, 3, 16, 28,
     93
     ACLU and, 57–58, 59, 61, 62, 67,
        70
     African Americans in, 34, 35, 38,
        40–41, 42–43, 45, 50–89,
        93–107, 169–170, 177
     Balmer Congress 6.2, 47, 57, 59,
        60, 70, 71, 77, 80, 154, 155,
        156, 157, 158, 159, 160, 161,
        162, 163, 164, 165
     Balmer Congress 7.8, 50, 57, 59, 71
     Balmer Congress 8.1, 59, 63–64,
        65, 66, 71, 83, 155, 156, 157,
        158, 160, 161, 162, 163
     Balmer Congress 9.1, 63
     Balmer Congress 10.1, 63
     Balmer Congress Block Level, 50,
        57
     Balmer Congress Final Version, 63
     Black Leadership Caucus of, 48,
        49, 52
     census and, 17, 35, 52, 99, 135,
        136, 138
     Civil War and, 34
     Compact 2-Minority Plan, 68, 71,
        87, 155, 156, 157, 158, 159,
        160, 161, 162, 163, 165

compactness in, 149–166, 174, 176
computers in, 45–46, 52, 53, 68, 98
Congressional Base Plan #1, 46,
47, 48, 49
Congressional Base Plan #2, 47,
48, 49
Congressional Base Plan #3, 50
Congressional Base Plan #4, 50
Congressional Base Plan #5, 50
Congressional Base Plan #6, 50,
51, 52, 57, 58, 59, 60, 65, 69,
71, 75, 77, 82, 100, 144, 150,
159, 160, 161, 162, 163
Congressional Base Plan #7, 68,
69–70
Congressional Base Plan #8, 68, 70
Congressional Base Plan #9,
69–70
Congressional Base Plan, #10,
69–70, 71, 72, 77, 89, 98, 137,
141, 144, 145, 150, 154, 155,
156, 157, 158, 159, 160, 161,
162, 163, 164, 165
Democratic Party in, 16–17, 37, 43,
45, 58, 60, 62, 63, 65, 67, 68, 69,
70, 72, 73, 75, 76, 77, 94, 95, 96,
98, 103, 149, 165, 166
federal courts and, 60, 61, 63, 77,
94–105
General Assembly of, 36, 40, 41,
45, 46, 96, 100, 134, 135,
141–142, 151
gerrymandering in, 45, 60, 70, 72,
93, 94, 98, 100, 103, 105, 106,
107, 109, 123–124, 138, 139,
151
Governor of, 63, 96, 123–124
Grofman Test in, 151, 152–156,
161, 164, 165
Hispanics in, 105, 108
history of, 34
Interstate 85 Corridor Plan and,
65–66, 68, 70, 144, 145
Lumbee Indians in, 47

majority districts in, 3, 4, 6,
46, 47–48, 49, 52, 53, 61–62,
63, 64, 65, 66, 67, 68, 69,
70, 72, 73, 74, 75, 77, 80,
81, 82, 83, 84, 85, 86, 87, 88,
89, 93, 95, 104, 106, 107,
113, 123–124, 141, 142, 144–
145, 149, 155n, 156n, 157n,
158n, 159, 160n, 163n, 165,
166, 171
majority-minority districts in, 6,
47, 61, 62, 73, 100, 149–151,
164, 165–166
minority districts in, 38, 48, 57, 58,
59, 60, 62, 63, 64–65, 67, 68,
70, 72, 73, 77, 102, 138, 139,
159, 177
NAACP and, 58, 61, 62, 65, 67,
69, 70, 103, 105
Native Americans in, 14, 47, 50,
51, 59, 60, 68, 69
92 Congress 1 and, 68, 71, 85, 155,
156, 157, 160, 161, 162, 163, 164
Optimum II–Zero Plan of, 66, 71,
73, 86
polygon area test and, 151, 152,
154–155, 159–160, 164, 165
polygon perimeter test and, 151,
152, 154, 155, 159–160, 165
population of, 35, 40–41, 45, 50
reapportionment in, 97–104
Reconstruction and, 17
Redistricting Committees in, 40,
42–44, 45–47, 48, 49, 50, 51,
52–53, 57, 59, 61, 75, 134, 135,
136, 137
redistricting in, 36, 40, 42–52,
59–77, 95–109, 118, 123–124,
133, 134–145, 149–166, 170
Reock Test and, 151, 153–154,
158, 159, 164, 165
Representative Flaherty's Congress Plan, 69, 71, 88, 155, 156,
157, 158, 160, 161, 162, 163

North Carolina, State of (*continued*):
  Republican Party in, 16–17,
    33–34, 37, 41–42, 46, 47,
    48, 49, 51, 52, 60–61, 62, 63,
    64, 67, 68, 69, 70, 72, 73, 74,
    75, 77, 94, 95–96, 97–98,
    103, 154
  retrogression in, 94, 95
  Schwartzberg Test and, 151, 153,
    157, 159, 162, 164, 165
  Shaw v. Barr in, 99–103
  Shaw v. Hunt in, 123–124, 127
  Shaw v. Reno in, 6, 103–109, 123,
    126, 127, 140, 141, 174, 176
  Sixty-five Percent Rule of, 75
  State Board of Elections of, 54, 96
  State Constitution of, 39, 40
  State Disenfranchisement Amend-
    ment (1900) of, 17
  State House of Representatives of,
    43, 44, 46, 47, 50, 51, 57, 58,
    59–60, 61–62, 63, 64, 65, 66, 95,
    96, 99–107, 133–135, 141–145,
    149, 159, 165, 166, 170
  State Senate of, 40, 43, 44, 46, 47,
    51, 57, 58, 59–60, 61–62, 63,
    64, 65, 66, 95, 96, 99–107,
    133–135, 141–145, 149, 159,
    165, 166, 170
  *Statistical Abstract of North Car-
    olina*, 144–145
  suburbs of, 21, 24–25, 36, 73, 144,
    150, 152, 155, 159–164, 165
  U.S. Congress and, 3, 16, 17,
    18, 34, 35, 73, 93, 94, 96, 97,
    99, 100, 104, 121, 124, 127,
    128, 133–145, 149–166,
    170–171
  U.S. Constitution and, 34, 39, 94,
    96, 97, 99, 101–102, 104, 105,
    107
  U.S. Department of Justice and,
    5–6, 40, 57, 59–60, 61–62, 63,
    64, 65, 66, 69, 70, 72, 75, 77,
    93, 95, 96, 99, 100, 101, 102,

    103, 104, 144–145, 149, 154,
    159, 170
  U.S. House of Representatives
    and, 35, 36–37, 74–75, 94, 96,
    97, 100
  U.S. Senate and, 74–75
  U.S. Supreme Court and, 93, 94,
    95, 96, 99, 101, 102, 103–109,
    133–134, 136–137, 140, 141
  urban areas of, 21, 23, 24–25, 36,
    64, 98, 106, 142, 144, 150, 152,
    154, 155, 156, 157, 158, 159,
    165
  veto power of Governor in, 63
  Voting Rights Act and, 3, 43–44,
    54, 57, 58–59, 61, 62, 70, 72,
    93, 94, 95, 100, 101, 102, 103,
    104, 105, 107, 119, 124, 135,
    137, 170
  Wilson Test and, 154, 155, 156,
    157, 158, 159, 160, 161, 162,
    163, 164, 165
North Carolina Legislative Black
    Caucus (NCLBC), 66–67
North Carolina State University, 97
Northeast:
  migration from, 35
  migration to, 22–23, 24, 178
  U.S. House seats from, 35

O'Connor, Justice Sandra Day,
    103–104, 107, 108–109, 123,
    129, 168
O'Hara, Congressman James E., 17
Ohio, State of, 35
"One person, one vote," 27, 36, 134
Optimum II–Zero Plan, 66, 71, 73, 86

"Packing," 38, 95
Paradox of Representation, The, 74n
Parker, Frank, 76, 106, 108–109
*Party Loyalty, Black Gains Clash in
    Redistricting*, 67
Peeler, Mary, 65, 68, 69–70
Pennsylvania, Commonwealth of, 35

Pildes, Professor Richard, 140, 151, 152
Plessy v. Ferguson (1896), 18
Politics of Congressional Elections, The, 98, 173
Poll taxes, 2, 18, 167
Polsby, Professor Daniel, 138
Polygon area test, 151, 152, 154–155, 159–160, 164, 165
Polygon perimeter test, 151, 152, 154, 155, 159–160, 165
Pope, Representative Art, 60, 72, 96
Pope v. Blue (1992), 96–99, 100, 102, 136–137
Popper, Professor Robert, 138
Powell, Congressman Adam Clayton, 19, 20
Powell, Jefferson, 103
Preclearance, 101
Price, Congressman David, 37
Professors Take Case to Court, 103

RNC, *see* Republican National Committee
"Race-based" districting, 1, 4, 5, 25–28, 126
"Race-blind" redistricting, 6, 176
Race Matters, 25
Racial apartheid, *see* Apartheid
Racial gerrymandering, *see* Gerrymandering
Raleigh News & Observer, 18, 67, 72
Ramsey, James, 170
Reagan, President Ronald, 44, 60
Reapportionment, 23, 113–130
  in North Carolina, 97–104
  and United States Constitution, 36–37
  and United States House of Representatives, 34–35
Reconstruction:
  African Americans and, 2, 5, 15, 16, 18, 121
  C. Vann Woodward on, 20

First Reconstruction era (1867–77), 11
  Hayes-Tilden Compromise and, 17
  Second Reconstruction era (1940–present),11, 20, 113
Reconstruction Act (1867), 15–16
Redistricting, 1, 3, 5, 23, 34–36, 38, 39, 41–42, 93, 113–130, 133–134
  Davis v. Bandemer and, 93–94
  federal court decisions and, 94, 107
  in North Carolina, 36, 39–40, 42, 43, 45, 46, 47, 48, 49, 50, 51, 52, 57–77, 95–109, 133, 134–145, 149–166, 170
  in South, 1, 3, 33–36, 113–130, 140, 165, 167, 168, 169, 170, 171, 172, 173, 177, 178
  U.S. House of Representatives and, 34–36, 133–134
  United States Supreme Court and, 36
  United States Supreme Court and, 36
  Voting Rights Act and, 37–38
Rehnquist, Chief Justice William, 99
Reock Test, 151, 153–154, 158, 159, 164, 165
Reock, Ernest, 138, 140, 151, 153–154, 158, 159, 164
Representation theory:
  African Americans and, 23–29
  cumulative voting and, 28, 142
  descriptive representation and, 23–29, 73, 74
  Lani Guinier on, 26–28
  substantive representation and, 24–29, 73, 74
  "winner-take-all" voting, 28
Representative Flaherty's Congress Plan, 69, 71, 88, 155, 156, 157, 158, 160, 161, 162, 163
Republican National Committee (RNC), 42, 103

Republican Party, 2, 3, 4, 5, 6, 16, 19, 20, 21, 22, 33–34, 37, 41–42, 46, 47, 48, 49, 51, 52, 60–61, 62, 63, 64, 66, 67, 68, 69, 70, 72, 73, 74–75, 76, 77, 94, 95, 96, 97–98, 103, 115, 118, 154, 168, 170, 173, 175

"Republican Revolution," 74

Retrogression, 94, 95

Reynolds v. Simms (1964), 133–134

Rice, Professor Mitchell, 24

Richardson, State Senator James T., 66

Rose, Congressman Charlie, 37, 48–49, 66

Rural areas, *see* Suburbs

Schwartzberg Test, 151, 153, 157, 159, 162, 164, 165

Segregation, xi, 4, 19, 20, 23, 24, 25, 104, 129

Shaw, Ruth, 99

Shaw v. Barr (1992), 99–103

Shaw v. Hunt (1994), 123–124, 127

Shaw v. Reno (1993), 3–4, 6, 103–109, 121, 122, 123, 124, 126, 127, 128, 140, 141, 152, 174, 176

Shimm, Melvin, 99

Sixty-five Percent Rule, 75–76

Sizemore, Representative Trip, 49

Slavery, 2, 13–14

Smith, Professor J. Owens, 24

Souter, Justice David, 105, 126

South:
    African Americans in, 1, 2, 3, 4, 5, 6–7, 15, 16, 17, 18–19, 20, 21, 33–35, 38, 42, 108, 109, 113–130, 137, 140, 165, 167–174, 178
    "cracking," 38, 95
    election to Congress from, 16, 18–19, 20, 21

gerrymandering in, 2, 121, 122, 123, 124, 128

grandfather clauses in, 2, 18

Hayes-Tilden Compromise and, 2, 17, 113

literacy tests in, 2, 18, 101, 167

majority districts in, xi, 1, 2, 3, 4, 6, 33, 113, 114, 115, 117, 118, 119, 121–130, 139, 171, 172, 173, 174, 176–177, 178

majority-minority districts in, 33, 114–130, 165–166, 167

migration from, 22–23, 24

migration to, 35

minority districts in, 37, 48, 122, 138, 139, 159, 168, 169, 171, 172, 173, 174, 177

"packing," 38, 95

poll taxes in, 2, 18, 167

reconstruction in, 2, 5, 11, 15, 16, 17, 18, 113, 121

redistricting and, 1, 3, 33–36, 113–130, 140, 165, 167, 168, 169, 170, 171, 172, 173, 177, 178

Shaw v. Reno and, 108, 109, 121, 124, 128

"stacking," 38, 95

see also individual states

South Carolina, State of, 3, 15, 64, 65, 76, 95, 114, 115, 121, 125, 128

Southeastern Business College, 170

Southern Politics in State and Nation (1949), 16, 65

Spaulding, Representative Kenneth B., 171

"Stacking," 38, 95

Statistical Abstract of North Carolina, 144–145

Statistical data:
    AIDS, 12
    birth rates, 75
    crime rates, 12–13

education levels, 12, 13
employment, 12, 13, 24–25
health care, 12, 13
incarceration rates, 13
life expectancy, 12, 75
net worth, 12
population, 18–19, 71
single parent families, 11–12
Stevens, Justice John Paul, 105
Stith, David W., 170
Stokes, Louis, 20
Substantive representation, 24–29, 73, 74
Suburbs, 21, 24–25, 36, 68, 73, 98, 106, 115, 118, 119, 121, 122, 124, 125, 139, 140, 143, 144, 145, 150, 152, 155, 159–164, 165
"Superman," 122
Swain, Carol, 4, 16, 23, 74n, 168–169

Taylor, Representative Charles, 37, 48
Taylor, Peter, 150
Tennessee, State of, 16, 33, 36, 122, 168, 174, 177
Texas, State of, 16, 21, 35, 76, 120–121, 127–128, 172, 174
Thernstrom, Abigail, 4, 26, 168–169, 172
Thernstrom, Stephan, 4, 169, 172
Thirteenth Amendment (1865), 2, 14–15
Thomas, Justice Clarence, 24
Thornburg v. Gingles (1986), 43–44, 62, 95, 137, 139, 171
Three-fifths Compromise, 14
Tilden, Samuel, 17
Truman, President Harry S., 19
Two Nations: Black & White, Separate, Hostile, Unequal (1992), 13
Tyranny of the Majority, The (1994). 27, 142

United Jewish Organizations of Williamsburg v. Carey (1977), 75, 102, 104–105
United States Armed Services, African Americans and, 19
United States Attorney General, *see* United States Department of Justice
United States Bureau of Labor Statistics, 25
United States Census, 2, 3, 34, 35, 40, 45, 48, 52, 99, 124, 135, 136, 138, 165, 174, 178
United States Congress, 33–34, 52, 93, 99, 113–121
African Americans and, xi–xii, 2, 3, 4, 5, 6, 16–19, 20–22, 25–26, 33, 34, 35, 36, 37–38, 39, 41–42, 73, 74–75, 76, 77, 93, 94, 96, 97, 99, 100, 113, 128, 129, 130, 133–145, 149–166, 169, 173, 174, 176, 177, 178
Brown v. Board of Education and, 20
Congressional Black Caucus and, 20–21
Congressional districts, xi, 1, 3, 4, 5, 39, 149–166
Congressional redistricting, 6, 36, 115–130
Hayes-Tilden Compromise and, 17
majority-minority based districts and, 22
North Carolina and, 3, 17, 34, 35, 73, 93, 94, 96, 97, 99, 100, 104, 123–127, 133–145, 170–171
race-based districting, 1, 3, 4, 25–26
redistricting and, 133–145, 149–166
Supreme Court and, 37–38
Voting Rights Act and, 2, 38, 167, 168

United States Congress (*continued*)
  see also United States House of
    Representatives and United
    States Senate
United States Constitution, 6, 13–14,
  97, 99, 100, 105, 107, 108, 121,
  126, 127, 140
  census and, 34
  Fifteenth Amendment of, 2, 15, 17,
    102, 135, 167
  First Amendment of, 97
  Fourteenth Amendment of, 2, 15,
    36, 94, 96–97, 101, 102, 104,
    122, 125, 134, 135, 177
  North Carolina and, 34, 39, 94,
    96–97, 99, 101, 102, 104, 105,
    107
  reapportionment and, 36–37
  redistricting and, 133, 134, 135,
    140–141
  Thirteenth Amendment of, 2,
    14–15
United States Department of Justice,
  2, 3, 5, 33, 34, 40, 43, 44, 48,
  52, 53, 54, 57, 59–60, 61,
  62–63, 64, 65, 66, 69, 70, 72,
  75, 76, 77, 93, 95, 96, 99, 100,
  101, 102, 103, 107, 117, 118,
  123, 125, 126, 128, 130,
  144–145, 149, 154, 159,
  165–166, 170, 176, 178
United States Department of Labor, 12
United States District Courts, *see*
  federal courts
United States Geologic Survey, 45
United States House of Representatives, 14, 16, 17, 20, 21, 22,
  35–37, 74–75, 94, 96, 97, 100,
  115, 117–118, 121, 128–129
  and census calculation, 34, 35
  and reapportionment, 34–35
  and redistricting, 34–36, 133–145
  see also United States Congress
United States Senate, 16, 17, 21, 22,
  74–75, 115, 129

nomination of Lani Guinier and,
  26–28
see also United States Congress
United States Supreme Court, 17, 26,
  36, 42, 43, 93, 99, 102–103,
  128–130, 167–168, 169, 177
Badham v. Eu (1989), 94
Baker v. Carr (1962), 36
Beer v. United States (1976), 95
Brown v. Board of Education
  (1954), 19, 20
Bryant v. Lawrence County (1993),
  140
Bush v. Vera (1996), 127
City of Mobile v. Bolden (1980),
  37–38
certiorari and, 102
Civil Rights Act of 1964 and, 19, 20
Colegrove v. Green (1946), 36
Davis v. Bandemer (1986), 39,
  93–94
*Daughtry v. State Board of Elec-
  tions* (1991), 61, 95–96
*Dillard v. Baldwin County Board
  of Education* (1988), 139–140
Fourteenth Amendment and, 36
gerrymandering and, 39
Hays v. Louisiana (1993), 122–123
Johnson et al. v. Mortham et al.,
  127–128
Karcher v. Daggett (1983), 93
*Kirksey v. Board of Supervisors of
  Hinds County* (1977), 75
Major v. Treen (1983), 118–119
majority districts and, 6, 102, 103,
  104, 122, 123, 128–130, 168
majority-minority districts and,
  105, 126, 127–128, 167
Miller v. Johnson (1995), 6,
  124–127
minority districts and, 39, 104,
  108, 109
Morris v. Gressette (1977), 101
nomination of Clarence Thomas
  to, 24

North Carolina and, 93, 94, 95, 96, 99, 101, 102, 103, 104–105, 133–134, 136–137

Plessy v. Ferguson (1896), 18

Pope v. Blue (1992), 102

redistricting and, 36, 133–134, 174, 176, 177

Reynolds v. Simms (1964), 133–134

"separate but equal" doctrine, 18, 19

Shaw v. Barr (1992), 102–103

Shaw v. Hunt (1994), 123–124, 127

Shaw v. Reno (1993) and, 103–109, 121, 122, 123, 124, 126, 127, 128, 140, 141, 152, 174, 176

Sixty-five Percent Rule and, 75–76

Thornburg v. Gingles (1986), 43–44, 62, 95, 137, 139, 171

United Jewish Organizations of Williamsburg v. Carey (1977), 75, 102, 104–105

United States Congress and, 37–38

Voting Rights Act and, xi, 43, 44, 93, 94–95, 100, 101, 102–103, 104–105, 107, 109, 125, 126, 167–168, 171, 177

Wesberry v. Sanders (1964), 36, 134

University of North Carolina, 124

Urban areas, 21, 23, 24–25, 36, 64, 98, 106, 118, 141, 142, 144, 150, 152, 154, 155, 156, 157, 158, 159, 165

Valentine, Representative Tim, 37, 66, 73, 170–171

Virginia, Commonwealth of, 3, 15, 35, 64, 65, 76, 95, 121, 128, 174

Voting Rights Act, 2, 33, 41, 124, 125, 126, 128, 129–130, 167, 169, 171, 172, 177, 178

history of, 5, 37–38, 128

majority districts and, 4, 6–7, 33–34

North Carolina and, 38, 43–44, 54, 57, 58–59, 61, 62, 70, 72, 93, 94–95, 100, 101, 102–103, 104–105, 107, 109, 124, 135, 137, 170

passage of (1965), 2, 19

redistricting and, 37–38, 135

renewal of (1982), 2

United States Congress and, 38, 167

United States Department of Justice and, 3, 43

United States Supreme Court and, xi, 43, 44, 93, 94–95, 100, 101, 102–103, 104–105, 107, 109, 125, 126, 129–130, 167–168, 171, 177

Walker, Thomas, 67

Wall Street Journal, 106

Washington Legal Foundation, 103

Washington, State of, 35

Watt, Representative Mel, 37, 106–108, 124, 142

Watts, Representative J. C., 22, 74–75

Wesberry v. Sanders (1964), 36, 134

West:

migration to, 22–23, 24, 35, 178

U.S. House seats from, 35

West Virginia, State of, 35

West, Cornel, 25

Wheat, Congressman Alan, 22, 168

White, Justice Byron, 105

White, Congressman George H., 17, 18, 171

Whites, xi, 3, 4, 18, 43, 44, 48, 53, 58, 64–65, 67, 69, 72, 73, 74, 75, 76, 104, 106, 107, 108, 115, 118, 119, 121, 122, 124, 125, 128, 139, 140, 143, 144, 145, 150, 152 168, 169, 170, 171, 172, 173, 174, 177

Whose Votes Count? (1987), 26
Wilde, Kathleen, 52, 57–58, 69, 67
Wilson, J. Matthew, 75
Wilson Test, 154, 155, 156, 157, 158,
     159, 160, 161, 162, 163, 164,
     165
Wilson, William Julius, 25
Winner, State Senator Dennis, 48,
     49–50, 61, 62, 137–138
Winner, Leslie, 61–62

"Winner take all" voting, 28
Winston Salem Journal, 60
Woodward, C. Vann, 20
World War I, 19
World War II, 19

Young, Congressman Andrew, 21,
     168

"Zero tolerance," 12–13